*The Palgrave Macmillan Animal Ethics Series*

Series editors: **Andrew Linzey** and **Priscilla Cohn**

In recent years, there has been a growing interest in the ethics of our treatment of animals. Philosophers have led the way, and now a range of other scholars have followed, from historians to social scientists. From being a marginal issue, animals have become an emerging issue in ethics and in multidisciplinary inquiry. This series explores the challenges that Animal Ethics poses, both conceptually and practically, to traditional understandings of human–animal relations. Specifically, the Series will:

- provide a range of key introductory and advanced texts that map out ethical positions on animals;
- publish pioneering work written by new, as well as accomplished, scholars; and
- produce texts from a variety of disciplines that are multidisciplinary in character or have multidisciplinary relevance.

*Titles include:*

Alasdair Cochrane
AN INTRODUCTION TO ANIMALS AND POLITICAL THEORY

Andrew Knight
THE COSTS AND BENEFITS OF ANIMAL EXPERIMENTS

Claire Molloy
POPULAR MEDIA AND ANIMALS

Siobhan O'Sullivan
ANIMALS, EQUALITY AND DEMOCRACY

Thomas Ryan
SOCIAL WORK AND ANIMALS: A MORAL INTRODUCTION

Joan Schaffner
AN INTRODUCTION TO ANIMALS AND THE LAW

*Forthcoming titles:*

Aysha Akhtar
HUMANS AND ANIMALS: THE NEW PUBLIC HEALTH PARADIGM

Mark Bernstein
HUMAN–ANIMAL RELATIONS: THE OBLIGATION TO CARE

Eleonora Gullone
ANIMAL ABUSE AND HUMAN AGGRESSION

Alastair Harden
ANIMALS IN THE CLASSICAL WORLD: ETHICAL PERCEPTIONS

Lisa Johnson
POWER, KNOWLEDGE, ANIMALS

Kay Peggs
AN INTRODUCTION TO ANIMALS AND SOCIOLOGY

The Palgrave Macmillan Animal Ethics Series
Series Standing Order ISBN 978–0–230–57686–5 Hardback
                       978–0–230–57687–2 Paperback
(outside North America only)

You can receive future titles in this series as they are published by placing a standing order.
Please contact your bookseller or, in case of difficulty, write to us at the address below with
your name and address, the title of the series and one of the ISBNs quoted above.

Customer Services Department, Macmillan Distribution Ltd., Houndmills, Basingstoke,
Hampshire RG21 6XS, England

# Popular Media and Animals

Claire Molloy
*University of Brighton*

First published 2011 by
PALGRAVE MACMILLAN

Palgrave Macmillan in the UK is an imprint of Macmillan Publishers Limited, registered in England, company number 785998, of Houndmills, Basingstoke, Hampshire RG21 6XS.

Palgrave Macmillan in the US is a division of St Martin's Press LLC, 175 Fifth Avenue, New York, NY 10010.

Palgrave Macmillan is the global academic imprint of the above companies and has companies and representatives throughout the world.

Palgrave® and Macmillan® are registered trademarks in the United States, the United Kingdom, Europe and other countries.

ISBN: 978–0–230–23924–1 hardback

This book is printed on paper suitable for recycling and made from fully managed and sustained forest sources. Logging, pulping and manufacturing processes are expected to conform to the environmental regulations of the country of origin.

A catalogue record for this book is available from the British Library.

Library of Congress Cataloging-in-Publication Data

Molloy, Claire.
    Popular media and animals / Claire Molloy.
      p. cm.
    Includes bibliographical references and index.
    ISBN-13: 978–0–230–23924–1 (alk. paper)
    ISBN-10: 0–230–23924–2 (alk. paper)
      1. Animal welfare – Moral and ethical aspects. 2. Animal rights.
    3. Animals in mass media. I. Title.

HV4708.M66 2011
179'.3—dc22                                                              2011007804

10  9  8  7  6  5  4  3  2  1
20  19  18  17  16  15  14  13  12  11


Transferred to Digital Printing in 2014

*For Louie*

# Contents

# Figures

# Acknowledgements

I am extremely grateful to the series editors, Andrew Linzey and Priscilla Cohn, and to the Fellows of the Oxford Centre for Animal Ethics for their insightful comments at the proposal stage and beyond, which helped to shape the broad themes and direction of this book. Thanks go to Yannis Tzioumakis, who read draft chapters and was both generous and enthusiastic in his observations. I am fortunate to have had the support of colleagues in the School of Arts and Media at the University of Brighton. Thanks to Sarah Atkinson and Kathleen Griffin for their thoughts and notes on Chapter 4 and to Julie Doyle for her encouragement during the writing process. I am especially grateful to my colleague Rebecca Bramall for her much-valued comments on various chapters.

Thanks to Sarah Wharton and David Sorfa, who made suggestions which helped in the sourcing of texts for Chapters 7 and 8 and to Tom Tyler for his notes on Chapter 4. A conversation with Richard Parkinson assisted in developing one of the themes in this book, and a discussion with Peter Krämer helped to refine some of the ideas in Chapter 9. Thanks to Louie, who was with me while I wrote, and to Andy, without whom this book could not have been written.

Acknowledgement is due to the following sources for their kind permission to reproduce their images and content:

Content from the TripAdvisor web site is used with kind permission from TripAdvisor.
Figure 1.1 Richard Austin, *Phoenix the calf*, 2001
Figure 3.1 Loomis Dean/Time & Life Pictures/Getty Images
Figure 3.2 Loomis Dean/Time & Life Pictures/Getty Images
Figure 4.1 Inaldo Perez, *Columbia Animal Shelter*, Associated Press
Figure 6.1 Image courtesy of the Advertising Archives
Figure 6.2 Image courtesy of the Advertising Archives
Figure 8.1 Frank Marasco/Milwaukee Journal Sentinel
Figure 8.2 *Them*, 1954. Dir. Douglas Gordon, Warner Bros./The Kobal Collection

# Series Preface

This is a new book series for a new field of inquiry: Animal Ethics.

In recent years, there has been a growing interest in the ethics of our treatment of animals. Philosophers have led the way, and now a range of other scholars have followed, from historians to social scientists. From being a marginal issue, animals have become an emerging issue in ethics and in multidisciplinary inquiry.

In addition, a rethink of the status of animals has been fuelled by a range of scientific investigations which have revealed the complexity of animal sentiency, cognition, and awareness. The ethical implications of this new knowledge have yet to be properly evaluated, but it is becoming clear that the old view that animals are mere things, tools, machines, or commodities cannot be sustained ethically.

But it is not only philosophy and science that are putting animals on the agenda. Increasingly, in Europe and the United States, animals are becoming a political issue as political parties vie for the 'green' and 'animal' vote. In turn, political scientists are beginning to look again at the history of political thought in relation to animals, and historians are beginning to revisit the political history of animal protection.

As animals have grown as an issue of importance, so have there been more collaborative academic ventures leading to conference volumes, special journal issues, indeed new academic animal journals as well. Moreover, we have witnessed the growth of academic courses, as well as university posts, in Animal Ethics, Animal Welfare, Animal Rights, Animal Law, Animals and Philosophy, Human–Animal Studies, Critical Animal Studies, Animals and Society, Animals in Literature, Animals and Religion – tangible signs that a new academic discipline is emerging.

'Animal Ethics' is the new term for the academic exploration of the moral status of the non-human – an exploration that explicitly involves a focus on what we owe animals morally, and which also helps us to understand the influences – social, legal, cultural, religious, and political – that legitimate animal abuse. This series explores the challenges that Animal Ethics poses, both conceptually and practically, to traditional understandings of human–animal relations.

The series is needed for three reasons: (i) to provide the texts that will service the new university courses on animals; (ii) to support the increasing number of students studying and academics researching in animal-related fields; and (iii) because there is currently no book series that is a focus for multidisciplinary research in the field.

Specifically, the series will

- provide a range of key introductory and advanced texts that map out ethical positions on animals;
- publish pioneering work written by new, as well as accomplished, scholars; and
- produce texts from a variety of disciplines that are multidisciplinary in character or have multidisciplinary relevance.

The new Palgrave Macmillan Series on Animal Ethics is the result of a unique partnership between Palgrave Macmillan and the Ferrater Mora Oxford Centre for Animal Ethics. The series is an integral part of the mission of the Centre to put animals on the intellectual agenda by facilitating academic research and publication. The series is also a natural complement to one of the Centre's other major projects, the *Journal of Animal Ethics*. The Centre is an independent think-tank for the advancement of progressive thought about animals, and is the first centre of its kind in the world. It aims to demonstrate rigorous intellectual enquiry and the highest standards of scholarship. It strives to be a world-class centre of academic excellence in its field.

We invite academics to visit www.oxfordanimalethics.com, the Centre's website, and to contact us with new book proposals for the series.

ANDREW LINZEY AND PRISCILLA N. COHN
General Editors

# 1
# 'Animals Sell Papers': The Value of Animal Stories

The continued proliferation of animal images across every area of popular media is both undeniable and inescapable. Indeed, animal narratives are widely dispersed throughout our daily interactions with popular media forms and have become established as well-recognized and easily consumable genres of entertainment, news and advertising. Vast numbers of animal videos, often tagged as 'cute', 'funny' or 'baby', as well as 'animal attack' clips populate social networking web sites. That so many of these animal videos 'go viral' and attract millions of online views suggests that our appetite for particular types of animal imagery is voracious. Pet programmes, wildlife films, natural history documentaries and specialist channels such as National Geographic and Discovery testify to the ongoing attraction of animal-based narratives in television whilst a snapshot of the box office figures, in mainstream cinema, for the first decade of the twenty-first century gives an indication of the popularity of animal stories, with at least one animal film appearing in the ten highest grossing films each year from 2001 to 2009.[1] Whilst box office returns reflect the enduring popularity of animal narratives, they also make apparent the economic dimension of such representations: animal stories are profitable. In short, animal narratives are economically significant for popular media industries, which, in turn, play an essential role in shaping the limits and norms of public discourses on animals and animal issues and so constitute a key source of information, definitions and images. From an industrial-economic perspective, the popular construction of animal imagery and narratives is part of, and intrinsically connected in multiple and diverse ways to, a wider set of processes by which animals are commodified and the norms of human–animal relations established and sustained. This book examines some of these discursive interconnections.

## Newsworthy animals

With regard to the worth of animal stories in news media, Bernard Rollin (2008) makes a succinct yet salient observation when he writes, 'Animals sell papers' (p. xvi). Indeed, animal stories account for a substantial proportion of soft news, where human interest stories about baby animals, albino animals, the bond between humans and animals or some entertaining animal behaviours are important elements in the news mix. Animal stories act as an antidote to hard news, which typically focuses on crime, politics, science, economics and war. Soft news about animals is designed to have emotional appeal, to arouse our sympathies, curiosity or fascination. In fact, news of this type has been so common that, in the UK, the title of a 1990s television series, *Drop The Dead Donkey*, parodied the use of animal stories as news filler. In this regard, Steve Baker (2001) makes a valuable point when he argues that the treatment of animals within popular culture has all too often been derisory, with the effect that animals have been trivialized, constructed as ridiculous or pathetic or as simple objects of entertainment. He writes, 'The animal is the sign of all that is taken not-very-seriously in contemporary culture; the sign of that which doesn't really matter. The animal may be other things beside this, but this is certainly one of its most frequent roles in representation' (Baker, 2001, p. 174).

It serves to consider some examples of soft news stories about animals here in light of Baker's comments.

In January 1998 the international media descended on Wiltshire in the UK to cover the story of two pigs, named Butch and Sundance by the press, that had escaped from an abattoir, swum across the River Avon and escaped into the countryside. Police and RSPCA officers were involved in the hunt and the five-month-old pigs were eventually caught a week after their escape. In the face of mounting public pressure for the pigs to be spared, press reports confirmed that the owner had agreed that they would not be slaughtered. The interest in the 'Tamworth Two', as the pigs were labelled, was so great that the BBC made a film about the incident entitled *The Legend of the Tamworth Two* and other companies exploited the commercial opportunities that the story presented. For instance, that year Butch and Sundance soft toys were produced for children and a mustard company placed print advertisements in the UK press with an image of a cartoon pig leaning over a fence with a speech bubble inside which was written, 'Butch, Sundance. It's worth it! Meet you at my place in the Algarve for a Barbeque' (Colman's Mustard advertisement, January 1998).

In April 2001 the front page of the *Daily Mirror* newspaper celebrated the reprieve of a 13-day-old calf from slaughter. The story came in the midst of the UK foot-and-mouth crisis and the cull of more than four million animals ordered by the UK government. The white calf, named Phoenix, was referred to as 'the symbol of hope for everyone who has suffered during this crisis' (*Daily Mirror*, 26 April 2001, p. 1). A photograph of the calf accompanied the article, which noted that 'her plight has touched the heart of this animal-loving nation already sickened by the sight of piles of slaughtered and burning carcasses' (p. 1). The *Daily Mirror* printed a quote from the Ministry of Agriculture, which, it claimed, had referred to the public outcry over Phoenix's impending death as 'hideous sentimentality' (p. 1). The paper mounted a public campaign to save the calf and reported that, as a result of the public response, the Prime Minister had personally ordered Phoenix's reprieve.

The story of Larry, a lamb born in an abattoir, caught the attention of the press in March 2006. Beneath the headline 'Saved from the chop' one paper described how none of the ten operatives at the facility had been prepared to slaughter the newborn lamb and her mother, leading the owners of the abattoir to appeal to the Department for Environment and Rural Affairs (Defra) to allow both animals to be removed to a nearby farm (*Daily Mirror*, 17 March 2006, p. 17). Although regulations governing slaughter in the UK state that any animal entering an abattoir must be killed, Defra granted the appeal and the ewe and lamb were sent to live on a farm in West Yorkshire. The owner of the slaughter facility was quoted saying, 'None of the lads would kill it – 10 lads all said no. No one was going to kill 'owt like that. Both the lamb and the ewe are fit and healthy and everything has a right to live' (*Daily Mirror*, 17 March 2006, p. 17).

In August 2007 the UK news media carried the story of 'Squeaky the piglet' who had been born in the back of a transport lorry on its way to a slaughterhouse in Derbyshire. The *Daily Mirror* report described how Squeaky had fallen from the animal transporter into approaching traffic. The piglet had been saved by a passing motorist and taken to an RSPCA centre where the paper reported that 'centre staff are hoping to find her a permanent home [...] "Pigs make great pets. They're as clever as dogs and can be housetrained"' (*Daily Mirror*, 11 August 2007, p. 3).

In December 2009 a stretch of motorway was closed for ten hours following an accident in which an animal transporter carrying pigs to a slaughterhouse overturned. Most of the 82 adult pigs had been trapped in the overturned wreckage but 12 managed to escape onto the carriageway. Police, fire-fighters and vets attended the accident where five pigs were euthanized because of their injuries. The 12 escaped pigs were caught and along with the remaining 65 that had been trapped in the lorry continued on to their destination and were slaughtered the same day (*Daily Mirror*, 31 December 2009, p. 31).

These five media reports of farmed animals who escaped en route to slaughter were all soft news stories and they illustrate the ambivalence which characterizes contemporary human–animal relationships. Such stories raise the question why, when the slaughter of many millions of animals for the global food industries continues unabated, should some newsworthy animals be classified as morally considerable and allowed to live? The answer to this question is, of course, far from simple. One response would have it that it is not the task of soft news stories to engage with questions of animal ethics. From an industry perspective this may well be true enough, but the point remains that Larry, Squeaky, Sundance, Butch and Phoenix were each constructed by news articles in ways designed to elicit public sympathy. In three cases the media coverage of the 'escapes' led to reprieves from slaughter, whilst the 12 unnamed pig escapees from the animal transporter in 2009 did not merit the same sympathetic media treatment. What these stories and their outcomes suggest is that there is an important connection between the aesthetic, ethical and economic dimensions of media representations of animals.

In the cases of the reprieved animals, the media coverage of their escapes shared common reference points. Each animal was young, they were individuated and named, and the reports of their 'escapes' were structured by familiar narrative conventions and utilized intertextual references. Press coverage of 'Butch' and 'Sundance' framed the escape story as paralleling that of the 1969 film, *Butch Cassidy and the Sundance Kid*, whilst the 'Tamworth Two' designation worked as an ironic reference to the media convention of assigning nicknames to criminal groups and social miscreants. On the day that the second pig was caught, the *Daily Mirror* newspaper offered another retelling of the escape story, publishing a short fictional interpretation written by Dick King-Smith, the author of *The Sheep-Pig*, and accompanied by an image of the character 'Babe' from the film adaptation of Smith's book. In the absence of available photographs of the actual animals, the media coverage overcoded the two Tamworth pigs as 'Babe-like', with a multiplicity of cultural references that contextualized their actions and assigned them with meanings of outlaw-like agency.

In the cases of Larry, Squeaky and Phoenix, the photographic images of the animals each demonstrated similar conventions of representation.

*Figure 1.1*   Phoenix the calf. Image courtesy of Richard Austin

The images covered more than half the available page space and each animal was photographed front-on, looking straight into the camera. Presented in this way the animals' gaze directly addressed the viewer, and the image was cropped so that only minimal background information was visible, thereby removing them from any specific context. The image of Phoenix in particular (Figure 1.1) was so striking that one journalist referred to it as 'iconic', but it is also worth noting that the photographer responsible for taking the picture, Richard Austin, remarked, 'if Phoenix had been a dark calf, the image just wouldn't have had the same impact' (Austin in Browne, 2001). In terms of the intertextual framing devices used, the article on 'Larry the lamb' recalled the children's character from the BBC series *Toytown*, and an additional picture of Larry was captioned 'Free wooly', a play on the film title *Free Willy* and yet another reference to an animal escape narrative. The report on Squeaky used the children's nursery rhyme *This Little Piggy* to frame the narrative of the pig's escape, and the 'Phoenix From the Ashes' headlines drew on potent mythological metaphors. These stand in contrast to the image used for the 2009 pig story which depicted the animals in context. A wide shot of the scene showed the overturned animal transporter in the background and a group of six pigs in the left side of the frame, whilst emergency vehicles and personnel made up the majority of the visual information. A further and much smaller inset picture showed three pigs being moved by two unidentified people along an embankment. The article ended with a reference to the case of Sundance and Butch in 1998 and cited a fact about the largest recorded weight for a pig. Other than these, the only other cultural references framed the pigs as food, and the article appeared under the headline 'Traffic Ham: Porkers Close Motorway after Lorry Crash' (*Daily Mirror*, 31 December 2009, p. 31).

The point of highlighting the modes of presentation is to note that the meanings attributed to each of the individuated and named animals called on a rich and complex corpus of cultural reference points to affirm their moral worth. Dramatic yet familiar narratives were employed to frame events and were coupled with a mode of visual presentation that connected the audience's gaze with that of the subject. In contrast to this, the photograph of the pigs who were slaughtered maintained a visual distance between the audience and the animal subjects, and the pigs were coded by the headline as 'food'. Whilst it is straightforward enough to point out how animals can be made to appeal to readers, through a combination of conventions of representation and intertextual references, the question remains as to why certain animals are favoured in this way. Certainly, much of the reason has to do with the editorial process. The popular press tends towards sensationalistic reporting, and stories are designed to be entertaining and to appeal to the reader. Animal stories fill up column inches on slow news days and during the summer period in 'silly season', a time when even the serious broadsheet newspapers traditionally indulge in frivolous reporting.[2] A life-or-death animal story can be used to mobilize public support, and if there is enough interest the story can run on over a period of days in follow-up articles. This was certainly the case with the stories about the 'Tamworth Two' and Phoenix the calf. If the animal does survive due to public and press intervention, the story has all the elements of a dramatic narrative: the innocent is saved at the eleventh hour and the public 'hero' is celebrated by the press for the act of kindness and compassion, thereby cementing a relationship between the paper and its readership. Animals are, in the context of tabloid reporting particularly, used as light relief or as characters in the reworking of familiar cultural narratives. They are apolitical and malleable in the sense that they can be made to conform to whatever anthropomorphic devices are used to frame the narrative, and, at the risk of sounding glib, they do not sue newspapers for misrepresentation. Animals are therefore easily constructed as characters in dramas, conflicts and romances. In the reports of the escapees described earlier, the animals were reduced to a series of humanized intertextual references. This process of reduction inevitably detaches animals from the classifications that define them as 'farmed' and therefore 'killable' and so avoids having to critique the industrial or economic discourses that sustain such categories.

The very fact that animal stories have been widely regarded by the media as soft news does indeed say much about the general way in which animals are perceived. Of course, not all news media representations trivialize animals. Public interest in conservation, animal welfare, animal rights, ethics and the environment has prompted the inclusion of animal stories that blur the line between soft and hard news in newspapers and on television.[3] Many such stories engage with issues about human–animal relations, and they are clearly important in that they question social practices (particularly in the mode of investigative journalism), inform public understanding and organize social meanings. Although popular media texts rarely present a direct challenge to the social order, they are nonetheless a crucial aspect of the cultural processes which set discursive limits on topics. As Brian McNair proposes, 'Journalists select aspects of the real world, then present them in a narrative form that allows them to be made sense of, but also prevents potentially disruptive readings of events being made by the audience' (McNair, 2009, p. 24). It is therefore unsurprising that the news stories about animal escapees did not challenge the ethical status quo on farming and animal slaughter. Even in the case of the Phoenix story, which prompted widespread public criticism of the government's decision to kill healthy animals under a contiguous culling policy during the foot-and-mouth crisis, the argument proffered by the Ministry – that the animals were going to be slaughtered anyway – demonstrated the degree to which practices of killing animals are normalized. The image of Phoenix did play a key role in mobilizing public attitudes against contiguous culling,[4] but the debate did not extend to a wider questioning of the ethics of animal slaughter in livestock farming, and in this way the moral–economic limits of the discourse of animal slaughter were never breached. To illustrate the point further, one journalist described the government response to public concerns in the following way: 'A Maff spokesman denounced the "hideous sentimentality". They had a point: after all, most of the animals being culled had been bred for slaughter' (Browne, 2001).

## News consumption

News is a commodity and journalism an industry that operates across print, broadcast and online platforms and which, through sales, advertising, subscription and syndication, generates billions in revenues (McNair, 2009, p. 2). News media is therefore shaped by advertising and audience demands as well as by editorial policies. Audiences are often cynical, media savvy and sceptical about news and, for that matter, other forms of commercial media. Inasmuch as journalism may attempt to regulate the polysemic nature of the news text, the construction of meaning is not a one-way street nor is the audience a homogenous mass. Instead, audiences are composed of active consumers who are able to negotiate the meanings of news and other media texts, and although far from being cultural dupes who passively absorb media messages that reproduce a dominant ideology, it is nonetheless apparent that popular media do, in multiple and diverse ways, shape public attitudes and beliefs about animals.

Whether audiences are consuming soft news, hard news or fictional texts, representations of animals are never neutral, and the cultural discourses that are constructed connect in direct ways with the realities of animal lives. Steve Baker reminds us of this fact when he writes, 'To emphasize questions of representation is not therefore to deny any particular animal's "reality," in the sense of that animal's actual experience or circumstances. Instead, the point is to emphasize that representations have a bearing on shaping that "reality," and that the "reality" can be addressed only through the representations' (Baker, 2001, p. xvii). Nigel Rothfels also elaborates on the significance of animal representations when he remarks that 'the perennial stories of whales, elephants, pandas, and other charismatic species, make clear that the stakes in representing animals can be very high. Who controls that representation and to what ends it will be used will be of profound importance in coming years [...]' (Rothfels, 2002, p. xi).

Cultural representations inform and shape public perceptions of animals, and this calls attention to the politics of representation, a theme that has occupied decades of media critique within the humanities.

In the main, the scholarly focus on representation has dealt with the thorny question of the relationship between representation and reality wherein that which is represented retains some connection to a referent in reality and acquires a set of meanings that are also inscribed across other representations. Representation has been conceived of as 'standing in for' something in reality and as part of a constitutive process of cultural meaning making. In this sense, media representations do not reflect the reality of animal lives but reconstruct animals within a set of discursive boundaries that delimit what can be said, visually and aurally, about them. For this reason, media discourses can shape public understanding of animals in ways that appear to be natural and normal. Yet, inasmuch as animals are discursively constituted as 'animal' within systems of production and through webs of relations, animals are embodied material beings with interests. What is at stake then is that there is a relationship between the discursive construction of animals and the material reality of animal's lives. For instance, in the 1920s the incredible success of the Rin Tin Tin films led to an extraordinary rise in the number of German Shepherds who were bought (and in many cases discarded) as pets. In fact, in 1926, at the height of Rin Tin Tin's fame, one in every three dogs registered with the American Kennel Club was a German Shepherd.[5] In terms of constructing public perceptions of animals, the repeated use of chimpanzees in films, television and advertising stands out for having fostered a popular misconception that chimps are plentiful and not, as is the case, endangered. And the media discourse on dangerous dogs, coupled with representations of 'hellhounds' in popular fictions, has led to the demonization of some breeds, including German Shepherds, Rottweilers, Dobermanns and, latterly, Pit Bull Terriers.

Discourses represent historically situated knowledge about a particular topic and define and reproduce animals as objects of that knowledge. The material existence of animals is therefore constituted as meaningful within discourses that govern what can be said about them, and this is linked directly to their treatment. For this reason, the representation of animals as morally considerable individuals can only appear as a meaningful construct within a definite historically situated discursive formation and through particular institutional apparatuses. In other words, where animals are not discursively constructed as having any moral worth, they are treated accordingly as property, objects, machines and things. However, the media industries involved in the circulation of these discourses are not, Stuart Hall points out, 'closed systems'. He writes: 'They draw topics, treatments, agendas, events, personnel, images of the audience, "definitions of the situation" from other sources and other discursive formations within the wider socio-cultural and political structure of which they are a differentiated part' (Hall, 2005, p. 119). In this respect it is vital that representations of animals are neither dismissed as *merely* human metaphors with little or no connection to the realities of animals' lives nor the media industries demonized for their role in the construction of discourses about animals. Instead we need to attend to the various relations between the economics of (media) production, the aesthetics and conventions of representational practices, the norms of human–animal relations and the historically situated discourses that connect and contextualize them.

## Connecting systems of production

In many cases media institutions are not unaware of the wider impact that particular representations of animals might have, and there are examples of organizations which have taken some measure of responsibility for the production of animal narratives. For instance, in 1996 Buena Vista released the Disney film *101 Dalmatians*, a live-action remake of the 1961 animated feature. Animal advocacy groups and Dalmatian breeders warned that the film would create a fad for the dogs, many of which they argued would end up in rescue shelters. Buena Vista and Disney responded to these concerns by creating brochures about responsible pet ownership, which were made available at Disney theme parks. The company also included a statement in the end credits of the film which said that no Dalmatians had been bred for the film and that all the puppies had been placed in suitable homes when filming had concluded. Despite taking these measures, a Disney executive still refuted claims that the film would make the dogs more popular and said that 'There can be no way to prove, though, that the film will create a demand for the dog. Dalmatians are a popular dog and the demand already is there. We believe that people seeing the movie will be more likely to go out and buy Dalmatian merchandize instead of the dog' (*Lodi News-Sentinel*, 13 November 1996, p. 2). The film made over $136 million at the domestic box office and was the sixth highest grossing film released in 1996. In 1997, newspapers reported that Dalmatian rescues across the US were inundated with unwanted dogs, with some centres seeing more than double the number surrendered than in previous years. The film represented Dalmatians as cute fun-loving family dogs, but experts pointed out that the breed was well-known for being strong-minded, destructive and requiring high levels of exercise.

A shelter in Los Angeles reported that one family had brought in a dog and 'complained it was nothing like the dog in the movie' (Associated Press, 1997b , p. 7B).

In the case of *101 Dalmatians*, there was an acknowledgement of responsibility for the idealized construction of the breed by the film studio and an attempt to counter the fictional representation with a factual statement framed by a discourse of pet welfare. Nonetheless, the circulation of the representation did shape public perceptions of the breed at some level and a minority acted on those and purchased Dalmatians as pets. Taking a wider view of this particular case it is clear that there were other factors at play. The Disney discourse that constructed Dalmatians as ideal pets operated within a culture of pet-keeping and a discourse in which dogs and other animals are constructed as disposable. A network of breeders and an institution such as the American Kennel Club legitimize the practices of dog breeding as well as sustaining a discourse of 'breed' in which an ideal 'type' of dog is produced. This ideal type was then available to be fetishized by the film discourse and through the commodification of the breed as Dalmatian merchandize. If the film mobilized certain public attitudes about Dalmatians and created a demand for the dogs, then it is also the case that there was a wider cultural and institutional infrastructure of dog breeding and pet ownership in place that facilitated and met that demand. The point here is that there is a broader context of human–animal relations that operate in addition to, as well as through, the media discourse. And although there is a case to argue for an acknowledgement of responsibility for the production of media representations of animals, it is also the case that the relationship between media discourses and the material treatment of animals has to be considered in relation to extant human–animal relations.

## Selling animals

The comments by the Disney executive about Dalmatian merchandize draw attention to the widespread commodification of animals as marketable products. Moreover, the cultural and economic values of particular animals demonstrate trends wherein certain species or individual animals become marketable and popular. A brief example here serves to illustrate the point further: 1980 saw a surge of international interest in the film *Bedtime for Bonzo* (1951), a Hollywood comedy that had been made some 30 years earlier about a college professor who attempts to prove that environment is more influential than heredity by raising a chimpanzee as a human child. Directed by Frederick de Cordova, *Bedtime for Bonzo* was released in 1951 and featured the future US President Ronald Reagan, then a young actor, in the role of the professor of psychology playing alongside a chimpanzee, the eponymous Bonzo. Although reasonably successful at the box office the film had a lukewarm critical response and sank into obscurity for nearly three decades to be later catapulted to the status of a comedy classic when, in the run-up to the presidential election, public and media attention turned towards Reagan's earlier acting career in Hollywood. The pairing of Reagan and Bonzo was a source of humour and derision for political opponents and satirists eager to remind the voting public that a presidential candidate had appeared on-screen with an ape. Rental companies reported a rush of orders from political fund-raisers for *Bedtime for Bonzo*, which was described by one journalist as a frivolity 'in which Reagan plays second banana to a chimp' (Wolf, 1980, p. 46). By way of a response to his critics, Reagan used the film to illustrate his claims of personal integrity saying:

> You must have credibility...Now, you take my role in *Bedtime for Bonzo*. I was a scientist who raised a chimp as a child in my home. It was a huge money-maker, terrific. But then the studio decided to make a sequel called *Bonzo Goes to College*. I refused to play in it. It bombed. Who could believe a chimp could go to college and play on the football team? [It] lacked credibility (Reagan quoted in Kramer, 1980, p. 27).

After the inauguration, interest in the film did not wane and in 1981 the *Bedtime for Bonzo* movie poster was reported to be the most popular film artwork featuring Reagan.[6] The film's screenwriters, Ted Berkman and Raphael David Blau, had retained the merchandizing rights to 'Bonzo the Chimp' since 1951 and were able to capitalize on the continued public fascination with the film. In 1980 they signed marketing deals for 'Bonzo T-shirts, posters, bumper stickers, decals, suspenders, baseball caps, belt buckles, toy dolls and syndicated comic strips', and it was reported that negotiations were underway for a Bonzo the Chimp TV series (*New York Magazine*, 3 November 1980, p. 11). In November 1980 *New York Magazine* and the *Los Angeles Times* declared that Bonzo was 'going to be the hottest merchandising vehicle since Lassie or Bambi' (*New York Magazine*, 3 November 1980, p. 11).

The vast range of products featuring Dalmatians, Bonzo, Lassie, Bambi and a host of other commodified animal characters as well as other trends for dolphin, meerkat and big-cat imagery reflect the extent to which media representations operate within an economic framework. Animals generate billions in revenues as stars, monsters, comedians, companions, food and so forth. In many cases, however, animals have an economic worth which takes precedence over their moral worth. In 1947, *Life* magazine published a lengthy article about Jackie the MGM lion, which lampooned the notion of animal stars. A few lines from the article serve to give a sense of its humorous intent:

> Jackie is a sensational victim of capitalist exploitation. All other Hollywood profiteers pale by comparison with Jackie's managers who collect his entire pay. [...] Jackie is the subject of considerable discrimination. Social pressures keeps him from living in such luxurious movie settlements as Beverly Hills and Brentwood and he is confined to an otherwise pleasant den some 20 feet square at the World Jungle Compound. [...] The hours are long. In addition, while working, Jackie is kept hungry in order to keep him frisky (Jenson, 1947, pp. 19–22).

Although meant as a joke, the article's treatment of Jackie's movie star life nonetheless reflects the exploitative nature of certain aspects of human–animal relations.

## Popular media and animals

Media discourses are important in sustaining a range of constructions of animals that are connected, appropriated or co-opted by other systems of production and so play a role in the normalization of particular practices and relations. The chapters of this book take up this issue and attempt to grapple with some of the industrial–social–ethical configurations of media discourses on animals. With a few necessary excursions into earlier eras, the remaining chapters examine the role that popular media play in constructing, informing and reflecting on human–animal relations after 1945. The media under discussion include television, film, print, video games and advertising, and the chapters explore, in the main, animal experimentation, animal performance, human–wildlife encounters, farming, hunting, animal threats and meat consumption. These larger topics intersect with recurring themes of suffering, sentimentality, authenticity and identity, and discussion of these is woven through explorations of the cultural processes by which each is managed. Animal experimentation is approached in two ways. First, chapter 2 considers press involvement in the production of popular discourses on vivisection; chapter 5 later returns to the topic to examine Hollywood's integration of animal experimentation into feature film narratives and maps the routes by which a fictional representation relates to the real lives of chimpanzees. The construction of legitimate social identities has been central to the ongoing contest over the validity of animal experimentation since the late nineteenth century, and chapters 2 and 5 consider the role that gender has played, particularly through the feminization of sentiment, in determining social credibility. The conflict between media representations and authentic animal encounters occupies chapters 3 and 4 which examine wild animals, firstly as animal stars in the Hollywood films of the 1950s and then in wildlife films for television. Creation of an animal movie star relied on fabricating the illusion of an autonomous, talented, humanized individual who had transcended their animal state. Yet, as chapter 3 discusses, the animal star was not created by a movie appearance alone but instead by the larger industrial apparatus that included trainers, publicity, advertising and marketing, all of which were necessary to sustain the on-screen and off-screen illusion. Chapter 4 then looks at television wildlife films and the depiction of 'authentic' wild animal behaviours which shape audience expectations of human–animal encounters. An economy of human–animal relations frames the discussion of the relationships between the symbolic and material–commercial value of farmed animals in chapter 6. Systems of industrial production and media production coalesce in the advertising and promotion of farmed animal products such as eggs, milk and meat where animal suffering is managed or denied. Chapter 7 takes up the theme of animal suffering again, this time in relation to hunting discourses where representations of 'pleasure in killing' and 'clean kills' in television, film and video game texts are explored. Monstrous animals feature in cultural fictions and social reality, and chapter 8 examines the overlap between the two and the material consequences for those animals that have been constructed as monstrous. With a focus on the cultural rules that regulate the consumption of animal flesh, chapter 9 concludes with a consideration of films that, in some sense, re-imagine or reflect on human–animal relations.

# 2
# Media and Animal Debates: Welfare, Rights, 'Animal Lovers' and Terrorists

Throughout the late nineteenth century, the mass media in Britain and America played a key role in defining and shaping the public discourse on vivisection. In Britain, newspapers reported cruelty cases, publicized upcoming gatherings and provided transcripts of speeches given at antivivisection meetings, whilst letters to newspaper editors gave certain commentators opportunities to reach a wide readership. In America, activists ensured that the details of cruelty cases made their way into the city newspapers, and some prominent members of humane societies used the press to gain public attention, sometimes by staging direct action to ensure media coverage. In New York, for instance, Henry Bergh, founder of the ASPCA, caused traffic jams on the streets, which brought areas of the city to a standstill, exploits designed specifically, he argued, to 'invoke the potent influence of the press' (Beers, 2006, p.62). Bergh believed that activists should actively seek out media attention through provocative direct action, a tenet which he himself followed by bringing prosecutions that sometimes had little hope of succeeding in the courts but were widely reported by the press of the time.[1] In Britain, Stephen Coleridge's denunciation of William Bayliss, which led to the 1903 'Brown Dog' libel hearing, was able to garner a high degree of publicity and was a chance for Coleridge to publicly criticize the 1876 Act, with little expectation that he would win the case in the courtroom (Lansbury, 1985, p.10). In short, for some animal advocates the losses in the courts were of little significance compared with the gains in media coverage and consequent marshalling of public support.

Press involvement in the antivivisection debates occurred as British newspapers moved into a free-market phase after 1860. This followed the repeal of stamp duty in 1855, legislation that had levied a tax on newspapers in efforts to prohibit the mass circulation of radical views. The effect of lifting the stamp duty tax was an increase in the numbers of newspapers and greater competition between titles, which then differentiated themselves in the marketplace by claiming specific political allegiances, interests and biases. Although they were free from the state censorship that had been imposed by stamp duty, newspapers now relied on advertising revenue. This did not, however, transform the press into an independent entity or 'fourth estate'. As Curran and Seaton (2003) argue, 'On the contrary, the development of modern political parties from the 1860s onward encouraged a closer interpenetration of party politics and commercial journalism' (p.6). Newspapers became central to the continuance and shaping of the debates on vivisection as different factions of the press aligned themselves with competing pro- or antivivisection interests represented by members of the political parties and social reformist movements of the time. In Britain the working class and liberal press asserted their sympathies with the antivivisection movement, and in America too various influential magazines and newspapers, which included *Vogue*, the *New York Herald*, *Life* and the *Nation*, supported antivivisection campaigns and regularly published articles and editorials on the subject.[2] The development of professional standards of news reporting was a driving force behind the establishment of many American newspapers in the latter part of the nineteenth century, and this occurred at a time when the antivivisection movement began to gain momentum. Papers had expressed formal political affiliations that appealed to a particular readership, but as the nineteenth century drew to a close there was a loosening of these allegiances in the drive for journalistic objectivity. In addition to the press, popular culture in a broader sense also played a part in mobilizing antivivisection feeling. For instance, animal narratives were prevalent within late nineteenth-century literature, arts and popular science; and alongside the popularization of pet-keeping, stories of dogs involved in live dissections that were dispersed through various newspapers and magazines met with public outrage. Dogs had a privileged position in late Victorian society, and the public clamour that arose over newspaper accounts of dogs licking the vivisectionist's hand revealed that there was little support for the use of canines for experimental purposes. In America, one of the most controversial issues that managed to rally widespread public support was that of dogs being seized or given up by shelters to laboratories for experimental purposes.

By the 1940s, opposition to animal experimentation had lost much of its press support as science defended its use of animal research with examples of medical advances, such as the development of new sulfa drugs and a treatment for diabetes.[3] Newspapers were keen to report on the new medical breakthroughs which in many cases mentioned the role of animal experimentation, and as a consequence the popular media interest in antivivisection rapidly diminished. The antivivisection movement also faced internal problems, as the concessions given to animal welfare were considered inadequate victories by many antivivisection supporters who sought an outright ban. Differences of opinion on the key objectives of the movement divided support and eventually fragmented its power in America and Britain. The women's movement, which had kept interest in the antivivisection debate buoyant, achieved the vote and lost much of its collective reformist momentum; and in the face of medical advances declared to be overwhelmingly beneficial to human welfare, the opposition to medical science, previously constructed as oppressive and brutal towards women, also dwindled. State funding for experimental research in Britain and America and the introduction of new legislation that sanctioned mandatory animal testing dealt a major and decisive blow to the restitution of the antivivisection movement after the war. In fact, experimental research and animal testing were considered fundamental to post-war economic and social restructuring, and the rebuilding of the post-war West was reliant on the sustained exploitation of animals.

Antivivisection debates did not disappear from newspapers, but there was a shift in popular engagement with the topic and a clear lessening of support when compared with coverage at the end of the nineteenth and beginning of the twentieth centuries. There were certain events that aroused sporadic press and public interest, such as the use of goats to test Air Raid Precautions (ARP) bomb shelters in the UK in 1939, and the Bikini Atoll nuclear testing in which 4,900 animals were used by American scientists in 1946 to record the effects of A-bomb blasts. In the UK, during the 1950s, reports about dogs and cats being stolen and sold to laboratories made their way into papers and vivisection reappeared in the news, albeit as a highly controversial topic, by the 1960s. The *Daily Mirror* with a readership of 14,000,000 (discussed later in this chapter) positioned itself as the newspaper for a nation of animal lovers and established the National Pets Club in 1957, which could count 345,000 members by 1969 and was influential in steering public opinion on the issue of vivisection in the UK. By the 1970s, leading proponents of the animal rights movement wanted to distance themselves from the identity of 'animal lover', which many regarded as a legacy of overly sentimental nineteenth-century welfare discourses. In *Animal Liberation*, a seminal text of the animal protection movement, Peter Singer wrote: 'The portrayal of those who protest against cruelty to animals as senti-mental, emotional "animal-lovers" has had the effect of excluding the entire issue of our treatment of nonhumans from serious political and moral discussion' (Singer, [1975] 1995, p. xi). Sentimentality and emo-tion were constructed in opposition to a rational reasoned discourse on animal ethics, and the 'animal lover' became a marginalized identity within late twentieth-century animal politics.

'Animal lover' remained part of the popular discourse on animal wel-fare in Britain, used by the press as shorthand to signal a normalized national moral orthodoxy: 'Britain is a nation of animal lovers'. In con-trast to the representations of animal lovers, animal activists received mixed press, with sympathetic reporting on early forms of direct action which was soon replaced by stereotypes and moral panics about deviant activities in the 1980s and labelled as terrorist practices after 9/11. In press reports and in films such as *Twelve Monkeys*, *28 Days Later*, *Lethal Dose* and *Rats*, and episodes of television series that include *Murder She Wrote* ('A Nest of Vipers', 1994), *Silent Witness* ('Schism', 1996), *Bones* ('The Tough Man in the Tender Chicken', 2009), *The Inspector Lynley Mysteries* ('Playing for the Ashes, 2003), *CSI* ('Loco Motives', 2006) and *Ashes to Ashes* (episode 3, 2009), antivivisection supporters have been depicted as dangerous, either in the sense of being intentionally villainous or by dint of being misinformed, and their activities are represented as being vio-lent or even potentially devastating to humanity. It is clear that popular media have had a key role in producing and sustaining particular social identities that have, in turn, become central to the political and public credibility of animal issues. This chapter attends to three aspects of the news media discourse on vivisection in America and Britain: the roles played by the *New York Times* and the *Daily Mirror* in debates on vivisec-tion and the construction of a gendered discourse of sentimentality.

## The *New York Times* and the ASPCA

As historical accounts of animal experimentation have made apparent, vivisection practices were not always hidden away from the public view. For instance, in his essay 'Vivisection in America' published in 1894, Albert Leffingwell wrote:

> Up to fifteen or twenty years ago, when agitation against cruelty had just begun, it was the custom not only to show results of experiments

but to perform even the most excruciating operations on living animals before a class-room of students, as aids to memory. There was no special secrecy about them; anyone able to find his way to the lecture-room could observe everything. If there were indefensible cruelties, they were at any rate as unconcealed and as openly done as in Paris to-day. Now, all this is changed. Experimentation has vastly increased; but it exists largely in comparative secrecy, behind locked doors, guarded by sentinels (Leffingwell in Salt, 1894, p.140).

From being practices routinely performed in public for educational and scientific demonstration purposes, experimental research on live animals in America retreated away from the public gaze as concerns about the pervasive nature of cruelty within society focused attention on a constellation of welfare issues during the nineteenth century. Some newspapers gave support to the welfare movement but took a more measured position on the subject of vivisection: The *New York Times* was one such publication and significant in that it supported the establishment of the ASPCA, the first humane society in North America. The paper, originally named the *Daily Times*, was established in 1851 by Henry Jarvis Raymond, a supporter of the radical anti-slavery wing of the Whig Party. Before the paper had gone into circulation there were criticisms that it would promote radical views. The first editorial answered its critics and claimed that the paper's position was somewhere between Conservatism and Radicalism saying, 'We do not believe that *everything* in Society is either exactly right, or exactly wrong; – what is good we desire to preserve and improve; – what is evil, to exterminate, or reform' (*Daily Times*, 18 September 1851, p.1).

In 1866 the *Daily Times*, now renamed *New York Times*, offered its support for the bill that legally incorporated the New York-based American Society for the Prevention of Cruelty to Animals (ASPCA), the first humane society in North America, and which gave the Society powers to enforce anticruelty laws. The paper estimated that the number of horses that were worked until close to death and then left to die in the streets numbered between ten and twenty per day in the city of New York, and it fully endorsed the formal establishment of an organization that was empowered to deal with the 'extent and diabolical character of the cruelty' (*New York Times*, 11 March 1866, p.4). In May of the same year the paper reported on the first annual meeting of the ASPCA, where it noted that the Committee was composed of some of the most prominent members of New York society. The paper was particularly keen to acknowledge the Society's decision to give female patrons the right to vote (*New York Times*, 22 May 1866, p.8). There was encouragement for the Society's work against animal cruelty, and editorial comments urged the ASPCA to continue with its mission despite facing hostility from city judges, who were initially unwilling to find in the Society's favour and would debate their interpretation of the law before dismissing cruelty cases.[4] Led by its founder, Henry Bergh, whose letters to the editors of all the New York papers regularly found their way into print, the ASPCA did eventually get its first successful prosecution for animal cruelty in 1866, and by 1879 the ASPCA in New York had prosecuted some 6000 cases (Beers, 2006, p.61).[5]

The *New York Times* played a key role in the promotion of the ASPCA during this time. In an effort to rally support for their cause the paper published long descriptions of horses dying in the streets and recounted incidences where horses had been starved to death or worked to the point of collapse, as well as accounts of drivers whipping, beating and kicking horses in public view. Indeed it was the very public nature of cruelty towards horses which was witnessed by the city's residents on a daily basis that needed to be addressed, and the paper pointed out that it was imperative that the public back the ASPCA, which could only tackle cruelty if 'public sentiment indorses the summary and signal punishment of offenders' (*New York Times*, 3 February 1867, p.4). At the request of Henry Bergh in 1867 the paper added its support to the Society's proposals to bolster the 1866 anticruelty legislation saying, 'The measures thus far put in operation at the instance of Mr Bergh's Society have been of most manifest advantage in the prevention and the punishment of cruelty to animals' (*New York Times*, 5 February 1867, p.4). However, much more was needed to be done, the paper argued, by the public and the Legislature.

The legislative changes proposed by Bergh brought criticism from the medical community, which took issue with the ASPCA's newfound power and felt impelled to make a case against Bergh particularly. Their concerns were that any strengthening of anticruelty legislation would impact directly on vivisection activities, and Bergh was accused by the Medical Society of the State of New York, in a letter to the *Times*, of 'the most extravagant misrepresentations, calculated to mislead the members of the Legislature and to injure in a serious manner the interests of medical science and the cause of medical education' (*New York Times*, 24 February 1867, p.5). Bergh's response to the accusations was printed in the *New York Times* in full; however, whilst the paper had been willing to support action to improve the welfare of animals, particularly horses, in the city it began to part company with Bergh on the subject of vivisection.

This is not to say that the *New York Times* endorsed vivisection. Indeed, the topic was used to illustrate national differences, and the paper was, similar to British newspapers, keen to make contrasts between humane American scientists and the inhumanity of continental vivisectionists. Discussing an Italian vivisectionist, for instance, the paper opined in 1875:

> [...] vivisection is often practised very unnecessarily, with no results and with not even the possibility of any results. Animals are tortured for the sake of illustrating by experiment facts which have been known and proved for a long time. They are tortured recklessly, and in a hap-hazard kind of way, for the sake of some impossible speculation. And this is done in the name of science by self-styled physiologists (*New York Times*, 30 April 1875, p.6).

Although it declared vivisection 'revolting' and 'dreadful', the paper supported such practices when undertaken by qualified expert American physicians who, the *New York Times* argued, worked in the interests of humanity. Although supportive of legislative change to regulate vivisection, the *New York Times* advanced a discourse that favoured vivisection practices as long as they were undertaken by credible authorities. The paper's position was made clear in the following way:

> We would not sneer at sentiment, even in regard to dogs and rabbits; but we must not allow even such a sentiment as compassion to stand in the way of the development and improvement of man, to diminish the rightful and the rational happiness of the human race. If to make men happy brutes must suffer and die, then so it must and so it should be (*New York Times*, 24 February 1875, p.4).

In 1885 the paper restated its position in response to an article in the British newspaper, *The Times*, saying that whilst it was in favour of prohibiting vivisection for the purposes of illustrating already known scientific facts, it was not opposed to 'true experimentation' that would further science and contribute to the alleviation of human suffering. Highly critical of Henry Bergh's condemnation of an operation on a sheep in Britain, which he had described as 'an abominable cruelty', the paper argued that Bergh 'labours under "a perversion of the sense of humanity"' (*New York Times*, 17 March 1885, p.4). Unable to endorse Bergh's demands for legislation to prohibit experimentation on animals, the paper suggested that people who supported antivivisection must suffer some form of misanthropy that would make them care more for the 'lower animals' than for 'their own species' (*New York Times*, 17 March 1885, p.4).

## Legislation in Britain

In some European countries, public vivisections continued to be undertaken well into the late nineteenth century and, as already mentioned, resulted in the experimental practices of many Italian, German and French vivisectionists being widely criticized by the American and British press as well as scientists and social reformers. Commenting on the treatment of live animals at the hands of European scientists, Leffingwell wrote that it was 'torture' and 'an abuse of experimental science' (Leffingwell in Salt, 1894, p.142). One French physiologist in particular, François Magendie, was condemned by the press, the public and the scientific community alike for the brutality of the dissections he performed on animals without anaesthesia. Magendie's experiments, and particularly those involving dogs, were cited as examples of excessive cruelty by the press and supporters of the antivivisection movement, and this criticism became crucial to the mobilization of public support against live dissections in British experimental research.[6]

However, despite the outrage over continental practices in the latter half of the nineteenth century, vivisectionists in Britain regularly experimented on dogs and cats. Such activities were difficult for the public to reconcile alongside the growth of pet-keeping, the cultural dominance of sentiment and the social significance of compassion towards animals as a marker of class and humanity. By the late 1830s animal welfare groups, particularly the Society for the Prevention of Cruelty to Animals (SPCA), had become popular with the middle and upper classes, and vivisection was one of the key issues of concern for welfare campaigners and supporters. With mounting pressure from the public, a Royal Commission on Vivisection was established, the findings of which resulted in the 1876 Cruelty to Animals Act, legislation that introduced a licensing and inspection system to regulate animal experimentation. The Act aimed to reassure the public that Government inspectors policed vivisection practices and that the experimental subjects were anaesthetized and therefore felt little or no pain. The legislation did not satisfy all campaigners, and it was argued by Stephen Coleridge, in his capacity as Secretary of the National Anti-Vivisection Society, in a letter to the editor of the *Daily News* that 'No one knows what actually takes place in laboratories, and it is part of our contention that until a Government inspector is present at every vivisection we can never know what sufferings are inflicted on the animals' (Coleridge, 1900, p.7). Coleridge's criticism of the implementation of the Act highlighted the issue of visibility: Vivisections were no longer open to public scrutiny and inspectors could not police each experiment.

Although regulatory measures had been put in place to license vivisection practices in Britain, the efficacy of the legislation was regularly called into question by Coleridge and other opponents. In 1903 the accounts of experiments performed by two physiologists, William Bayliss and Ernest Starling, on a brown terrier-type dog between December 1902 and February 1903 escalated the debate. Stephen Coleridge publicly condemned the failings of the 1876 Act following the publication of *The Shambles of Science: Extracts from the Diary of Two Students of Physiology* (Lind af Hageby & Schartau (*sic*), 1903), which described vivisections performed at University College.[7] In particular, he expressed outrage about multiple procedures performed over a period of two months on the dog without adequate anaesthesia; practices which, he argued, contravened the 1876 legislation.[8] Quoting from the observations of Lind-af-Hageby and Schartau, Stephen Coleridge denounced the practices of Bayliss and Starling in a speech to the National Anti-Vivisection Society. Coleridge's comments were subsequently published in national newspapers, which led Bayliss to bring a charge of libel against him. Coleridge was quoted in The *Daily Mirror* newspaper saying: 'If this is not torture, let Mr Bayliss and his friends [...] tell us, in heaven's name, what torture is?' (*Daily Mirror*, 14 November 1903, p.5).

The libel hearing was a bonanza for the press, although newspapers were divided in their support for Coleridge. At the hearing, the case for the prosecution hinged on undermining the credibility of Lind-af-Hageby and Schartau's observations as well as establishing both the legality and validity of the experiments. The jury found in favour of Bayliss, and the judge admonished Coleridge for accepting the women's description of events without further corroboration. The day after the verdict the *Daily Mirror* printed a front-page comment on the case stating that the outcome was 'a most courageous vindication of sanity as opposed to sentimentalism and ignorance' (*Daily Mirror*, 19 November 1903, p.1). It continued:

> The case for the defence rested almost entirely on the evidence of two Swedish ladies who, it was elicited, had never witnessed a vivisection before, but who gained admission to London demonstrating theatres

on the grounds that they were students interested in research. It transpired, however, in the course of their evidence, that they came with minds already prejudiced, and prepared to discover negligence and cruelty in the operator's methods (*Daily Mirror*, 19 November 1903, p.1).

The outcome of the case polarized the press, with the *Daily News*, the *Star*, the *Sun*, the *Standard* and *Tribune* declaring their support for Coleridge whilst the *Telegraph* and *Daily Mirror* sided against him (Lansbury, 1985). Despite the libel case finding in favour of Bayliss and undermining the credibility of Lind-af-Hageby and Schartau's account, the Brown Dog Affair did demonstrate that, even with the 1876 Act in place, legislative intervention did not fully placate the public. Their support for Coleridge was amply demonstrated when, after being fined £2000 by the court, Carol Lansbury notes, 'The *Daily News* immediately opened a subscription fund to pay Coleridge's damages, and the money was oversubscribed within the month' (Lansbury, 1985, p.12).

## Challenges for the antivivisection movement

In the US the case for legislation to protect experimental animal subjects faced substantial opposition from the medical community, particularly the Council on Defense of Medical Research formed in 1908, as well as from earlier coalitions between the American Physiological Society, the American Society of Naturalists, the American Society of Physicians and the American Society of Surgeons formed in the 1890s. The Council on Defense of Medical Research attempted to defuse public support for antivivisection by drawing up 'Guidelines for Laboratory Animal Care' and pledged to tackle issues such as anaesthesia and unsanitary kennelling, concerns that the campaigners and the press had used to rally public opinion. The Council's strategy was successful and, coupled with the Spanish–American War, World War I and the economic depression of the 1930s, public attention was directed away from the issue of vivisection at a time when antivivisection organizations experienced a significant drop in their membership.[9] A further blow was dealt to the antivivisection cause in 1937 when, following the sale of an untested medicine, Elixir Sulfanilamide, 107 fatalities resulted among the public from ethylene glycol toxicity (Lesch, 2006, p.178). The national press followed the story as the number of fatalities increased and published regular reports that updated the public on the rising death count. In the face of mounting public anxiety about the safety of drugs in the marketplace, Congress passed the Food Drug and Cosmetic Act of 1938 under which all pharmaceuticals had to undergo premarket safety testing on animals (Gad, 2006, p.3). The standardization of toxicity and potency testing led to the widespread adoption of the $LD_{50}$ test, a procedure developed in 1927 by a British pharmacologist, J.W. Trevan, by which various doses of substances are typically administered orally or by inhalation to groups of between 50 and 100 mice or rats until 50 per cent of the animals die, thereby establishing the lethal dose, and hence the name $LD_{50}$.[10] In addition to applying tighter regulation to pharmaceutical testing, the legislation also addressed public concerns about the safety of cosmetics after press reports about products that had been on general sale and which were claimed to have resulted in conditions such as ulcerated eyes and blindness (Rowan, 1984, p.217). One consequence of including cosmetics under this tightened regulatory control was that it produced a requirement to find new forms of testing which would provide the evidence of product safety now demanded by the 1938 Act. This resulted in the development of the Draize irritancy tests in 1944, procedures that used a scoring system to determine the degree of irritancy of a substance after 24 and 72 hours of being administered to the eyes or skin of groups of albino rabbits. This became the standard testing procedure employed throughout the contracted laboratories used by the cosmetics industries.[11]

The movement for regulation to protect animals used in experimentation lost significant ground in America by the 1940s; and in Britain too there was a discernible shift in public attitudes towards vivisection, which began at the end of the nineteenth century. As the scientific community emphasized the advantages of animal experimentation in aiding the expansion of medical understanding, emotion and sentiment towards animals began to be popularly constructed as opposed to human progress and scientific advancement; a point which the 1903 *Daily Mirror* comment made clear when it referred to antivivisection as being derived from 'sentimentalism and ignorance'. Although the Brown Dog Affair did rekindle the debate on vivisection, and whilst it was also acknowledged within the pro-vivisection discourse that animals suffered at the hands of the vivisectionist, the idea that the potential benefits to human knowledge and welfare outweighed the pain and suffering inflicted on animals gathered support from the public and the national press. As a result, although animals were granted some degree of moral worth by many pro-vivisectionists, it was proposed that human welfare had greater moral significance and that the acquisition of medical knowledge via animal experimentation was not only needed but was an entirely noble pursuit. Typical of this stance, a letter to the editor of the *Weekly Dispatch* in 1886 argued:

> The history of physiological research teaches us that almost all the great discoveries relating to the origin and manifestation of animal life are owing to experiments on the living subject. Humanity is one of the noblest attributes of an intelligent being. But when we consider that pain is minimised in order that the maximum amount of good may result therefrom, we argue that vivisection is beneficial. Brief pain in the individual confers happiness to the whole species [...]. If this subject is examined calmly and dispassionately, there is but one conclusion – viz., vivisection is needful if we would enlarge our scientific knowledge (Maxwell, 1886, p.9).

A similar line of reasoning was expressed in the conclusion to the *Daily Mirror* comment on the Coleridge libel case, which used the verdict as a platform to articulate the newspaper's support for, and the growing public faith in, vivisection as a means to greater human knowledge. The comment was also positioned as a vindication of the scientists who performed live dissections, who the paper argued were 'men who are conspicuous for kind heartedness and humanity':

> Vivisection, as we have said, is not a pleasant necessity, but that it is a necessity no one who has ever benefited by surgical or medical treatment should doubt. What mother would not save her child's life at the cost of a painless operation on a dog or cat? [...] The lower animals, who are our unwilling but valuable allies in research will be the last to suffer from the inculcation of that wider and truer humanity which is the lesson of all science (*Daily Mirror*, 19 November 1903, p.1).

Harriet Ritvo (1987) proposes that there were two determining factors for the shift in public attitudes towards vivisection in Britain: The 'extreme and rigid positions' adopted by antivivisectionists and 'proofs of the medical benefits of research on living animals [with] the discovery of the diphtheria antitoxin in 1894' (Ritvo, 1987, p.162). In short, the antivivisection movement became incompatible with new concerns about disease control that dominated late nineteenth-century society, and there was a resultant change in public feeling towards vivisectionists, who were recast by the press as 'noble scientists'. Within the popular media discourse, the identity of 'vivisectionist' was eschewed in favour of the 'professional scientist' and a corresponding change in popular feeling about the moral status of experimental animals. Characteristic of the support for the role of the professional scientist, one 1886 newspaper article opined: 'vivisection [...] ought to be in the hands of bona-fide professors of irreproachable character, whose objects are noble, whose principles are high, and who have approved by past deeds their devotion to the cause of humanity' (*Weekly Dispatch*, 6 June 1886, p.9). The antivivisection discourse was marginalized as 'anti-scientific' and criticized for holding misplaced sentimental attitudes towards animals; and although the movement had appeared to garner enough public support to succeed, Ritvo argues that 'by the early twentieth century antivivisection had become a fringe movement, appealing to an assortment of feminists, labour activists, vegetarians, spiritualists, and others who did not fit into the established order of society' (Ritvo, 1987, p.162). A factor that contributed to this marginalization was that 'sentimental' attitudes towards animals were conflated with emotion and irrationality, which were, in turn, constructed as feminized characteristics and considered irreconcilable with the rational pursuit and production of scientific knowledge.

## The feminization of sentiment

In Britain the relationship that was established between women and irrational sentiment towards animals emerged at a time when the independent women's movement had managed to gain ground and women became increasingly active in the spheres of both animal advocacy and suffrage. With key individuals such as Frances Power Cobbe having a well-publicized presence within both arenas, it was apparent that many women involved in support for political and economic reform were also active in campaigns against vivisection. This is not to suggest, however, that there was a straightforward relationship between the antivivisection movement and the women's movement. Although Cobbe did indeed argue that antivivisection was a female concern and despite the fact that the majority of executive posts within the movement were held by women, antivivisection was a social reform movement without specifically feminist objectives (Hamilton, 2004, p. xl). For these reasons, Susan Hamilton argues that 'Victorian feminism and anti-vivisection are not easily reconcilable protests' (Hamilton, 2004, p. xlii). Carol Lansbury also points out that there was a complex and sometime incongruous relationship between suffrage and antivivisection but argues that women closely identified with the suffering and pain of animals (Lansbury, 1985). Nicolaas Rupke also finds points of overlap between women's involvement with antivivisection and the campaigns against the Contagious Diseases Act and smallpox vaccination and argues that 'all three were campaigns against the increasing claims of science and medicine to the right to dictate morality and personal behaviour' (Rupke, 1990, p.274). Although it is problematic to assume that antivivisection and the various concerns of the women's movement were entirely compatible in their motivations or aims, the role of women in both was indicative of the newfound presence of a female voice within the public sphere. What is of interest to this discussion then is the extent to which the antivivisection debate was constructed by the media as a gendered issue whereby emotion and sentiment were configured in opposition to rational science.

Women's involvement in the vivisection debate was criticized when it was suggested in some periodicals that female opposition to animal experimentation was motivated by emotion, hysteria, sentimentalism or ignorance, all of which were opposed to the rational scientific acquisition of knowledge. For instance, following the introduction of the 1876 Act, the Editor of *Popular Science Review* wrote, 'a number of well-intentioned and equally uninformed old women have raised a banner with "cruelty to animals" inscribed upon it. This, of course, has been followed by an ignorant and withal a very noisy crowd [...]' (*Popular Science Review*, January 1876, p.398). Pointing towards the particular strategies employed by those who were opposed to vivisection, one commentator argued that they, 'appeal to the emotions [...]' and 'put themselves at once in opposition to that method by which science has won most of its triumphs; the method of experiment' (Wallace, 1892, p.246). The 'appeal to the emotions' made by the antivivisection movement met with the disapproval of the physician Sir William Gull, and in an article for *Nineteenth Century* he expressed his condemnation for a woman who had accused the French physiologist Claude Bernard of inventing a stove for the purpose of 'baking dogs alive'. Gull declared, 'there is in the language and statements of the opponents of vivisection an almost unbroken harmony of exaggeration' (Gull, 1882, p.1882). Critical of women's suffrage and their involvement in the antivivisection movement, a weekly London newspaper argued in 1884 that if women were allowed to participate in politics then matters such as vivisection would 'be governed by hysterical impulse or even amiable prejudice' (*Saturday Review of Politics, Literature, Science and Art*, 1884, p.800), and the *Pall Mall Gazette* censured, 'evils are likely to accrue to the common-sense and scientific interest of the age, if legislation is to be interfered with by sentimental feminine agitators' (Mitchell, 2004, p.244).

The association between female emotion and the criticisms of women for their role in the antivivisection movement was far from straightforward. Whilst Broomfield and Mitchell remark that 'supposedly driven by instinct and emotion, women's "virtue" – their ability to empathize and sympathize – was also their greatest weakness' (Broomfield & Mitchell, 1996, p.485), women such as Lind-af-Hageby and Schartau declined to be ruled by their feminine impulses and instead held in contempt those sentimental women 'who drowned themselves and their listeners in floods of tears when they spoke about the sufferings of animals under the vivisector's knife' (Lansbury, 1985). For other female activists the emotional response to animal suffering was welcomed as it set them apart from the 'cold rational materialism of science' which threatened to 'freeze human emotion and sensibility' (Cobbe cited in Groves, 2001, p.221). Consequently, it is important to recognize that the associations made between women and emotion did not reflect a disproportionate level of sentimentality in women as compared with men. Instead the relationship revealed the construction of a gendered discourse that attempted to normalize a specific nature for females and, in turn, legitimize particular roles for women in society. Accordingly, a discourse of feminized emotion was mobilized by both sides of the debate to argue from a position of empathy against the unfeeling and morally redundant practices of vivisection carried out by men and simultaneously also to bolster the opposing argument by positioning women's stance as irrational, sentimental and anti-scientific.

Women could and should, it was argued, control their emotional impulses. For instance, as women became established in nursing after the Crimean War, distinctions were drawn between the need for them to be 'tender-hearted' and the requirement for them to control unwanted emotions lest they lead to lapses in judgement. Empathy and sympathy could be accommodated within the female character but emotional control was something to be acquired through training, as the physician and vivisection supporter Sir Thomas Lauder Brunton contended when he wrote: 'The power of controlling one's emotions, of disregarding one's own feelings at the sight of suffering, and of thinking only of the relief which we can give, varies in different individuals, but it can be greatly increased by training' (Brunton, 1882, p.480). Brunton, like others, considered it possible for 'even delicate women' to disregard their feelings to ensure that '[t]hey are guided no longer by emotion, but by judgement' (p.480). The acquisition of judgement and the suppression of emotion could then be applied to the observation of vivisection and, in doing so, trained professionals – men and women alike – would, Brunton argued, 'subordinate their feelings to their judgement, and make them willing to purchase future good at the expense of pain' (p.480).

The feminization of sentimental attitudes towards animals was also present elsewhere, and it is significant that women played a key role in antivivisection movements in both France and America. For example, Kathleen Kete notes that women had a part to play in the early animal protection movement in France, where it was considered that sentiment was a specifically gendered attribute and women's concerns with the protection of the weak created 'a logical connection between women's interests and animal protection' (Kete, 1994, p.8). Sentiment, it was warned, should not be allowed to become irrational sentimentality, though until the 1860s women's role in animal protection in France was predominantly 'decorative, symbolic and marginal' (Kete, 1994, p.9). As in Britain, antivivisection connected with other social reform concerns, and from the late 1860s women took a more active role in the movement, with representatives from societies such as the Lingue populaire contre les abus de la vivisection directly confronting the vivisection practices of 'male science' (p.16). In America women played an influential role in the antivivisection movement, but in some quarters their activities were considered indicative of mental health problems (Buettinger, 1993). Craig Buettinger (1993) notes that 'American antivivisection was eastern, urban, and female, led by such women as Caroline E. White of the AAVS' (p.277). However, in America the 'irrational sentiment' of a predominantly female-led antivivisection movement was constructed as pathological, and charges of mental instability were levelled at those involved. Buettinger writes:

> In 1909, at a time of great controversy over the practice of vivisection, American neurologist Charles Loomis Dana proclaimed heightened concern for animals to be a form of mental illness, which he called "zoophilpsychosis." Advocates of animal experimentation immediately employed Dana's diagnosis in vivisection's defense, claiming that antivivisectionists were afflicted by this malady (Buettinger, 1993, p.277).

The charge of 'zoophilpsychosis' went further than other discourses in establishing a derogatory relationship between female emotion and antivivisection. In general, those who defended experimental practices argued that antivivisection campaigners had little or no knowledge of science, over-exaggerated the suffering caused or were plainly anti-scientific.[12] What is significant is that in Britain, America and parts of Europe the majority presence of women within the antivivisection movement was eventually assimilated into a dominant gendered discourse that aligned women with emotion, misplaced sentiment towards animals and anti-science attitudes.

## The *Daily Mirror*

In Britain, the topic of vivisection returned to the public sphere in the post-war period and demonstrated a shift from the gendered discourse of previous decades. The *Daily Mirror* newspaper played a key role in shaping popular ideas through the promotion of an ideology of human–animal relations that aligned pet ownership with the identity of 'animal lover', part of a larger discourse of national identity which claimed that Britain was a nation of animal lovers.[13] Pet ownership was on the rise in post-war Britain, and greater affluence led to a boom in the commercialization of pet-keeping. In 1957 the *Daily Mirror* founded the National Pets Club (NPC). The NPC articles appeared every two weeks and, as their popularity grew, part of the page was given over to advertising pet products. In the early years following its launch, the weekly pet column gave the newspaper a lucrative advertising space from which it could generate revenue from the expanding pet-product market. Apart from the commercial benefits, the *Daily Mirror* Pets Club was established with a key goal: 'to bind together the great British family of animal and bird lovers' (*Daily Mirror*, 4 November 1957, p.11). In constructing a specific identity for its readership, the paper pointed out that it had 14,000,000 readers and that 'most of them love animals' (p.11). Members were issued with badges, membership cards and given free advice on pet welfare, and they were also able to attend NPC pet shows. The paper promised that 'The aims of the club will be to protect all animals from unnecessary suffering, to create a closer link between pet owners and to provide a platform for an exchange of news and ideas about pets' (p.11). Each member was bound by a code of conduct which included helping sick, injured and lost animals, reporting cruelty and undertaking responsible pet-ownership practices. The overarching discourse that the Club promoted was thus one of a collective national identity that could be defined by its animal-related practices.

In 1958, National Pet Club members were warned that 'pet-pirates' were operating across Britain, taking unwanted dogs and cats from owners, which were then sold to research laboratories.[14] The paper was careful to avoid any criticism of vivisection and acknowledged that it was legal for animal traders to sell dogs and cats to laboratories, but the problem, it argued, was that the animals obtained by dealers were acquired under false pretences and people giving up their pets were not aware that they would end up in medical research facilities (*Daily Mirror*, 16 August 1958, p.7). In the nascent discourse on vivisection that would be developed later by the paper, 'pet-pirates' were cast as deviant underhanded individuals who were profiteering from the sale of innocent pets. However, animal dealers were not consistently referred to in these terms, though they figured in another animal-related scandal which received a great deal of publicity at around the same time: cat stealing. In this case, the dealers were regarded in news coverage as honourable people who were misled by thieves from whom they bought stolen cats in good faith, which were then sold to universities and research laboratories.[15]

In the same year there were reports about an outbreak of cat thefts in the south-east and that 'hundreds of Britain's pet cats' had been stolen over a three-week period, which began to focus public attention on vivisection.[16] When a further spate of cat thefts was reported in 1959, there was a small yet significant change to the discourse on pet theft from previous years. In the 1959 newspaper article, pet owners were warned that they should do all they could to guard against their cat falling into the hands of a cat thief and ending up in a laboratory. Taking precautions, the paper remarked, 'may help to save your pet from a painful death' (*Daily Mirror*, 25 April 1959, p.11). In previous articles there had been no mention of what a laboratory animal experienced in a research facility, but in this article the explicit reference to 'a painful death' began to change the dynamics of the debate. Yet another article in 1960 returned to the subject of pet-pirates and called on National Pet Club members, as animal lovers, to be active in the prevention of 'pet-pirating'. On this occasion the subheadline read: ' "Good Home" adverts can mean DEATH to animals ...'(*Daily Mirror*, 16 July 1960, p.9, emphasis in original). The paper expressed its support for the work of the RSPCA and the British Union for the Abolition of Vivisection (BUAV) in finding ways to end the trade in 'pets-for-experiments', which the paper acknowledged was still legal (16 July 1960, p.9).

As it ran a scheme for homeless dogs, the BUAV figured prominently in the National Pet Club (NPC) articles, where appeals were made by staff writer Betty Tay seeking homes for dogs held at the BUAV rescue centres. Within the NPC articles the BUAV was identified largely as a canine rescue organization, although this changed in 1961 when key differences between the BUAV and the RSPCA on the subject of vivisection were reported as part of the *Daily Mirror* campaign against pet-pirates. Tay wrote, 'The RSPCA are not an anti-vivisection organisation because they say some experimental work with animals is deemed necessary both for the health of other animals and of humans' and further on, 'the British Union for the Abolition of Vivisection (Dog Rescue Scheme) actually buys pet dogs and cats to prevent them from getting into the hands of laboratory agents' (Tay, *Daily Mirror*, 4 February 1961, p.7). The NPC claimed affiliations with both organizations, and it was not the purpose of the article to make comparisons between the BUAV and RSPCA. However, because of its stance on animal experimentation at that time, the article noted that the RSPCA did not join the BUAV in lobbying the Home Office to tighten up regulation on the issuing of pet shop licences. The BUAV also campaigned to force animal traders to display notices on their premises informing the public that they sold animals for experimental purposes, and the organization called on the government to force traders that collected animals from private homes to be required to give notice to owners that their pet might be used for vivisection (*Daily Mirror*, 11 March 1961, p.9). In a follow-up article, Tay reported that the RSPCA was, on the basis of her article, taking other action in the form of a national poster scheme to deter people from giving their pets to anyone other than a representative of an established welfare society. Although supportive of vivisection in principle, a spokesperson for the RSPCA asserted, 'it is wicked to mislead people into believing an animal will go to a new home when, in fact, it is destined for a laboratory' (*Daily Mirror*, 11 March 1961, p.9), and the poster issued by the organization stated, 'Many unscrupulous dealers advertising from private addresses buy for laboratories carrying out cruel experiments' (RSPCA poster, 1961).

The discourse on pet-pirating was firmly linked with vivisection, and the *Daily Mirror* articles on the subject left their readers in no doubt as to what happened to animals that entered a research facility. In an article that sparked the 1961 campaign, Tay recounted the story of Millie, a dog who had been given unknowingly to an animal dealer by her pensioner owner due to a change of circumstances. When the owner changed his mind and contacted the dealer, he was told that Millie had been sold to a laboratory for 45 shillings. The *Daily Mirror* declared, 'now Millie is dead – murdered by Pet Pirates' (*Daily Mirror*, 4 February 1961, p.7). In the article, blame for the suffering and death of animals in laboratories was displaced onto rogue animal traders. Whilst some might have acquired animals by misleading the public, animal dealers were also official sales agents; but as the *Daily Mirror* remained unwilling to openly criticize the legal vivisection of animals, the media discourse tended to demonize the dealers. As the paper's coverage of rogue animal traders progressed, more details about research labs and discussion of state responsibility for the regulation of all aspects of animal experimentation began to be debated. In an interview with a 'cash-for-cats man' the animal trader was identified as 'one of a group of Government-backed collectors who paid cash for cats', and the paper warned that 'there are still men collecting cats for research' (*Daily Mirror*, 9 March 1963, p.5). In a later article the newspaper gave graphic details of chemical testing on dogs that had been undertaken in Agriculture Ministry laboratories (*Daily Mirror*, 6 January 1964, p.5). With so little information about vivisection available in the early 1960s, newspaper accounts such as these were a key source and in this sense were absolutely central in shaping public views about animal experimentation.

There was a strong public response to the 'pirate' campaign, which was reflected in a growth in the number of members of the NPC, an increase in letters to the paper that reported suspected pet-pirates as well as further general public commentary on the topic of vivisection. For instance, in response to the paper's coverage of US scientists who had exploded an out-of-control Atlas rocket which contained a golden squirrel monkey in November 1961, one reader wrote, 'Let's not raise a wail at the Americans for sending a monkey to its death in a Spaceship. We should dry our crocodile tears and inquire how many monkeys died in British vivisection laboratories during the past few months' (*Daily Mirror*, 15 November 1961, p.10). And, following articles about stag hunting and animal experimentation in the paper, another reader wrote, 'penalties for cruelty to children and animals should be drastically increased and should always include a prison sentence. I agree. Let's start with huntsmen and vivisectionists' (*Daily Mirror*, 28 November 1963, p.10).

With growing fears about the theft of pets and the fate of those that ended up in experimental labs, the Government response was to attempt to reassure the public that they had nothing to fear from 'pet-snatchers'. The Home Office Under-Secretary, in reply to the *Daily Mirror*'s claims, stated that there was 'no truth in the idea that animals were obtained by irregular means', and he stated that all dealers were asked to confirm that animals supplied to labs had been 'properly obtained' (*Daily Mirror*, 7 July 1962, p.4). A 1962 Government paper on live animal experimentation, which noted that the number of animals being used was increasing year on year, was widely criticized by welfare groups for 'whitewashing the facts' about vivisection.[17] The criticisms were reported by the *Daily Mirror*, which continued to campaign for an end to the trade in dogs and cats and for changes to regulation which allowed pets to make their way into the system. As news broke in the early 1960s that the drug Thalidomide, which had been tested on animals, was responsible for birth defects when taken during pregnancy, the *Daily Mirror* offered the following comment:

> Their drugs are painstakingly tried on animals. But testing them on a New Zealand white rabbit (the animal that gave an important clue to the dangers of Thalidomide) can never be the same as trying them on a human being. Eventually, WE must be the guinea-pigs. That is the risk we have to take for all medical research and progress (*Daily Mirror*, 29 August 1962, p.11).

Due to continued press interest, public anxieties about vivisection did not dissipate, and pressure was put on the Home Secretary to respond to questions about animal experimentation. In response, a Departmental Enquiry chaired by Sidney Littlewood was set up in 1963. In 1965 the Littlewood Committee published a series of recommendations but nothing was done with the Committee's findings, and its Report was not debated until the following decade. The issue of vivisection continued to be discussed in the *Daily Mirror*, although as the decade came to a close the term 'pet-pirate' disappeared from the discourse. In a shift of emphasis the newspaper began to focus on critiquing the system and the weak regulation that allowed pets to be sold for vivisection purposes. A renewed boost of public support was given to the *Daily Mirror's* ongoing campaign when ten dogs were seized on their way to a university laboratory in 1969, all of which were claimed to be pets. The newspaper aroused strong public feeling when it printed photographs of each dog. This story was significant in that it provided visual proof to the newspaper's readers that pets were being sold to laboratories; and when some of the dogs were identified by former owners, the paper was able to claim that it now had concrete evidence that the present system for supplying animals to labs was not working. Plans for a pet register to permanently identify dogs and cats in an effort to curb, what the paper described as, 'the callous trade in pets for vivisection' were presented by the BUAV the following year, but their plans were declared impractical by the Home Office. The same year the Littlewood report was discussed in the House of Lords, following newspaper reports that over 5,200,000 live animal experiments had taken place in 1969, 4,600,000 without anaesthetic. During the Lords debate it was noted on more than one occasion that newspaper coverage of vivisection issues was driving public opinion on the matter; however, legislative change was not forthcoming, a situation that was blamed, in no small part, on the fact that the Littlewood report had been initiated by the previous government.

## 1970s and 1980s campaigns

The *Daily Mirror* openly opposed cosmetics testing on animals in the mid-1970s and began a campaign that gathered momentum towards the end of the decade. It also renewed in 1978 its opposition to legislation that allowed animal dealers to supply pets to vivisection laboratories. The paper began to employ a sensationalistic name-and-shame strategy, and in November 1978 the front page carried the headline 'Pets for Slaughter'. The article named an animal dealer and printed his photograph on the front page stating that he was involved in supplying dogs and cats to vivisection laboratories. The paper then followed its investigative report with a series of articles on vivisection that included a debate about the rights of animals between the author Richard Adams and David Smyth, Emeritus Professor of Physiology at Sheffield University. The *Daily Mirror's* investigation into animal dealers was debated in the House of Lords, and the paper reported that the RSPCA chairman, Richard Ryder, had asked the Home Secretary to take action over the paper's allegations. A second and more aggressive name-and-shame campaign was pursued in 1988 in which details of companies that sold toiletries and cosmetics tested on animals were published. A front-page headline asked readers: 'Guilty: But do YOU care?' (*Daily Mirror*, 19 November 1988, p.1). Over the next decade, the paper published a series of articles that described, in detail and with pictures, toxicity and irritancy testing on animals, until the ban on cosmetics and ingredients in the UK in 1998. In the year prior to the ban, the newspaper in conjunction with the BUAV bought 50 beagles bred for laboratories and ran a successful campaign to rehome them. When the ban was announced, the *Daily Mirror* claimed it was a victory for the campaigners, who had fought for 20 years, and for the paper itself, which had backed antivivisection groups and had 'published heartrending pictures of rabbits and monkeys suffering for human vanity' (*Daily Mirror*, 16 November 1998, p.4).

Whilst it is clear that the *Daily Mirror* was not the only newspaper reporting on the subject of vivisection, it did exert a degree of influence on public opinion, not least because by 1975 the National Pets Cub had 500,000 members and the paper was active in developing a particular discourse that forged a relationship between pet ownership and the issue of vivisection, in effect bringing the debate squarely into the field of popular concern. Because of the emphasis placed on the pet trade and due to the collective identity of 'British animal lovers' that the paper wished to foster, its treatment of the activities of animal activists changed when some groups began to engage in illegal direct action in the 1980s. In 1964, a man had been found guilty of stealing three dogs from a vivisection laboratory at Newcastle University. The *Daily Mirror* identified him as an 'anti-vivisectionist' who had broken into the lab and freed ten dogs, three of which he had taken home, and he was fined £21. This incident was described in neutral terms, but in later coverage of antivivisection issues from the 1960s onwards, the paper tended to refer to those involved as 'pet lovers' or 'animal lovers'; both of which sat comfortably with the vocabulary of the National Pet Club, under whose auspices many of the articles were published. Initially in 1981, direct action claimed by the Animal Liberation Front (ALF) was referred to in sympathetic terms, and the paper identified the activists as 'animal lovers'. Later in 1981, the tone changed in a report on threats that were alleged to have been made by ALF members, now referred to as 'militant animal lovers', to staff at a laboratory in Kent. In another article the same year about paint raids on fur shops, ALF supporters were described as 'fanatical animal-lovers'. In 1984, in the wake of the 'Mars Bar poisoning action', the *Daily Mirror* made a statement that distanced the paper's antivivisection actions from those of the ALF and referred to the ALF as a 'crazed organisation', describing the members as 'demented' and declaring that their actions bordered 'on insanity' (*Daily Mirror*, 20 November 1984). From that point forward, 'fanatic' and 'maniac' were typically used to refer to animal rights supporters. In a history of direct action, Kim Stallwood writes that the early to mid-1980s was the time when the ALF 'moved from a position of nonviolence to support violence toward people', and the shift from non-violent action to violent direct action 'cost the ALF its sympathetic media coverage and growing public support. It also forced other animal advocacy organisations to defensive positions' (Stallwood, 2004, pp. 84–85). Certainly this was the case with the *Daily Mirror*, which, in setting out its opposition to the ALF, began to reclaim the identity of animal lover and deploy it in ways that reinscribed differences between a general welfarist stance and a rights direct action position.[18]

The *Daily Mirror* showed a marked change in its position on live animal experimentation, from its opposition to Coleridge during the Brown Dog Affair at the beginning of the twentieth century to its support for the BUAV and action to effect change to legislation from the 1950s onwards. Claims that Britain was 'a nation of animal lovers' were exploited by the paper keen to utilize a collective identity that could create a relationship between the *Daily Mirror* and its readership, establish a regular advertising space that could capitalize on the commercialization of the pet market and, at the same time, give the paper an identity that differentiated it from its competition. With the animal lover identity being so closely associated with pet ownership and a tabloid readership, as well as having former links with a gendered discourse of sentiment and emotion from the previous century, it is unsurprising that there were those who felt it necessary to distance themselves from animal lovers in an effort to reclaim some sense of seriousness to the vivisection debate. Although the coverage of animal traders brought the topic into a public forum, the paper's discourse on vivisection privileged pets to the extent that dogs and cats became the key symbolic victims of animal experimentation. Later articles did begin to focus on monkeys and rabbits, but other animals were notably absent from the discourse. Rats and mice, which in fact represented the greater proportion of animals used in experimentation, were effectively erased from the debate.

## Identities

A brief review of some of the most popular television crime dramas demonstrates the extent to which animal rights remain associated with violent direct action. *Murder She Wrote, Silent Witness, Bones, The Inspector Lynley Mysteries, CSI* and *Ashes to Ashes* each have an 'animal rights' episode which depicts antivivisection proponents engaged in violent and illegal activities. Often the characters are stereotyped as young, misinformed, angry, aggressive, sometimes insane, social deviants. In most cases the programmes tend to avoid dealing with the suffering of animals and instead focus on the illegal activities, thereby reducing animal advocates to a stereotype of criminality and destructive behaviours. The repeated presence of activists as criminals in crime drama continues to sustain a relationship between violence and animal rights that effectively obscures the issue of vivisection. In films, the stereotype is usually taken further such that activists are represented as responsible for releasing some type of virulent disease from a laboratory, which has apocalyptic consequences. Such representations are not unique to the contemporary era, of course, and the social marginalization of animal advocates has a long and sometimes disturbing history. The antivivisection movement of the late nineteenth and early twentieth century faced charges of being anti-scientific to the extent that it had to counter criticisms of misanthropy and accusations that humans would suffer if vivisection was ended. Animal advocacy has been, and remains, a battleground where the normalization and marginalization of positions on the issue of vivisection has been tied up, in no small part, with the cultivation of culturally legitimized identities.

# 3
# Stars: Animal Performers

On 6 March 1951 the first Patsy awards, arranged to coincide with the premiere of *Bedtime for Bonzo*, took place at the Carthay Circle Theatre in Los Angeles. Organized by the American Humane Association (AHA), the awards were created to honour the top animal movie star of that year, as voted for by film critics, columnists and editors. The AHA had approached the Academy of Motion Picture Arts and Sciences with a request to include an award for animals at its annual Oscar ceremony that year, but their suggestion had been met with a firm refusal. Following the Academy's rejection the AHA decided to hold the Patsys two weeks before the Oscars, and Bonzo the chimpanzee, star of *Bedtime for Bonzo*, was scheduled to present the awards with co-star Ronald Reagan. Voters were polled in February 1951, and the following month it was announced that Francis, the star of *Francis the Talking Mule*, had won the inaugural annual 'picture animal top star of the year' award.

Bonzo died two days before the 1951 Patsy awards. Trapped in a cage during a fire at the World Jungle Compound, Bonzo suffocated from smoke inhalation despite the best efforts of fire fighters who, it was reported, 'worked unsuccessfully for 30 minutes with a resuscitator' (*Billboard*, 17 March 1951, p.37). In the days that followed the fire, newspapers reported the loss of 'one of Hollywood's most engaging comics' (*Pittsburgh Post-Gazette*, 6 March 1951, p.12). The news was reported as far away as Australia, where the *Sydney Morning Herald* commented, although not without irony, that 'Hollywood is in general mourning over the death of a monkey actor named Bonzo' (*The Sydney Morning Herald*, 17 March 1951, p.2). In the mainstream press, Billy Richards, one of the owners of the World Jungle Compound, was quoted saying that the loss 'could not be measured in dollars and cents' (*Pittsburgh Post-Gazette*, 6 March 1951, p.12). Despite Richards's comment, the trade press were nonetheless keen to report on the costs of the fire, which also claimed the lives of three other chimpanzees and a young kangaroo, and stated that the animals were 'valued at over $100,000' (*Billboard*, 17 March 1951, p.37). In breakdowns of the losses it was reported that the unnamed kangaroo had been worth $500, whilst a movie columnist for the *Sunday Herald* commented that 'The death of Bonzo the Chimp means a loss of $75,000 for his trainer. Bonzo had a tight contract at U-I for three years at $500 a week' (Graham, 1951, p.39). Press reports also revealed that Bonzo was not, as the promotional discourse for *Bedtime for Bonzo* had claimed, a 'new star' but had worked extensively in the entertainment industry under the names Tamba, Pierre, Jo Jo and Rollo and was in fact 'a veteran of scores of movie and television shows' (*Pittsburgh Post-Gazette*, 6 March 1951, p.12). Moreover, although referred to exclusively as male in all publicity and press prior to her death, it also came to light later that Bonzo was a female chimpanzee.[1] According to the media discourse, Bonzo was an animal actor, a star and a commercial commodity, and it is to the interrelations between these constructions that this chapter now turns.

## Animal labour

Within the spectrum of animal issues, onscreen animal performance has attracted substantially less concern than vivisection, hunting or intensive farming. There are obvious reasons why this should be the case: first, the scale of suffering involved in experimentation, hunting and factory farming is of a different magnitude from that experienced by animal actors; second, there is the reassurance in the end credits of many films and television programmes that 'No animals were harmed', the statement being a registered trademark of the American Humane Association, which monitors the use of animals during productions; third, there is a certain glamour associated with the film and television industries that lends credence to the idea that the animals who appear onscreen enjoy the benefits that are bestowed on all those who work in 'show business'; fourth, animal performances are an undeniable source of entertainment and pleasure, a point borne out by the box office success of stars such as Rin Tin Tin, Strongheart, Beethoven, Francis, Bonzo, Lassie, Benji, Flipper, Willy and many others, and there is a tacit assumption, perpetuated by publicity and promotional discourses that include 'behind-the-scenes' glimpses, that the actors, who are especially talented, enjoy what they do. These points are neither arbitrary nor unrelated. They are intrinsically connected by a cinematic apparatus which sustains the production of animal narratives and animal stars through organized systems of regulation, production and promotion and through the employment of recognizable patterns of editing, narrative, genre and conventions of representation.

With the exception of the regulatory body, in this case the American Humane Association, which began monitoring the use of animals in productions after 1939, the above description of the cinematic apparatus is, by and large, a general sketch of Hollywood during the studio system. Indeed, it was between the 1920s and 1950s that some of the most popular animal stars rose to fame. In their study of the Hollywood mode of production to 1960, Bordwell, Staiger and Thompson identify relationships between the labour force and the means of production, which I want to call on here to briefly consider the place of animals in the economic system of relations specific to this era (Bordwell et al., 2005, p.91–2). Under this mode of production the labour force was organized into a hierarchy by work functions, where a management position was assigned with responsibility for supervising part of the total labour process (Bordwell et al, 2005, p.92). For instance, in the case of MGM from 1931, the hierarchical specialization of labour, known as the 'producer-unit' system, meant that a central producer would be in charge of a group of associate supervisors, one of whom had responsibility for all 'animal films'.[2] With the associate, the producer would decide on a writer, a director and the leads for a film on a project-by-project basis. The associate would then make decisions about costs, costumes, remaining staff and so forth, which were then sent for approval by the central producer. Animal trainers were part of the specialized labour force and integral to the production of animal films, which were, in turn, a specific type of commodity. At MGM, from 1932, George W. Emerson was the studio's head animal trainer with responsibility for sourcing animals, managing the MGM zoo, training animals and doubling for stars during animal sequences.[3] Animals were thus part of the physical capital – that is, the tools and materials – of the studio.

In 1940 changes to the Motion Picture Production Code, the regulatory system that was enforced by the Hays Office, specifically attended to the issue of animals in films. These were the 'Special Regulations on Cruelty to Animals'; changes made to the Code in December of that year which stated that 'Hereafter, in the production of motion pictures by the members of the Association such member shall, as to any picture involving the use of animals, invite on the lot during the shooting and consult with the authorized representative of the American Humane Association' (Motion Picture Production Code, 1940). What is crucial about this particular regulatory change is that it redefined animals as a morally considerable category of physical capital within a framework that sought to protect the dominant values of a society.

It serves here to briefly outline the events that led to the MPPC changes. In 1939 the American Humane Association (AHA) protested to the president of the Motion Picture Producers and Distributors' Association of America, Will Hays, about the excessive cruelty that had been inflicted on horses during the filming of *Jesse James*. The chief concern was that two horses had been blindfolded and forced over a 73-foot-high cliff during the filming of a getaway scene. The AHA claimed that the horses had been put on greased slides to ensure that they went over the edge and, as a result of the fall, one of the horses died. There was a public outcry which forced Darryl Zanuck, Vice-President of Twentieth Century Fox, to write an open letter to newspaper editors, in which he claimed 'the mishap in "Jesse James" was purely and completely accidental and not wanton cruelty' (Zanuck, 1939, p.10). The incident was finally resolved by an agreement between Richard C. Craven, western director for the AHA, and the Hays office that a representative of the AHA would be present by invitation of the studios to inspect practices and ensure the welfare of animals during production.[4] These changes to the MPPC were contextualized within a specific moral framework. Concerned that films would affect and undermine social values, the MPPC stated that motion pictures had 'a most important moral quality' for two reasons: 'They reproduce the morality of the men who use the pictures as a medium for the expression of their idea and ideals' and 'They affect the moral standards of those who, through the screen, take in these ideas and ideals' (Motion Picture Production Code: Preamble, 1940). Framed in this way, the regulations pertaining to animals were part of the wider policing of morality in twentieth-century America, but this should not obscure the fact that, following the public outcry, studios became increasingly aware of the commercial implications of having their industry branded as 'cruel'.[5]

Post-war, industry awareness of public feeling about animals was reflected in the types of animal imagery depicted onscreen, where a balance between public tastes, dramatic necessity, regulation and commercial interests had to be achieved. Negotiation of these various factors was amply demonstrated by the different versions of *Fiesta* which were produced and released by MGM in 1947. In the domestic release and the version distributed in England and Scandinavia, bullfighting sequences were heavily edited and no bull was shown being injured or killed, whilst the version released in Spain and Latin America included scenes of bullfights shot on location in Mexico in their entirety. The reason given by the studio for the difference in the versions was that 'bloodletting' of this nature went against the tastes of US audiences and those of 'other English-speaking nations' (*St Petersburg Times*, 24 August 1947, p.29). Furthermore, to be distributed in America, MGM would have had to clear the bullfighting scenes with the AHA, which could have proved problematic. Despite such examples of circumventing the regulations in order to maximize market viability for a film, studios were keen to assure audiences that the industry was animal friendly. This resulted in claims that, when treated well, animals worked better on set, and as a result the studios suggested that welfare issues were assimilated into the economic logic of production. The practices of animal trainers remained something of a mystery though, and whilst it was repeatedly claimed that chimpanzees, lions, tigers and elephants could only be taught to respond to commands on set with the application of gentle training techniques, later accounts of the methods employed revealed that many trainers relied on harsh physical intimidation. For instance, an account published in 1980 by a trainer who had worked at the World Jungle Compound during the 1950s described how he had been instructed to use the 'whip approach' to training, which had resulted in him being mauled several times. The trainer explained, 'They [the trainers] thought they were right then. But their training was based on mutual fear and distrust. The animals actually hated them' (Simross, 1980, p.9). Studios were conscious of public feeling and unwilling to disclose the methods by which wild animals were captured, trained and then controlled during productions. Consequently, in the creation of the film product, studios constantly negotiated a position between economics and ethics, and this was also true in the creation of animal stars, which relied on the manufacture of an illusion that individuated animals were no longer merely physical capital but were instead active, autonomous members of the labour force.

## Stars

Animal stars, in much the same way as human stars, are manufactured fabrications. The point to be made here is that the 'animal star' is a cultural construction and as such is differentiated by the publicity and promotional processes of the industry from the 'real animal' and their animality. The animal stars of the 1950s are particularly interesting as they emerge at a time when, as the previous chapter discussed, certain animal issues (such as vivisection) had receded in terms of importance in the public mind (see chapter 2). For the American film industry of the mid-twentieth century, animal stars were absolutely vital. Their significance was in large part because the 1950s were a difficult point in Hollywood history, as legislation that would break the monopolistic control of the major studios was coming into force and television was beginning to encroach on box office profits as it claimed a significant portion of audiences' leisure time. To appreciate how economically significant animals stars were to the industry, one need only look back to Rin Tin Tin and Francis the talking mule for examples of animals whose films alone brought in profits that kept two studios, Warner Bros. and United International, financially solvent. Cases such as these leave little doubt that animal stars were a major box office draw and therefore highly attractive to studios.

Writing about human stars, Richard Dyer has argued that they are 'as much produced images, constructed personalities as "characters" are' (Dyer, 1998, p.20). He asserts:

> Thus the value embodied by a star is as it were harder to reject as 'impossible' or 'false', because the star's existence guarantees the existence of the value s/he embodies [...] the roles and/or performance of a star in a film were taken as revealing the personality of the star (which was then corroborated by the stories in magazines, etc.). What was only sometimes glimpsed and seldom brought out by Hollywood or the stars was that that personality was itself a construction known and expressed only through films, stories, publicity etc. (Dyer, 1998, p.20).

In much the same way, the 'animality' of animal stars was seldom depicted by Hollywood, and animal stars and the characters they portrayed embodied humanized qualities such as wit, intelligence, loyalty and tenderness and relied on cultural stereotypes of animals for their meanings.

In general, stars were important to the film industry because they helped to sell a film. As Dyer remarks, 'The star's presence in a film is a promise of a certain kind of thing that you would see if you went to see the films' (Dyer, 2004, p.5). In the case of the animal star, their presence was often declared in the title: *Bedtime for Bonzo, Lassie Come Home, Francis and the Haunted House* and so on. In constructing the star, publicists created a personality that meshed a devised backstory with some aspect of the character which was to be played onscreen. As a result, the access that audiences had to stars was via the publicly available star image and personality, which, in the case of animal stars, rendered the 'real' animal redundant. Being little more than a character, it was standard practice for multiple individual animals to be substituted for one 'animal star'.

This is not to suggest that audiences were manipulated into believing every aspect of the humanized star personas created for animals by studio publicists. However, it is possible to read across the publicity discourses that constructed various animal stars to find two discernible strategies. The first of these promoted the star image through a discourse of 'talent': a particular set of attributes that separated the star animal from others and in doing so distanced them from their animality. In these cases, animals transcended their animal state. The second strategy utilized a discourse which I will refer to as 'camp', in the sense that the term is used by Susan Sontag (1982) to describe an aesthetic sensibility that delights in artifice, exaggeration, trivialization and theatricality. Camp is, Sontag writes, 'a love of the exaggerated, the "off", of things-being-what-they-are-not' (Sontag, 1982, p.108). Part of the pleasure of the animal star for the audience was thus derived from the artifice perpetuated through the publicity discourse, which offered audiences images of dogs in chauffeur-driven cars, chimpanzees in tuxedos and lions at cocktail parties: animals living the Hollywood lifestyle. Such images became part of the conventions of representing the animal star, which resonate with Sontag's notion of camp as extraordinary, glamorous and the glorification of 'instant character' (Sontag, 1982, p.114). As 'nothing in nature can be campy' (Sontag, 1982, p.108), the production of the star image was a process that reshaped animals – things of nature – into culturally accessible humanized commodities. This process of commodifying animals meant that only very rarely did Hollywood reveal the animality of animal stars, preferring instead to represent the animal star in human terms. Following from Dyer's analysis of human stars, the animal star was thus a representation that expressed particular qualities which were inevitably humanized by processes that sought to exploit their marketable function. Constructing the camp artifice of animal stars and employing a discourse of 'talent' thus provided two mechanisms by which animal stars were distanced from their animalness and made available for audience consumption, processes that were evident in the construction of Fearless Fagan and Bonzo in the early 1950s.

## Fagan

1951 was a time of change for Universal International (U-I). U-I was created in 1946, the result of a merger between Universal and International

Pictures Corporation that had been orchestrated in the hopes of producing better quality films. Following the merger, the company did gain some prestige from literary adaptations such as *Letter from an Unknown Woman* but nonetheless found itself in serious financial trouble by 1949. In November 1951, negotiations that had been underway for some time finally came to fruition, and Decca, a company better known to the public at the time as a music recording label, announced that it had bought a majority share of the studio. With control of the company changing hands, U-I shifted its attentions away from 'quality' products and towards movies with a wider appeal. The change proved to be beneficial and, with the focus on the balance sheet, by 1953 the company's common stock had increased by 200 per cent and U-I had become 'the darling of Wall Street'.[6] One of the reasons cited for the change in the company's fortunes was its investment in 'gimmick' movies.

Despite the ventures into 'quality' films, by the early 1950s U-I was known for its 'gimmick pictures', which were defined by the press as 'cheap to make, easy on the eyes and the mind and, while unimpressive to critics, a great hit in small towns' (*Life Magazine*, 15 June 1953, p.109). Amongst these gimmick movies, films such as *Francis*, and *Bedtime for Bonzo* showed strong profits, and as a result the studio invested in a number of sequels: *Bonzo Goes to College* (1952), *Francis Goes to the Races* (1951), *Francis Goes to West Point* (1952), *Francis Covers the Big Town* (1953), *Francis Joins the WACS* (1954), *Francis in The Navy* (1955) and *Francis in the Haunted House* (1956).[7] The Francis films proved to have more audience appeal than the Bonzo movies, a fact that was reflected at the box office, where, unlike *Bedtime for Bonzo*, *Bonzo Goes to College* was a flop in 1952, thereby ending any hopes of further sequels. Francis, on the other hand, continued to be a big hit, so much so that the trade press reported in 1952 that U-I had been able to pay off the studio's overheads with profits from the Francis films alone.[8]

There was no doubt in the industry that animal stars were extremely lucrative, and one newspaper stated, 'There is no better, or more consistent, moneymaker in the business than a series picture with an animal star. Lassie, Rin Tin Tin and now Francis are top examples' (Bacon, 1952, p.14). Other studios wanted to emulate the success that U-I had with Francis and sought out new animal stars that would draw in audiences. In 1952, in an effort to compete with U-I, MGM introduced a new animal star named 'Fearless Fagan, the wandering lion'. MGM's publicity department worked quickly to introduce Fagan to Hollywood and to the press by staging an impromptu arrival of the lion at a cocktail party. The official story released by MGM was that Fagan had been hand-reared from the time he was a cub by a young man, Floyd Humeston. Drafted by the army in 1951, Humeston could not bear to be separated from Fagan and asked the warrant officer at the base for a 14-day furlough to find a home for 'his cat'. After much searching, Humeston finally managed to find Fagan a home with the Humane Society of Monterey, which was located seven miles from the army base at Ford Ord. The story was reported in *Life* magazine and accompanied by photographs of Humeston in bed with Fagan, the two walking on the beach together and a series of pictures of their journey to find the lion a new home.[9] The *Life* article caught the attention of MGM assistant producer Sidney Franklin Jr, who arranged to bring Humeston and Fagan to the MGM studios, where a screenplay based on Fagan's story was developed. MGM bought the screenplay and Fagan the lion for $10,000, of which Humeston received $3,300. Humeston was reported to have said that the money was 'of minor significance'. What was important was that Fagan had a home at MGM. Humeston remarked, 'The very least I could do for the lion is give it a good home' [...] 'Look what he's done for me. He only needs 16 pounds of horsemeat a day. What other MGM star works that cheap?' (Bacon, 1952, p.14).

Fagan's move to Hollywood was covered in a sequel story printed in *Life* magazine in July 1951, in which the MGM studio was cast as the hero, rescuing Fagan from a circus in Ohio where, the article stated, 'a keeper was trying to alienate his affections from his old master' (*Life*, 23 July 1951, p.107). In the five months since the publication of the original story, *Life* explained, Fagan had been expelled from the Monterey Humane Society 'because he couldn't pay for cage and board'. In between the two *Life* articles, syndicated newspapers reported that Fagan had spent six weeks with the Mills Bros. Circus before being given by Floyd in March 1951 to his brother and animal trainer Earl Humeston.[10] Earl had used Fagan in a nightclub act in Ohio, in which he wrestled the lion on stage. Fagan was kept in a cage at the back of the Palm Gardens nightclub and in a garage when it rained, until the police stopped the act after only four days citing an ordinance that stated it was illegal to lead a dangerous animal on a leash. From the nightclub, Fagan was moved to Columbus Zoo from April until May 1951 when he was finally flown to San Francisco by MGM to be reunited with Floyd Humeston as part of a major publicity event.[11] Press coverage of Fagan's flight into San Francisco referred to him as 'an orphan', whilst the MGM publicists introduced the press to various Fagan-related merchandize and services that included peanuts and a moving and storage company.[12] The second *Life* article excluded any details about the nightclub act or Fagan's time at Columbus Zoo and instead reworked the story so that MGM producer Franklin stepped in at the point where Fagan was still at the Mills Bros. Circus. Rescued from his wanderings, it was noted, Fagan was free to enjoy all the trappings of the Hollywood lifestyle. Accompanied by a picture of Fagan looking at another MGM star, Esther Williams, from his chauffeur-driven convertible car (Figure 3.1), and an image of his screen test on the MGM back lot with an assistant holding a sign saying 'Mr Fagan', the *Life* article noted that 'Fagan is being introduced to those alterations of luxurious ease and hard work which make up a movie star's life' (*Life*, 23 July 1951, p.107).

Thomas Harris's 1957 article 'The Building of Popular Images' outlined the process of promoting a Hollywood star who, he wrote, 'becomes a symbol to an unseen mass audience whose only contact

*Figure 3.1*  Fagan the lion. Loomis Dean/Time & Life Pictures/Getty Images

with him/her is through the indirect means of the media' (Harris, 1991, p.40). Harris makes the point that there is a separation between the star and audience which is bridged through studio-controlled publicity, advertising and exploitation. Audience knowledge of the star and the star image were constructed, he argued, by a publicity process that followed similar patterns (irrespective of the studio) and which included an initial publicity build-up before the star's screen debut. The build-up focussed on a story of their 'discovery' usually devised by studio publicists and accompanied by a series of pictures and a rumoured romance or starring role in a film. When the actor had been cast in a film, the studio worked on a pre-sale campaign for the film and the star personality by 'planting' items in national magazines and newspapers followed by the creation of stunts and merchandizing tie-ins: 'Especially important in this total process is the perpetuation of the star stereotype. It is the publicist's job to interpret the new film in terms of the pre-established stereotypes and to communicate the image through a variety of means at his [*sic*] disposal' (Harris, 1991, p.41). Although Harris discussed the system in relation to human stars, the Hollywood publicity apparatus functioned in much the same way whatever the star's species. The star and star personality were thus not constructed by the films in which they appeared but were instead intertexual, the totality combined from a complex image-making process that incorporated multiple media instances beyond the textual limits of the movie.

In the case of Fagan, the two *Life* articles provided the 'discovery story', the background to the lion's life and his relationship with Humeston, as well as the public announcement of his role in an upcoming film. Publicity shots of Fagan in a chauffeured car, head lolling over the door looking at an already established star, worked to promote his star status and equivalence with human stars, a well-established publicity convention used with other animal actors. Stunts such as Fagan's unannounced appearance at a Hollywood cocktail party and arrival by plane in San Francisco were used to promote merchandize and guarantee that the 'Fagan story' was repeated in newspapers, thus ensuring that audiences became familiar with the 'wandering lion' narrative as well as the star's personality prior to the film's release.

The film, *Fearless Fagan*, based on the *Life* magazine story was released in 1952, and with it the retelling of Fagan's story merged with the dramatized adaptation in the publicity discourse. Following the film's preview for the press, it was reported that Humeston had originally taken Fagan to Ford Ord and had been promptly told to remove the lion or face serious consequences, an addition to the original *Life* story which had made no mention of Fagan on the army base.[13] Details of Humeston's pre-draft job, working as an animal trainer in circuses, were also omitted, the publicity discourse preferring to identify Humeston and Fagan not as 'lion trainer' and 'performing lion' but instead as 'soldier' and 'pet lion'. In print media, *Fearless Fagan* was advertised using stills from the film that replicated the images of Humeston and Fagan from the original *Life* article with the headline 'LIFE inspires a Movie! M-G-M's "FEARLESS FAGAN" A unique film comedy based on a true story' and the text:

> Movie fans owe Life Magazine a debt of gratitude for having printed the true story of Private Floyd C. Humeston and his pet lion, Fearless Fagan. On this page are photographs from the hilarious comedy that M-G-M has made, entitled 'FEARLESS FAGAN', inspired by the unique adventures of a boy drafted into the Army, who found no rest until he could provide a home for his pet. In the film, following a series of thrilling episodes which almost cost the lion his life, Fate in the shapely form of a Hollywood starlet, played by Janet Leigh, arranges for the lion to be taken to Hollywood where he joins his illustrious predecessors Lassie, the dog, and Francis, the mule, in the roster of screen favourites (*Fearless Fagan* advertisement in *Toledo Blade*, 17 September 1952, p. 23).

The publicity and promotional discourse worked hard to blur the factual and fictional aspects of the Fagan stories and in doing so to manufacture a narrative which charted the rise of a new animal star, one that MGM hoped would compete directly with Francis the talking mule. The critical response to the film was positive and described in one review as 'a movie of honest-to-goodness charm, and a nice touch of sentiment'. The reviewer referred to Fagan's performance in equally upbeat tones: 'it is big lovable Fagan who walks away with the movie lock, stock and barrel' (*Pittsburgh Post-Gazette*, 17 October 1952). The good critical response to *Fearless Fagan* was reflected in the 1953 Patsy awards when Fagan was voted overwhelmingly as the top animal star of 1952. Second place that year went to Bonzo the chimpanzee and in third place was Trigger the horse. However, doubt was cast over which lion had actually appeared in the film when the well-known animal trainer Mel Koontz turned up with a lion named Jackie to receive the main award for *Fearless Fagan*. The confusion over whether the film role had been played by Fagan or Jackie was further compounded by the lack of screen credit for either of the lions, an unusual decision for a studio to take with an animal star who, having been so heavily promoted, would usually receive a full onscreen credit. The trade press suggested that Jackie had been used in addition to Fagan and there was some speculation that a sequel to *Fearless Fagan* was in the pipeline, but the film did not materialize. By June 1953, Fagan was no longer on the MGM lot and instead promotion elsewhere for the Clyde Beatty Circus listed Fagan and Humeston as their new 'side attraction'.[14]

Apart from mapping out the process by which an animal was produced and promoted as a star, Fagan's story illustrates a difference between the production of animal stars and human stars in Hollywood: the established practice of substituting different individual animals for the star. In addition, one animal was often reused and promoted as a 'new star' when they had, in fact, appeared in other film roles under different names. Whilst human stars were part of a cultural production process that manufactured, for instance, one 'dumb blonde' after another – the stars differing in some ways but always constructed to fit with, what Harris refers to as, the pre-established stereotype – animals were much more versatile and able to be shaped into various star personalities. They were interchangeable and this interchangeability was concealed by a discourse of talent in which animal stars had transcended their animal nature and were represented as unique, distinctive and irreplaceable individuals. In Fagan's case the discourse emphasized the gentleness and sensitivity of his character. Although a fully grown lion weighing a reported 410 pounds, Fagan behaved 'like an overgrown kitten' (*Reading Eagle*, 8 July 1952, p.14). Fagan's unique nature was constructed through publicity images which depicted him lying in a bed of flowers, listening to music and having his make-up and 'hair' tended to, whilst press reports and reviews recounted stories of Fagan drinking from the same milk bottle and sleeping in the same bed as Humeston and marvelled at Fagan's ability to communicate through 'growls and gurgles' (*Life*, 12 February 1951, p.31). The discourse of talent was thus constructed primarily through promotion, publicity and critical reception. Studio publicists released images and orchestrated stunts that were designed to emphasize the exclusive attributes of the animal star, and when the film was released the star's talent onscreen was assessed by film critics. To further illustrate the extent to which the discourse of talent enabled the separation between animal and their animality, it is worthwhile mentioning one report on the 1953 Patsy awards which stated, without irony, 'Second place went to Bonzo the chimp for his convincing portrayal of a chimp in *Bonzo Goes to College*, a

Universal-International production' (*The Modesto Bee*, 21 March 1953, p. 5). The promotion of 'Bonzo the chimp' as an animal star thus provides a suitable case study to examine the processes by which the discourse of talent and the employment of a camp aesthetic distanced animals from their animality, and it is to Bonzo that this chapter now turns.

## Bonzo

Bonzo was imported to America from Liberia in 1948, part of a large shipment of wild animals, by Isaac 'Trader' Horne and Billy Richards, the owners of the World Jungle Compound, which was based in Thousand Oaks, California. Horne and Richards were animal traders, involved in the import, export, breeding, buying and selling of wild animals, and by 1950 they were established as the main supplier of animals to the film industry as well as to carnivals and circuses across the US. The World Jungle Compound, a 20-acre animal farm 35 miles north of Hollywood, housed around 200 animals at any one time. These were largely lions, tigers, leopards, cougars, panthers, elephants, kangaroos, bison, hyenas, camels, monkeys, apes, water buffaloes, ostriches and coyotes, many of whom were prepared for the entertainment industries by the 20 or so resident trainers. The World Jungle Compound had been a centre for the supply of wild animals to the entertainment industry since 1926 when it had been established by Louis Goebel and originally named Goebel's Lion Farm. Starting with five lions purchased from Universal Studios following the closure of the Universal zoo, Goebel supplied wild animals to the burgeoning movie industry, the most famous of these being Queenie and Sally the 'movie elephants' and Leo 'the MGM lion'.[15] Goebel's Lion Farm expanded to meet the requirements for wild animals in the entertainment industries and by 1940 more than 100 lions, 15 tigers and 15 elephants were kept at the facility.[16] Goebel's faced financial difficulties during the war years and a fire at the farm in 1940 resulted in the deaths of Queenie and Sally, who had been under contract to Paramount studio, as well as the loss of eight tigers, two lions, and two camels. The animal losses were added to building damage and the total losses from the 1940 fire were estimated at $100,000.[17] As soon as the war ended, Goebel's Lion Farm was bought by Richards and Horne, both of whom were well known for their work in circuses, zoos and the animal trade, and it was renamed the World Jungle Compound. From 1945 until the sale of the World Jungle Compound to two executives from Twentieth Century Fox studios in 1956, wild animals were imported by Richards and Horne to the compound, where one newspaper reported 'their trainers break and train beasts fresh from the jungle and develop acts which the owners book with circuses and carnivals' (*Toledo Blade*, 25 June 1950, p.74).[18]

The success of Horne and Richards' enterprise was due to the size and diversity of the operation, which included hiring out animals on short- or long-term contracts to film studios; putting together acts and arranging bookings in nightclubs, circuses and carnivals; opening the compound up as a public attraction as well as importing, exporting, selling and breeding wild animals which were supplied to zoos and private clients. Averaging several hundred visitors per day, and particularly popular as a destination for large groups of school children, the public flocked to the World Jungle Compound to watch 'big cat' and ape trainers working with the animals. By 1950 the animal farm was one of the 'must-see' attractions in California. Profits from visitors to the farm alone averaged around $100 per day, but films were the most lucrative work and many of the highest paid animal performers in the industry were housed at Richards and Horne's facility. In 1951 film studios paid $600 per week to hire 'tame big cats' such as Jackie the lion, Dynamite the black panther, Satan the tiger or Sherry the puma. On average, a camel would earn $50 per day and an elephant $100 per day for Richards and Horne.[19] The highest earner at the compound was Bonzo, also known as Tamba, who received a three-year contract with Universal International in 1950 which paid $500 per week, a sum that increased to $1000 per week when Bonzo was required to work.[20]

On arrival at the World Jungle Compound from Liberia, Bonzo was trained by Hank Craig, an experienced trainer who had worked with apes for 23 years. In 1949 the first major publicity photographs of Bonzo (named Tamba at that time) making telephone calls from the World Jungle Compound appeared on the front pages of some syndicated newspapers. Wartime material shortages meant that telephone service providers were unable to meet the need for private lines, and people were given shared party telephone lines and encouraged to 'be a good telephone neighbour' by making short calls and hanging up quickly.[21] The four images of Tamba depicted her listening on the phone and 'telling the other party off' for not getting 'off the line' (*St. Petersberg Press*, 24 April 1949, p.1). Each image of Tamba showed a different facial expression which, framed by the 'party line' narrative, could be read as a humanlike emotion. The following year, and now named 'Pierre', she received her first screen credit for the role of 'Tamba' in the Paramount film *My Friend Irma Goes West* (1950), starring Dean Martin and Jerry Lewis. In promotion for the film, a sequel to the 1949 movie *My Friend*

*Irma*, 'Pierre' was widely acknowledged as the 'new cast addition' (*The Deseret News*, 5 July 1950, p.13). Reviews of the film repeatedly made comparisons between the comic performances of Tamba and Lewis. For instance, the *Los Angeles Times* critic stated, 'There are several hilarious gags, one of which teams Lewis with a chimpanzee. The trained simian and Jerry ape each other with honors about even' (*Los Angeles Times*, 30 June 1950, p. A6), and elsewhere another reviewer noted that the high-light sequence of the film was 'a bit of byplay between a monkey and clown Lewis' (*Sunday Herald*, 24 September 1950).

The World Jungle Compound capitalized on Tamba's role in *My Friend Irma Goes West* and the publicity gained from the reviews of her scenes with Jerry Lewis. In July 1950 Richards and Horne ran an advert in the trade press advertising Tamba as a 'Wild Animal Act' and available for bookings with circuses, fairs and carnivals either alone or as part of an act with three other unnamed chimpanzees and her trainer Henry Craig.[22] Only two months after the World Jungle Compound advert had appeared in the trade press *Bedtime for Bonzo* began filming with Tamba, now renamed Bonzo, in the lead role and under a three-year contract with Universal International. U-I invested $50,000 in promotion and advertising for the film, which included a full publicity campaign for their new animal star. In the construction of her new personality the studio emphasized 'his' exceptional acting abilities, which, it was pro-posed, set Bonzo apart not only from other animal actors but also from other human performers. Introducing the press to their 'new star' for the first time, a publicist from Universal International stated during the filming of *Bedtime for Bonzo*, 'You must meet Bonzo. He can pull more faces than Andy Hardy' (*Reading Eagle*, 24 September 1950). In constructing her as a male animal star, and in much the same way that Tamba's abilities had been compared to those of Jerry Lewis, con-trasts between Bonzo and the fictional character Andy Hardy, played by Mickey Rooney, aligned her comic acting skills with those of the established human comedians of the time. Unsurprisingly, contrasts were also made between Bonzo and other animal stars, and Bonzo was variously referred to as 'an outstanding Hollywood animal actor' (*The Deseret News*, 14 February 1951, p.11); 'a talented 5-year-old chimp actor' (*Times Daily*, 15 March 1951, p.8); and 'the greatest scene-stealer since Rin Tin Tin was a pup' (*Reading Eagle*, 24 September 1950). The press were also happy to go along with the publicist's stories of ongoing rivalry between Bonzo and U-I's other animal stars, Harvey the rabbit and Francis the talking mule. One report revealed, 'Bonzo has a low opinion of a rabbit that is too bashful to let himself be seen and of a mule that has to hire a human to do his talking [...] He also considers the fact that they do not dress as indicating a lack of civilization' (*The Deseret News*, 14 February 1951, p.11).

During filming, stories that Bonzo's co-stars, Ronald Reagan and Diana Lynn, were upset at being upstaged by Bonzo and even intimidated by her acting skills were fed to the press by publicists. One article claimed that Diana Lynn was heard to complain, 'Who's going to look at me when Bonzo is on screen?' (Berg, 1950, p. G10) and elsewhere Hollywood gossip columnist Erskine Johnson wrote:

> Ronald Reagan, generally a Mr. Patience about his fellow actors, is muttering under his breath on the 'Bedtime for Bonzo' set. The reason: A scene-snatching chimpanzee who plays Bonzo. Wails Reagan: 'It's worse than working with Errol Flynn. The only difference between this monkey and Flynn is that if you have a good line in a Flynn picture, Flynn goes to the front office and takes the line away from you. The monk [*sic*] is too good an actor' (Johnson, 1950, p.65).

The *Los Angeles Times* devoted a full page to the discovery of U-I's new star under the headline 'Monkey of the Year' and claimed that Bonzo should be awarded an Oscar for 'his' performance in *Bedtime for Bonzo*. The article moved beyond the emphasis on Bonzo's comic talent to suggest that her acting ability exceeded that of most contemporary stars in Hollywood. Bonzo only needed one take, refused stand-ins and had the skill to bring emotion to a scene and to laugh, weep and show affection or hate on cue (Berg in *Los Angeles Times*, 17 December 1950, p. G10). Her ability to maintain the emotional tone of a scene was applauded, and it was noted, for instance, that during the 'vaccum scene' in *Bedtime for Bonzo*, 'Bonzo acted for three minutes without stopping' producing the 'longest single sustained take for any animal in any movie' (Berg in *Los Angeles Times*, 17 December 1950, p. G10). Such skill surpassed that of the current top animal star, Francis the talking mule, who 'could only sustain his mood for two minutes and 18 seconds' (p. G10). It was also maintained that reports of Bonzo's talent had spread to the wider Hollywood community and human stars came to the set to watch 'him' working:

> When Bonzo was performing during the making of the picture, actors from other sets, and even other studios, flocked to the Universal sound stage, to learn what they could in the line of

genuine histrionics. Bonzo drew a bigger crowd of visitors than Laurence Olivier or Vivien Leigh – the other current sensations of Hollywood (p. G10).

The discourse of talent produced a set of meanings that legitimized claims to stardom for Bonzo who was constructed by studio publicity and promotion as able to transcend her animal behaviour. This rhetoric relied on the trainer's role being somewhat ambiguous so that the illusion of animal autonomy and emotional authenticity could be stressed. Although, on set, the trainer cued Bonzo from the offscreen space, the apparatus of control received little acknowledgement in press or promotion, and the human–animal relationship between trainer and chimpanzee was reworked so that Craig was recast as Bonzo's spokesperson or friend. That Bonzo understood 1000 words was used to reinforce claims for her exceptional intelligence, and training commands were referred to as 'direction' and 'cues', thereby reconfiguring Bonzo's actions as an actor's performance that surpassed the trained imitation of an animal and reproduced authentic humanized emotional states. As Michael Peterson notes, 'At its simplest level, however, most animal acting involves framing trained behaviors in a "non-animal narrative"' (Peterson, 2007, p.34). Beyond the filmed performance it was thus imperative that Bonzo's actions appeared to remain autonomous, and therefore the publicity discourse, which included still images, also functioned to frame her behaviours as meaningful.

Whilst it is clear that studios applied many of the same conventions used to manufacture a human star in the fabrication of an animal star, audiences did not believe the publicity discourse in its entirety. As Peterson argues (2007), audiences have knowledge of how an animal act is produced, and therefore the way in which it is read is never on a symbolic level alone. In other words, the audience will always have some awareness that the animal has been trained, and therefore it is problematic to assume that spectators accept the framed behaviour as independent and intelligent. In the case of chimpanzees in the early 1950s, however, it is nonetheless salient to point out that stories of chimpanzee intelligence were widely reported in newspapers, and the chimpanzee was claimed to be the most intelligent animal other than humans by members of the scientific community. A typical report explained:

Scientists have speculated for years about which is the brainiest creature in the animals world. The evidence now indicates that, at least on the basis of tests made, the chimpanzee heads the class. Chimps can perform feats of reasoning that are beyond some primitive human beings. And in tests they have out-reasoned typical five-year American youngsters (*The Southeast Missourian*, 15 March 1950, p.20).

As a result, these accounts offered a further framing device for the construction of Bonzo as a self-directed, autonomous star personality. The illusion of animal autonomy is, however, always unstable, and Hollywood was often at risk of taking the fabrication too far so that audiences found it overly manipulative or ridiculous. This is in accord to some extent with Richard Dyer's argument that the authenticity of the star is always unstable, an ongoing balance between the 'star-as-image: star-as-real-person nexus' (Dyer, 1998, p.136–137). Dyer argues, 'There is more to authentication – there is a rhetoric of authenticity. This too has its own in-built instability – yesterday's markers of sincerity and authenticity are today's signs of hype and artifice' (Dyer, 1991, p.137). Dyer's idea can be extended to account for animal stars as an ongoing slippage between the animal-as-star and the star-as-animal, which in the case of Bonzo was managed by a discourse of talent and the camp aesthetic. If the rhetoric of authenticity was employed to maintain the illusion of Bonzo as a talented pseudo-human and animal-as-star, then it was the knowing inauthentic camp sensibility that could be relied on to relocate Bonzo as the star-as-animal. Both positions offered pleasures to the audience and at the same time denied Bonzo's animality and necessarily obscured the practices that were employed to capture and control real chimpanzees.

## Star-as-animal

The route by which Bonzo came to be in America was offered though two narratives. One clearly fictional story recounted Bonzo's 'discovery' by the studio and the second offered an apparently factual account of how Bonzo and other wild chimpanzees were captured. The publicity discourse stated that 'He was discovered five years ago in the Liberian jungle, and was lured to Hollywood by the offer of a bunch of bananas' (Berg, 1950, p. G10), whilst Henry Craig, the trainer, described Bonzo's capture in the following way: 'the natives set out a kettle of beer. Later they return and toss the passed out chimps into cages' (*Reading Eagle*, 24 September 1950, p.22). Whilst there is little need to comment on the publicist's 'discovery' narrative, the factual account from Craig is worth further consideration. According to Bonzo's trainer, chimps enjoyed capture, and Craig pointed out that since being introduced to alcohol in Liberia Bonzo 'hasn't lost his taste for the stuff. When an admirer recently offered him a full tumbler of bourbon, the ape gulped it down. And, like any other drinker, was tipsy' (*Reading Eagle*, 24 September 1950, p.22). Craig's description was a commonly repeated one, and in *Visions of Calaban*, Dale Peterson and Jane Goodall (2000) note that the methods for capturing wild chimpanzees were seldom discussed by importers or animal traders. Instead the practices were considered 'trade secrets'. It was usual, however, for traders to tell stories about how the chimpanzee's food was spiked with alcohol so that the captured chimps became stupefied and did not suffer any physical damage. According to Peterson and Goodall, the way in which wild chimpanzees were caught bore no relation to the stories told by traders. Hunters acquired chimpanzees for the animal trade by killing individual mothers either with shotguns or by poisoning and then pulled the infant chimpanzees from their bodies. In Liberia, where Bonzo was said to have been captured, hunters often shot adult chimpanzees for food and sold any surviving babies to animal dealers (Peterson & Goodall, 2000, p.102). Whilst it is unsurprising that Hollywood favoured the drunk chimp story or the 'discovery' narrative, the point to be made here is that the processes by which an animal was commodified for public consumption as a star relied on circumventing the realities of a range of animal practices, not only those of the trainer. Moreover, the same systems, practices and trade routes which supplied the entertainment industries also provided chimpanzees for research purposes. In this regard, the fictional *Bedtime for Bonzo* dealt with the subject of chimp capture and the animal trade with a greater degree of realism than the publicity discourse that constructed Bonzo as a star, a point which is elaborated in chapter 5.

In October 1950, U-I announced that Bonzo had been insured for $10,000. This was a publicity ploy common in Hollywood where stars had various body parts insured, often for amounts in excess of one million dollars and usually by Lloyd's of London, a company which claimed that it would 'insure anything' and was referred to in the press as 'one of Hollywood's favourite publicity helpers' (*Sarasota Herald-Tribune*, 14 April 1956). Once the filming of *Bedtime for Bonzo* had completed, a promotional tour started in February 1951, beginning with a highly publicized stunt in which U-I invited two psychologists to give Bonzo an intelligence test in front of the press. As already mentioned, the scientific accounts of chimpanzee intelligence had appeared in newspapers during the previous year and, coupled with Bonzo's ability to understand more that 1000 words and 500 commands, expectations were high that she would produce an exceptional result. The outcome of the tests was not as impressive as the press agents had anticipated, and instead of finding her to be a genius or comparable with a five-year-old (as had been claimed for other chimps) the psychologists equated Bonzo's intelligence with that of a two- to three-year-old child.[23] The stunt was declared a failure by the media, but publicists suggested that Bonzo had purposefully failed, continuing to frame her actions as intelligent, independent and self-directed.

The intelligence test stunt was followed by a series of personal appearances, for which Bonzo was taken to the east coast to appear on the television programmes *Broadway Open House, The Steve Allen Show* and *Blind Date*. During her television appearances in New York, Bonzo bit the host of *Blind Date*, Arlene Francis. Reports of the incident were mixed, and ranged from the bite being a minor accident:

> Actress Arlene Francis gave Bonzo, a movieland chimpanzee, a hand last night – and he bit it. It happened on Miss Francis' television show, 'Blind Date.' Bonzo meant well. He meant to kiss the actress' hand, but in his enthusiasm he bit one of her fingers. The show went on, however, and Miss Francis received medical treatment after the program (*The Southeast Missourian*, 10 February 1951, p.6).

to an attack:

> On 'Blind Date', a chimpanzee named Bonzo expressed a vehement opinion on this newest branch of show business by biting the mistress of ceremonies, Miss Arlene Francis, so severely in the third finger that she sat down hard while the chimp's trainer pulled the beast away (*Pittsburgh Post-Gazette*, 26 February 1951, p.33).

When interviewed about the incident, Bonzo's trainer trivialized the incident suggesting that the bite, now referred to as 'nibbling', had been a stunt engineered to attract 'extra fancy publicity' (*The Deseret News*, 14 February 1951, p.11). In this manner, the aberrant behaviour was framed as meaningful within the context of the star discourse, and it was explained that the appearance with Arlene Francis had offered the only opportunity to perform the stunt and, for various reasons, it had not been possible to bite the other television personalities, Steve Allen and Jerry Lester. Trainer Craig stated that Bonzo was 'actually quite fond of Miss Francis, he's going to send her passes to his new picture' (p.11).

The three interpretations of the incident reveal the instability of the rhetoric of authenticity that configured her as an animal star. Bonzo was variously represented in accounts of the 'bite' as an enthusiastic performer, a publicity-seeking star and as a 'beast', the latter of these sitting outside of the talent/camp nexus that was so central to the meaningful construction of Bonzo as a star personality. Referring to Bonzo as a 'beast' reconnected her to a sense of animality that publicity discourses worked hard to circumvent. Whereas the performance of biting could be understood within the discourse of talent – an animal could be praised for their ability to reproduce such behaviours on cue and within the context of a human-centred narrative – an act of recalcitrant biting animalized the star and returned her to being a thing-of-nature, wherein, following from Sontag, she could no longer be read as 'camp'. Only rarely in Hollywood was there an admission that animal stars were anything other than completely tame, and although chimpanzees became too difficult to handle and often began to bite after the age of six or seven, trainers usually reported that they retired chimps from show business at around eight years of age because they were 'too big'.[24]

In an unusual acknowledgement of the realities of chimpanzees in the movie industry, a *Life* article on the work of producer Sam Katzman in 1953 listed the problems that he faced on a daily basis. One of these was 'worry over hearing that his star ape, Tamba, is starting to bite people. ' "We're going to have a real casting problem in another year" said Sam' (*Life*, 23 March 1953, p.82). A photograph of Katzman (Figure 3.2) holding the hand of a chimpanzee with a collar on and the attached chain leading out of the frame was accompanied by the caption: 'Sam and Star confer on the lawn. She is known as Tamba in Sam's films and Bonzo at another studio but her real name is Peggy. She earns $25,000 a year' (*Life*, 23 March 1953, p.82). With the technologies of control on display (the collar and chain), the acknowledgement that biting was a recognized behaviour which developed in chimpanzees as they grew older, the multiple constructions of star personas (one chimp could be Peggy, Tamba and Bonzo) and the 'value' of animals as industry commodities, this hurriedly staged shot buried in the pages of *Life* can be reread as revealing much about animal stars than the star discourse was ever willing or able to disclose. Indeed, the Hollywood apparatus

*Figure 3.2*   Bonzo and producer Sam Katzman. Also named Bonzo, the chimpanzee pictured here appeared in *Bonzo Goes to College* following the death of the chimpanzee who starred in *Bedtime for Bonzo*. Image courtesy of Loomis Dean/Time & Life Pictures/Getty Images

worked hard to construct the illusion of wild animals such as Fagan and Bonzo as movie stars: that is as autonomous, talented and willing agents and not merely part of the physical capital of the studio, and the success of studio publicity relied heavily on the suppression and reframing of animal behaviours within human-centred narratives both onscreen and offscreen.

# 4
# Wild: Authenticity and Getting Closer to Nature

In 'The Work of Art in the Age of Its Technological Reproducibility', Walter Benjamin ([1935] 2008) argues that the organization of human perception changes over time and is conditioned by the mode of technological reproduction.[1] Filmmaking reproduces a reality that is entirely different from that of painting, he argues, because it diminishes the distance between the viewer and the subject/object and assembles a particular field of vision from fragmented filmed action through the processes of editing. Demand for the mass reproduction of images as photographs, in magazines or as films, Benjamin proposes, is driven by the desire of audiences to ' "get closer" to things, and their equally passionate concern for overcoming each thing's uniqueness ... by assimilating it as a reproduction. Each day the urge grows stronger to get hold of an object at close range in an image ... , or, better, in a facsimile ... , a reproduction' (Benjamin, [1935] 2008, p. 23). The previous chapter discussed the illusory construction of wild animals as movie stars in the Hollywood publicity discourses of the 1950s and their reliance on notions of star talent which were coupled with the pleasures of camp aesthetics. Following from Benjamin's point that audiences develop an appetite for imagery that bring things closer, this chapter shifts focus to examine how notions of reality, realism and authenticity in wildlife filmmaking and associated technological and cultural processes have facilitated a desire to 'get close' to wild animals.

## Ethics and wildlife filmmaking

In a book that elaborated on the professional practices and techniques of wildlife filmmaking, BBC Natural History Unit filmmaker Christopher Parsons wrote in 1971, 'Somewhere between tiger beetles and tigers there is a boundary marking what is permissible from what is not. The position of that boundary varies with each filmmaker. It is a purely arbitrary line, but it is necessary to observe it if a man is to go ahead with a clear conscience' (Parsons, 1971, p. 21). What Parsons was referring to was one of his 'first principles' of wildlife filmmaking: the obligation to the subject. Under this obligation, Parsons advised filmmakers that they must consider whether or not their actions caused distress to the animals being filmed. Taking a non-interventionist stance, Parsons argued that the filmmaker was fully entitled to film animal suffering if that suffering was the product of 'natural incidents'. It was not cruel, for instance, to film one animal killing another even if the prey appeared to be suffering. Such events were part of the natural world and the wildlife filmmaker could and should record them 'with a good conscience' (Parsons, 1971, p. 20). But what about events that were deliberately created for filming purposes? Here, Parsons advised, the line became blurred. He wrote:

> Some will justify this on the grounds that it happens in nature, and in a large number of cases this is answer enough. If you wish to film a spider catching a fly, for example, or a tiger beetle catching an ant, the only sensible method is to stage-manage the incident. I also tell myself that the fly and the ant are among the lower forms of life with simple nervous systems that rule out the experience of pain as I know it. But when it comes to applying the principle that 'it happens in nature anyway' to other and higher forms of life, I find myself faltering (Parsons, 1971, p. 21).

According to Parsons, deciding where the boundary between what was ethical and what was morally unacceptable lay was a decision that each filmmaker had to wrestle with alone. There were, he noted, no hard-and-fast rules to prevent filmmakers from introducing live prey to predators under controlled or semi-controlled conditions. The question was at what species a line should be drawn. As long as filmmakers could satisfy themselves of the necessity for the shot, Parsons implied, that was enough. In short, the level of intervention that was permissible was a matter of personal ethics.

The second obligation that Parsons outlined was to the audience. This obligation ventured to set out guidance for what could be referred to as an ethics of representation. In this regard he wrote, 'the film-maker's only obligation to his audience is to ensure that his film is true to life, *within the accepted conventions of film-making*' (Parsons, 1971, p. 14, emphasis in original). In memoirs of his career with the BBC Natural History Unit, notably entitled *True to Nature*, Parsons described some of the dilemmas he faced as a filmmaker and recalled a time on location in southeast Melbourne filming opossums when, unable to get suitable close-up shots under night-time conditions, he had to resort to filming captive animals the following day and cut the shots together with the footage from the previous night. Regarding this as 'an ethical problem', Parsons reasoned, 'We *had* seen them in the wild and it was only a technical problem which had prevented us from taking satisfactory pictures; it was, therefore, permissible, I argued, to film captive animals *under similar light conditions* so that the shots could be incorporated in our night sequence' (Parsons, 1982, p. 155, emphasis in original). Creating a composite sequence from footage shot in different locations and at different times was not the issue for Parsons; this, he accepted as standard wildlife filming practice. For the same reason, he was not troubled by the fact that the final sequence would comprise shots of different individual opossums. Instead, Parsons was voicing his concerns about staging action with captive animals and presenting it to an audience in such a way as to appear that the opossums were wild. The problem was thus one of identifying where the boundary lay between the realism of wildlife filmmaking and the highly constructed performances that could be found in dramatic live-action animal films. At issue was the question of whether controlled filming with tame or semi-tame animals could ever accurately capture natural behaviour, and Parsons was highly critical of films such as the Disney True-Life Adventures which used staged action. Such films, Parsons argued, 'are usually intended to provide pure entertainment [...] but the implication that they show natural animal behaviour is misleading' (Parsons, 1971, p. 16).

In *Wildlife Films* Derek Bousé expands at length on the representation of 'the real'. When it comes to wildlife, he asks, what reality is being represented? Bousé (2000) argues that, in adopting the structuring conventions of mainstream cinema, wildlife films will always present nature in ways that bear little relation to the day-to-day realities of animal's experience. For instance, he argues, continuity editing coupled with music and narration are designed to deliver a cohesive, and often dramatic, narrative but may well present a distorted version of nature (Bousé, 2000, p. 17). In the case of the dilemma Parsons faced when filming the opossums, the conventions of mainstream narrative (which are structured through a combination of particular shot types) dictated that close-ups were required to properly integrate the animals into the story. The ethical dilemma thus arises from the practices that filmmakers employ at each stage of production to meet the demands of viewers and the industry for commercial narrative-driven films. In short, the filmmaker must present a version of reality that meets particular cultural and industrial expectations and norms. As Bousé maintains, 'Film and television do not and cannot convey reality in its fullness, but have become quite adept at *realism* – that is, at giving convincing impressions of reality' (Bousé, 2000, p. 7, emphasis in original). Realism, in this sense, is culturally relative and an outcome of stylistic devices and conventions which produce a feeling of authenticity. For Parsons, manipulation of the natural world in this way was entirely allowable as long as the filmmaker presented an overall impression of 'truthfulness' to the audience. He argued, 'every cut and join is a distortion of the truth; but if the film story as a whole is truthful then the means used in the making of the film are justified' (Parsons, 1971, p. 19). Bousé agrees, but cautions:

> The use of formal artifice such as varying camera angles, continuity editing, montage editing, slow-motion, 'impossible' close-ups, voice-over narration, dramatic or ethnic music, and the like should by no means be off limits to wildlife filmmakers, but by the same token we should not avoid critical reflection on the overall image of the nature and wildlife that emerges, cumulatively, from the long-term and systematic use of such devices (Bousé, 2000, p. 8).

One outcome of adopting 'Hollywood' conventions is that wildlife filmmaking has been 'suspended somewhere between representation and simulation of nature – between truth and fiction, science and storytelling' (Bousé, 2000, p. 16). What troubles Bousé is that there may be consequences that arise from this state of affairs, and whilst he acknowledges that wildlife films are not, in themselves, deceptive, 'repeated exposure to wildlife films through a shroud of cinematic conventions may make us less, not more, sensitive to it' (Bousé, 2000, p. 8). These are not isolated concerns, and they are echoed by Nigel Rothfels (2002) in his introduction to *Representing Animals* where he argues that nature films, although highly constructed, suggest themselves to viewers as 'an unmediated, unedited experience of "Nature"' (Rothfels, 2002, p. x). Wildlife films follow the logic of commercial narrative and create dramatic moments and obstacles in which animals 'are manipulated into becoming performers' (Rothfels, 2002, p. x). One consequence of the employment of mainstream film conventions, Rothfels argues, is that they create and promote 'a culture in which tourists go to Africa to see the Discovery Channel live' (Rothfels, 2002, p. x).

## Tourism

Reports from the travel industry bear out Rothfels concerns. Indeed one study by a UK travel firm has claimed that television programmes are one of the main sources of 'travel inspiration'.[2] In 2007 there was a marked increase in safari holidays to Kenya, a trend that was claimed by tour operators to have been influenced by the BBC programme *Big Cat Diary* (Henderson, 2007). When concerns were raised about the impacts of tourism on wildlife in the Masai Mara, the same programme was cited by UK travel operators as being responsible for making 'clients believe that it is possible to get very close to the big cats' (Travel Foundation, 2008). At the same time, however, the programme was used by holiday companies to promote the area as a destination and to establish expectations of the experience that awaited travellers when they arrived. Brochures and web sites were explicit in pointing out that the Masai Mara was where the programme had been filmed and that visitors could expect to see the big cats who had been featured on television. For the same reason, a travel article published by a UK broadsheet recommended Kenya as one of the 'best family destinations for spotting six favourite beasts' (*Times*, 2006). The article claimed:

> The Masai Mara is the greatest animal show on earth: 1,800 square kilometres thick with wildebeest, gazelle and impala, every one of them a lion-sized lunch. But what makes Little Governors' Camp extra-special for youngsters is that they're likely to meet celebrities. It is famous for hosting the BBC's *Big Cat Diary*, a feline soap opera packed with violence, adultery and infanticide (*The Times*, 2006).

The article also included quotes from children who had experienced the destination firsthand and whose comments added to the veracity of claims for its similarity to the programme experience. A 13-year-old visitor to the area was reported to say: 'We saw eight lion cubs playing with their mother and scoffing a buffalo – very cute. The next day, we got within five metres of a battle, when the young males from one pride attacked the lionesses from another. Gory and amazing' (*The Times*, 2006).

Public reviews of Kenyan safari holidays suggest that wildlife programmes inform decisions about travel destinations and expectations of places. They also imply that there is value placed on witnessing the animals at close quarters: in other words, with the same sense of proximity that is achieved using television cameras that are often fitted with telephoto lenses. The gaze of the television camera and the intimacy that is gained from close-ups provides a framework within which expectations are formed about the degree of closeness needed for a satisfactory, and therefore authentic, experience of animals. John Urry has argued that tourism is an act of consumption that operates through the 'tourist gaze' (Urry, 2002). There is, he argues, an anticipation that is constructed and sustained through television, film, magazines and so forth, which influences the selection of places that are chosen to be 'gazed upon' (Urry, 2002, p. 3). Such places are marked out by their difference from the 'everyday' and are appropriated to the tourist experience: captured as photographs, on video or as postcards and then recirculated as a form of visual objectification (p. 3). The desire to experience places in this way is derived from a fascination with 'other lives'. For Urry, this attraction is related to the quest for authenticity, and he argues, 'Tourists show particular fascination in the 'real lives' of others that somehow possess a reality hard to discover in their own experiences' (p. 9). A definition of the 'authentic holiday experience' from the industry perspective has much in common with Urry's ideas and is considered to involve experiencing local culture and places of local interest, eating the same food as 'locals' and meeting local people (Nunwood, 2007, p. 16). On one hand, this suggests that getting close to wild animals with a local guide is an important aspect of the authentic experience, a way of encountering wild animals as a 'local'. On the other hand, although both Urry's and the travel industry definitions of authenticity focus on the 'real lives' of local people, the point also remains valid for another type of 'authenticity', one that is constructed by the animal's humanization in a wildlife programme such as *Big Cat Diary* which individuates animals as named characters. In this sense, tourist fascination with the everyday lives of individual cheetahs and lions results in the construction of an authentic experience as one which involves those animals performing the behaviours that meet the expectations set up by the television programmes.[3]

## Getting close

Attempts to get close and have authentic experiences of animals in Kenya have resulted in distress for the animals, young becoming separated, and animals becoming habituated to being fed by tourists and abandoning their normal hunting and feeding habits (International Tourism Services, 2008). Tourists banging on the windows and doors of guide vehicles and clapping to goad animals into action, coupled with the volume of vehicles taking visitors on game drives, have also been cited as major concerns by stakeholders keen to promote sustainable tourism in the Masai Mara (Tribal Voice Communications/Mara Conservancy, 2009). One of the main impacts on wildlife in the Masai Mara Game Reserve has been poor driver guide habits, which have been encouraged by tourists who want to see the animals at very close range (Travel Foundation, 2008). Yet, a 2007 survey on sustainable tourism showed that when asked to rank five factors in order of importance, the majority of respondents (26 per cent) listed the conservation of wildlife and plants as 'most important' (Nunwood, 2007, p. 25). This was followed by the preservation of the destination's culture and heritage (23 per cent), reduction of carbon emissions (23 per cent), reduction of pollution (16 per cent) and fair-trade benefits for local people (11 per cent). These attitudes seem to be at odds with the actions of tourists that have been cited as detrimental to wildlife. Two reasons that present themselves for this apparent contradiction are, first, that tourists are simply unaware that their activities are potentially harmful to animals and, second, that their actions reflect the expectations that are informed and endorsed by their television experience and which they attempt to replicate. A third reason for the gap between the attitudes that people hold about wildlife and their actions, and which is suggested by Nunwood (2007), is that their stated values do not reflect practical choices but a desire to claim certain social identifications that are associated with ethical consumerism and sustainable tourism.

Sustainable tourism has been an attempt by the travel industries and other stakeholders, including local communities, to address the impact of travel on the environment and wildlife conservation. The literature in this area acknowledges the widespread marketing of animal encounters as a fundamental aspect of promoting tourist destinations. Although only 2 per cent of holiday-makers reported that the main reasons for their choice of holiday was 'to see wildlife and enjoy nature' and a further 3 per cent said that a key reason was 'to experience adventure and excitement in natural environments', it is nonetheless the case that animal attractions remain a key feature of tourist experiences (Nunwood, 2007, p. 67). Animal contact has become a marketable commodity where people can have their pictures taken with wild animals as well as stroke, hold, touch or 'swim-with' them. Whilst many of these activities have been promoted as ways to encourage people to become more engaged with animal welfare and conservation, there is little evidence to suggest that this has been the outcome. Arguably, it is difficult to see how manipulating a trained wild animal into posing for a photograph with a tourist has any benefits for the animal. In many cases the animals used as photographic objects have been removed from their mothers at a very young age, are often subject to long-term psychological problems, are usually declawed, drugged or have their teeth removed or their mouths wired, and, once they become difficult to handle, are destroyed, given to research laboratories, or to poorly run zoos and circuses (International Tourism Services, 2008). In this sense animals have become fetishized objects of the tourist experience. The animal encounter all too often involves reducing the complexity of an animal to a 'touchable' curiosity, and the value of the encounter is determined by a cultural overloading of emphasis on the relationship between proximity, contact and authenticity. The tourist gaze is therefore not solely a visual experience, and in the act of consuming the experience as a photographic image, animals are often reconfigured as sensual objects. Photographic mementos of animal encounters are thus often seen to record and fetishize the moment of touch.

A 2002 video of 'Christian the lion' being reunited with the two men who had originally owned him in 1969 has produced a wide cultural engagement with the visual fetishization of contact with lions. The 'reunion' which had taken place in 1972 had been filmed and showed the lion approaching the two men then standing on his back legs to 'embrace' and nuzzle them. An edited version of the film went viral when posted on YouTube and, by 2009, had 11 million views. When counted together, the various versions of 'Christian the lion' on YouTube, MySpace and Google Video had garnered 20 million hits by March 2009 (Jarboe, 2009, p. 151). The video was said to show 'the unbreakable bond between man [sic] and beast' and was the most talked about viral of 2008 (Jarboe, 2009, p. 150). Circulated under the title 'lion hug' or 'lion embrace', many different versions of the reunion condensed the story of Christian to a single moment that functioned as an iconic and symbolic visual, in other words, as representing the event itself and as a symbol of a bond between humans and animals. The same visual rhetoric was used in a 2007 Associated Press report, initially broadcast on syndicated US news programmes, about Ana Julia Torres and a lion named Jupiter (Figure 4.1). Using the same signifiers, the story of Jupiter being rescued by Torres from a travelling circus was reduced to the image of the lion embrace, which was also repeatedly

*Figure 4.1*   Jupiter the lion and Ana Julia Torres. Image courtesy of Associated Press

described in news reports as 'hugging and kissing'. 'Give me a kiss, you big softie' was the headline used to report the story in a UK newspaper which included a quote from Torres saying 'this hug is the most sincere one that I have received in my life' and was accompanied by a photograph of Jupiter 'kissing' Torres through cage bars (*Daily Mail*, 2007). Various versions of the Torres/Jupiter video taken from different syndicated news reports were posted on YouTube and, like the video of Christian, also went viral.

Other videos of embraces between lions and humans, such as Craig Busch (*Lion Man*), Kevin Richardson, the owner of a private reserve in Johannesburg and known as 'the lion whisperer', and Marlice Van De Vuuren (*Marlice: Eine Vision für Afrika*), have a presence on the Internet, which seems to testify to a fascination with visualizing human–lion contact in very specific ways. It is also the case that the same visual rhetoric is employed as a spectacle, in the sense that it is utilized in sensationalistic ways to express the moment of a lion attack. For instance, at the same time that the images of the Christian reunion were being circulated, the story of a schoolteacher, Kate Drew, who received wounds to the head from a 12-month-old lion whilst on a 'walking with lions' experience at a private wildlife establishment in Zimbabwe, also gained international media attention. The experience that Drew took part in included touching, stroking and having photographs taken with the lions, in addition to walking with them. Press reports described how the lion had attacked the woman from behind, standing up on his rear legs and holding on to her head with his paws. Some accounts suggested that the lion cub had been attracted by the woman's hair and was playing, and Drew herself was quoted as saying that the incident was play and not an attack. Accompanied by photographs of the incident taken by a fellow tourist, most news coverage, unsurprisingly, took the opportunity to present the incident as a sensationalized mauling.[4] Similarly, a writer with the *Daily Telegraph* who was injured when he agreed to go into an enclosure with a 12-month-old lion in Limpopo Province, South Africa, to make 'tourist videos' was caught on camera, and the video was later circulated online in an edited version as an 'animal attack' video. Writing about the incident in an article for the newspaper, the journalist describes the moment of touch contact when, 'I slipped inside and the gate locked behind me. I approached slowly and bent down to stroke Mapimpan's wiry underbelly', and at the moment of attack: 'It rose on to its haunches, towering above me and I was spun into a waltz with a 300lb predator – as I pushed desperately at its throat to keep away its jaws. This did not feel like playing' (Smith, 2009). In the written account the lion shifts from an individuated and named being (Mapimpan) to a predatory object whilst the visual accounts of the incident repeated the familiar embrace/attack imagery. The many online video accounts of lion–human encounters suggest that visual rhetoric works to fetishize inter-species touch through constructions of behaviour that are culturally configured as affection, play or ferocity.

Such imagery stakes out the polarized stereotypes of human–lion inter-action that continue to circulate, and in doing so the meanings of animal behaviour are reduced to a normalized binary. Stories that frame the visual imagery depict lions as either grateful recipients of human assistance within 'rescue narratives' or as predatory beasts. In both cases lion behaviour is reduced to visual rhetoric in which the embrace/attack moment is a single image that functions as an iconic, symbolic and spectacular sign.

## Authenticity and authority

The quest for an authentic wildlife tourist experience is not only deter-mined by television programmes, news and YouTube clips but is also structured through, for example, tour operators, travel guides, bro-chures and various other organizational and institutional discourses which are concerned with selling wildlife as a product. A discourse of authenticity is thus highly organized and sustained through a range of different signs and narratives. Travel review web sites, where holiday-makers publish independent accounts of their trips, form part of this discourse of authenticity, and it is clear from comments posted that many have a sophisticated understanding of the construction of the tourist experience. For example:

> The set up of the camp is designed to bring you close to the wildlife – which it did: Zebras graze outside the dining tent of an evening; whilst hippos graze on the banks of the Mara River, which is closely overlooked by the bar terrace. This is not a blight on the landscape of park, the camp has been created extremely sympathetically to blend in with its surroundings. This camp is home to the *BBC Big Cay* [*sic*] *Diary*, and it was a pleasure to see the lions from the prides we had seen on TV. Indeed we did see the team filming and photographing the game whilst we were there.[5]

The extent to which viewers' perceptions of animals are shaped by nature films and programmes is therefore difficult to assess. At a general level, industry studies indicate that television is considered by the major-ity of people to deliver the most accurate information when compared with radio, Internet and newspapers (Ofcom, 2010, p. 24). Fifty-two per cent of UK respondents agreed that the information found on television was 'reliable and accurate', followed by information from radio (50 per cent), Internet (25 per cent) and newspapers (23 per cent). With regard to nature and wildlife programmes on television in particular, there are clear indications that viewers find such texts to be accurate, reliable and truthful. When children aged between 8 and 15 were asked whether nature and wildlife programmes, such as the blue-chip natural history programme *The Blue Planet* and the documentary series *Big Cat Diary*, were 'truthful', 76 per cent said that such programmes were true 'always or most of the time' (Ofcom, 2006b, p. 23).[6] The perceived accuracy of nature and wildlife television programmes was even greater in a survey of adults, 91 per cent of whom agreed that such programmes are accurate 'always or most of the time' (Ofcom, 2004, p. 13). Of this number 40 per cent considered nature and wildlife programmes 'always' accurate. In comparison, only 24 per cent thought that news programmes were always accurate, and other types of factual programming – current affairs, documentaries, dramatized reconstructions and consumer advice programmes – fared even worse for perceived accuracy.[7]

Although these studies suggest that wildlife films tend to be regarded as truthful accounts, they neither indicate what people are willing to accept within the bounds of accuracy nor do they provide a sense of how such programmes shape perceptions and expectations of animals. They do however provide a snapshot of the general regard that viewers continue to have for the authenticity of such programmes. Given that contemporary television viewers are considered to be highly media literate, it is reasonable to suppose that the perception of accuracy is, in part, due to the inclusion of location webcams, 'behind-the-camera' footage and blogs on web sites, DVD extras, and 'making of' programmes (featurettes) which appeal to viewers' interest in the practices and technologies involved in wildlife filming. These various insights into wildlife programme-making offer a sense of transparency by appearing to expose the production process to the scrutiny of viewers. Blue-chip wildlife films[8] tend to offer fewer opportunities for such transparency, as the characteristic features of blue-chip programming are intended to have a universal appeal and nature appears to unfold without intervention as a dramatic and glorious narrative on the screen. Blue-chip wildlife films feature high production values, an absence of humans and human influence, a sense of timelessness, visual splendour, depictions of mega-fauna, dramatic storylines and an absence of politics (Bousé, 2000, p. 14–15). They are also costly to make and so are often funded as co-productions. The role of the filmmakers in the main text is therefore minimized or erased, so it has become quite usual for the programmes to include a supplementary programme, diary, or 'making of' which details the extensive time frames (usually expressed as 'years in the making'), the difficulties of trying to capture the 'never-before-seen' aspects of animal behaviour that are exclusive to that programme, the ground-breaking technologies employed, the enormity of the project and the numbers of personnel and animals involved. Supplementary texts offer reassurance about the value of the programme as a cultural artefact and scientific document, emphasize its authenticity and make mention of the conservation issues that the programme avoids but are organized as dramatic narratives in their own right.

For the blue-chip natural history series *Life*, a BBC, Discovery Channel, SKAI and Open University co-production narrated by David Attenborough and broadcast by the BBC in 2009, 'diaries' followed at the end of each programme episode. These diaries were 10-minute featurettes which explained some aspects of the filming of that particular episode.[9] In the first episode, the featurette explains that the series has taken over three years to film and that the recording of footage in Antarctica had only been made possible through collaborations with various individuals and organizations. Information about the types of transportation used to reach inhospitable Antarctic regions are coupled with enthralling images of helicopters dwarfed against awe-inspiring snowscapes, and the methods used to gain underwater access are accompanied by images of the film crew jumping through holes drilled in the ice and into magnificent marine environments. These shots typically coded by blue-chip aesthetics are interspersed with some looser hand-held camerawork depicting the crew at work and suggestive of other traditions of documentary realism that express immediacy and 'being-there'. The narration, again by Attenborough, then moves on to introduce the story of 'the hardest and most ambitious shoot [which] involved four camera crews, a celebrated French yachtsmen and the Ministry of Defence'. After an introduction to the main 'characters', the narrative continues as a race against time and nature to get exclusive footage of leopard seals hunting chinstrap penguins, and killer whales hunting off the Antarctic peninsula. Music is used to indicate tension as crews work 'against the clock', whilst shots from cameras as they reframe and refocus as well as wind noise and sound distortion, always excluded from blue-chip programmes, are included, each acting as a signifier of authenticity and emphasizing the accuracy of the account.

Interviews with the film crew contribute to the sense of reliability and give firsthand accounts of the technical difficulties faced, the dramas witnessed and the personal problems encountered. In particular the featurette for the second episode offers the audience some sense of the emotional burden placed on crew in an account partly narrated by

Attenborough and partially by the cameraman and researcher tasked to track the full process of Komodo dragons hunting a buffalo, one of the never before seen exclusives caught on camera for the series. Attenborough's voice-over explains that the crew expected the filming to be 'a physical challenge' but had not realized that it would also involve 'emotional turmoil'. The cameraman and researcher are shown lying on the ground filming a Komodo dragon before the shot pulls back to reveal three men 'armed' with forked sticks behind them, the only protection that the crew has against the world's largest lizards, the narration informs us. The team move inland to capture the elusive footage of the dragon kill but have to wait more than a week before first sighting a dragon and a buffalo at the same watering hole. They describe their 'frustration' and boredom whilst they wait for something to happen. When the dragons finally attack one buffalo and the crew capture it on film, the cameraman turns to look at the camera and says, 'I've definitely got two heads at the moment; one as a cameraman saying "yes, brilliant" and the other's thinking "that poor animal", you know that's not nice, that's really not nice'. The crew then follow the buffalo as he dies slowly over a period of days, and Attenborough's voice-over informs the audience that 'this begins to take a toll on their emotions'. A researcher worries that the buffalo will think of the crew as 'death' and he voices his concerns to camera that he may not be 'cut out' for wildlife filming, Attenborough then explains that 'the event has become personal', and the researcher describes how the crew has 'built up a relationship' with the buffalo who eventually dies and is eaten by the dragons; the whole process is caught on camera. Reflecting on the process, and as a voice-over to the images of the dragons eating the buffalo, the researcher revises his concerns and finally realizes that what he has witnessed is, in fact, 'astonishing' and 'primeval' and that the dragons are 'the most fantastic things to be with: scary, 'awesome' and like 'something from *Jurassic Park*'. The featurette is infused with the danger that is posed to the crew and buffalo by the Komodo dragons and inflected with the emotional drama that the crew face in having to follow a dying animal over a period of days. The Komodo dragons are not demonized by the end of the programme as the event is contextualized by the authority of Attenborough's narration, which informs viewers that the event is a fact of nature and the only way the dragons can 'get large prey', and through the researcher's commentary of the buffalo's death, which is restated as part of the awe-inspiring grandeur of the natural world. In this way, whilst the featurettes do give some sense of the methods and techniques involved in filming for the series, they are presented as dramatic narratives in their own right.

A different strategy was used for the 2008 BBC television series *Big Cat Live*, where the live broadcast of the programme and its extensive use of webcams were designed to emphasize the unmediated nature of the programme. The exclusive 'never-before-seen' trope described the programme's use of technology that could record animal behaviour using methods that had not been attempted before. Although broadcast live from the Masai Mara Nature Reserve in south-west Kenya, the programme also incorporated edited footage of events from preceding days and weeks. The first episode of the programme opened with the presenters walking towards the camera telling viewers that the production crew had already been on location for some time and had been able to film 'some of the high octane drama that makes this place such a wonderful stage for this natural soap opera'.[10] A montage of action shots of the various big cat characters running, attacking, playing and roaring then followed, accompanied by a fast-tempo contemporary music track. The episode continued with a presenter explaining that roving cameras were filming action as it happened, which was, in turn, being broadcast live to viewers. Then turning to the live monitor screens he noted that the lions were 'doing what lions do best which is very little'. The viewer response to the programme revealed the extent to which the programme met audience expectations about what wildlife films should do: One viewer wrote, 'i didnt [sic] like it, filmed mostly at night, and with IF cams, i was bored and gave up after the 2nd day, we want more action, out there in the jeepy things all day!' whilst other viewers commented that 'i [sic] loved this one it was actually live and you could see wat [sic] the cats were doing', and another wrote, 'I am so far from those big cats living in Montana it's my only way of feeling like I am connected on some small way'.[11] The web site which accompanied the series devoted five pages to images taken by the production team on mobile phones, described as 'a snapshot of Big Cat life from both sides of the lens. Glimpse the whole team from cameramen to presenters and of course the animal stars' (BBC *Big Cat Live*, 2008).[12] With the use of live cameras constantly being foregrounded, the overriding discourse of the programme suggested that it gave access to an unmediated and direct experience of big cat life. Unsurprisingly, the programme makers were thus keen to stress the 'liveness' of a 'lion kill' which was eventually caught by the webcams and broadcast on the Internet. A statement by the team on a social networking web site claimed, 'We believe this is the first live lion kill broadcast on the internet. Recorded at approximately 16.15 BST, 3 October 2008'.[13] Social networking web sites thus also provided an important dimension to the sense of liveness and immediacy that the programme wished to cultivate, and in addition to posting video, photographs and updates between episodes, it also allowed viewers access to the production team.[14]

*Big Cat Live* highlighted one of the central issues of wildlife filmmaking: for the majority of the time, animals do very little that is of interest to a television audience. The promise of 'high octane drama' at the opening of the first episode and the montage of action shots was immediately at odds with the first live images that viewers were offered: lions lying on the ground. To appeal to audiences, wildlife films have relied on offering a compelling series of action events edited together to appear as if the day-to-day lives of animals are a non-stop drama of life and death, eating, breeding and birth. Writing some three decades before *Big Cat Diaries,* Christopher Parsons noted that, for commercial reasons, many films have tended to cram 'in as many incidents and confrontations with other species as time will allow. It may be argued that these confrontations *can* happen in nature, but it is probable that they occur only very occasionally, even when they are direct predator/prey relationships' (Parsons, 1971, p. 16). Although he was writing in 1971, Parsons' comments highlight the gap between authentic animal behaviour and that which fulfils the requirements of a wildlife film narrative. In this regard, Gregg Mitman suggests that the debate over drama versus authenticity in wildlife filmmaking is far from new, although the sources of concern have, in the past, been quite different. In *Reel Nature* he gives an account of the tensions that haunted early twentieth-century wildlife filmmaking with, on one hand, educators and religious leaders who agreed that natural history films could offer educational and moral value and, on the other hand, commercial filmmakers whose sensationalized animal films attracted large audiences. Mitman explains that those who wished to develop natural history films for 'a more serious-minded audience' could not simply eliminate emotional drama, as this would alienate popular theatre-goers, but what was at issue was whether the drama 'had been authentically captured in the wild or had been created through artifice to elicit thrills and generate mass appeal' (Mitman, 1999, p. 10). Distinctions between live-action animal narratives and wildlife films remain imprecise. If anything, Bousé's observation that they lie somewhere between fact and fiction and representation and simulation alerts us to the liminal position that they occupy in a cultural continuum of what can be broadly described as factual film and programme making. It is here that familiar tensions over definitions of wildlife films struggle to assert some firm ground between the slippery poles of documentary and entertainment.

## Genre

Contemporary wildlife films are the cinematic legacy of the late nineteenth-century appropriation of camera technologies to document scientific observations. Whilst cinema offered science a new-found apparatus of truth, commercial animal adventure films found large audiences, and jungle films such as the travelogue *Simba* (1928) combined the spectacle of dangerous wild animals with the popular appeal of comedy and titillation.[15] By the 1950s the Disney True-Life Adventure series monopolized the market for commercial nature films and offered sentimental portraits of nature and animals that were suited to a family audience. After the financial failures of *Pinnocchio*, *Fantasia* and *Bambi*, the studio had turned first to educational films and then to nature films, finding success with the True-Life Adventure films that were packaged with one of the studio's feature-length films and which provided the studio with the financial lifeline it needed. To present a pristine version of nature, all evidence of humans was excluded from the frame. Landscapes were presented as timeless and uncorrupted by human presence whilst the animals were stereotyped and anthropomorphized to enhance the dramatic aspect of the narrative. At the time of their release, the films were well received by scientists and the public, but True-Life Adventures were later criticized for their anthropomorphic depictions of animals, overuse of music and dramatic narratives, which were considered to be more in keeping with the world of fiction filmmaking than with documentary. Such criticisms were not without basis: the origins of the films were to be found in both the studio's animation classics and wartime information films (Mitman, 1999, p. 111). The films were marketed as educational and the studio targeted schools across the country with mass-market mailings and sent pamphlets to teachers to use in the classroom (Mitman, 1999, p. 113). At the same time, themes from *Bambi* – that nature could be portrayed as innocent in the absence of humans – informed the True-Life Adventures, and the profit margins generated by the films reinforced the studio's confidence in its approach to depicting nature.[16] Key objections to the Disney films emerged from critics who were opposed to the staging of some action where animals would be filmed under controlled conditions, and to the trivialization of animals, depicted as cartoonish characters set to music.[17] In his guide to making wildlife films, Christopher Parsons wrote, 'Music should be used sparingly in any documentary film, but even more carefully in wildlife films; in strictly scientific behaviour films it is out of place in any case' (Parsons, 1971, p. 190). Parsons' point regarding the institutional classification of wildlife films as 'documentary' was at the core of debates surrounding the legitimacy of True-Life Adventures, and genre definitions have continued to inform questions of authenticity in wildlife filmmaking into the twenty-first century.

It is useless to think about wildlife films and genre removed from their institutional context. Bill Nichols rightly points out that the institutional framework 'imposes an institutional way of seeing and speaking, which functions as a set of limits, or conventions, for the filmmaker and audience alike' (Nichols, 2001, p. 23). The institutional framework will always reflect the wider broadcasting environment and the demands that are placed on programming to find an audience. The commercial broadcasting environment and programming has had to alter to accommodate the requirements of broadcasters, audience tastes and public concerns, as well as shifts in scientific discourses and changes in technologies. Moreover, the 'community of practitioners' that work within institutional parameters have a considerable influence on the type and style of programming that is produced. For instance, Disney employed an array of naturalists and commercial filmmakers, editors and producers for the True-Life Adventures of the 1950s, whereas, during the 1970s, the BBC Natural History Unit and Oxford Scientific Films were very clear about the status of their practitioners as scientists first and filmmakers second, underpinned by an explicit commitment towards objective, factual production regulated by the discourses of science and the practices of scientific observation. Following a downturn in audiences for wildlife programmes in the 1990s, finding the balance between entertainment and documentary styles and approaches that met all the various demands put on wildlife filming resulted in the blurring of genre boundaries between, for instance, the mixing of soap opera formats and wildlife documentary in *Big Cat Diary* and *Meerkat Manor*.

Debates about the authenticity of wildlife programmes were brought to public attention in the 1980s and with even greater vigour in the 1990s when accusations of 'fakery' were levelled at the programme *Tale of the Tides*, broadcast in the UK as part of the ITV Survival series in 1998. Before this, reports in the 1980s had revealed that the lemming suicide scene in the Disney True-Life Adventures film, *White Wilderness*, had not only been faked but had involved forcing the animals over a cliff. During the 1990s there was a phenomenal growth in factual television, particularly documentaries and docudramas, which led to public outrage when stories began to emerge in the press that many such programmes used staged shots or re-shot some scenes. Attention was turned towards wildlife films when the controversy over *Tale of Tides* erupted, as the issues revolved around accusations that the filmmakers had used tame hyenas, porcupines and wildcats to simulate wild behaviour. A well-renowned wildlife cameraman, Hugh Miles, came forward to reveal that captive animals had been used in wildlife filming for years. Miles maintained that 'It is always a last resort and it is certainly something I try to avoid' and admitted that 'on one or two occasions I have had to fall back on it myself. The truth is that all films are a cheat. We get as close as we can to the scientific truth and 99 per cent of the work is genuine' (*The Independent*, 1998). Defending the use of staged action, the commissioning organization, Anglia Television, stated that 'the behaviour shown is authentic and the relevant sequences are not possible to obtain in any other way. Survival, along with other UK-based natural history producers, has never made any secret of the fact that these techniques are occasionally employed' (*The Independent*, 1998). In 2001, the BBC had to defend the inclusion of shots of lobsters spawning in tanks, filmed at Anglesey Sea Zoo in North Wales, in the blue-chip natural history documentary *Blue Planet*. The position taken by the BBC in response to criticisms that the footage was fakery was that 'It would have been unethical and physically impossible to shoot this physical process in the wild as it would have caused unnecessary and unacceptable disturbance, while doing it at Anglesey did not cause this' (BBC News, 14 October 2001). In 2007 the programme *Born Survivor* (re-titled *Man vs Wild* for non-UK markets) also had to respond to accusations of fakery and staged action, and the Discovery Channel admitted that 'isolated elements' were not 'natural to the environment' (BBC News, 19 March 2008). And, in 2008, *Big Cat Diary* faced criticisms of misleading viewers when it did not reveal that one of the main characters depicted in the 2007 series, a cheetah named Honey, had been killed before the series was broadcast. She had died two weeks before the programme aired when a vet accidentally shot her in the wrong place with a tranquilizer dart (*Daily Mail*, 2 February 2008).

Questions of fakery, lack of integrity and authenticity are framed by the expectations that genre inheres within the audience. Institutional genre classifications have defined many blue-chip programmes, such as *Blue Planet*, as natural history or wildlife documentaries, and, according to Bousé, this presents a major problem. He argues, quite rightly, that blue-chip wildlife films should not be conceived of as documentaries but instead as creative interpretations of nature that are more suited to the realms of art (Bousé, 2000, pp. 20–28). In 2008, and following the success of *March of the Penguins*, Disney returned to producing and distributing nature films and established the independent label Disneynature. The second release under the new label was *The Crimson Wing: Mystery of the Flamingos*, which was promoted as a wildlife documentary with all the characteristics of contemporary blue-chip nature films, which, in turn, have borrowed heavily from Disney's 1950s True-Life Adventure films. The film featured burlesqued head-bobbing to music, pristine nature, spectacular images of thousands of flamingos and vast natural vistas, as well as individuated bird characters. It is unsurprising therefore that Disney claimed that with Disneynature the company had returned to its origins in wildlife filmmaking.

In television wildlife programming, the blurring of genre boundaries and formats in the quest for dramatic entertainment has added to the complexity of defining nature or wildlife films with clarity or certainty. Trends in the industry have been a response to declining audience numbers and changing consumer demands. From the late 1990s onwards, this has resulted in a massive diversification in wildlife filmmaking with ever more varied formulas that have variously foregrounded technologies (*Walking with Dinosaurs*, *Walking with Beasts*), human–animal confrontation (*Born Survivor*, *The Crocodile Hunter*, *Rogue Predators*), individuated animal characters (*Big Cat Diary*, *Meerkat Manor*), predation (*Predator X*, *Animal Face-Off*) and so forth. Nature films have laid claim to cultural authority that has been derived, in no small part, from a history of institutional genre classification. The example of *Big Cat Diary* illustrates that wildlife programmes have some degree of influence in shaping expectations and perceptions. What such programmes do is relocate 'wild nature' into the domestic and culturally organized spaces of media reception – the living room, the cinema and so forth – and in doing this, they construct a relationship between viewer and animal that reduces distance and fulfils a desire to bring animals closer. But it is also easy to overstate their influence and, for instance, ignore tourism discourses which amplify particular aspects of wildlife programmes. This reminds us that wildlife programmes are part of a wider cultural mix where a myriad of other messages and signifiers compete to reinforce and challenge meanings about wild animals.

# 5
# Experimental: The Visibility of Experimental Animals

In post-war America and Britain, increased federal and state sponsorship of science brought scientists into the public spotlight, but with little understanding of scientific methods the public relied on popularized forms of science for information about scientific practices. Whilst much of this information was gleaned from popular science writers who published in magazines, newspapers and other periodicals, films also played their part by producing narratives about scientists for movie audiences.[1] Terzian and Grunzke (2007) argue that the link between the increased public interest in science and the types of representations of scientists that were typically found in Hollywood films between the 1940s and 1960s can be accounted for because 'people looked to experts – and particularly scientists – to apply their intellects to intelligent ends: to enhance the security of the nation, shield the nuclear family, and elevate the standard of living' (Terzian & Grunzke, 2007, p. 408). There was a general fascination with science although public feeling about scientists was ambivalent, and this was reflected in the range of representations on offer. Hollywood films established the various clichés of the mad, heroic, morally bankrupt, eccentric, arrogant or absent-minded scientist, and in doing so it was inevitable that their practices, methods and experimental subjects would also become important aspects of the films' narrative. The depictions served more than one purpose: they opened up a seam of story possibilities based on the prevailing scientific discoveries of the time and offered audiences a series of representations of science, scientists and experimental methods that, although fictional, were unavailable elsewhere.

Because of the lack of popular knowledge about science, the scientists' private experimental space – the laboratory – could be imagined within films as a mysterious, dangerous and fascinating site, a place of intrigue where the fictional scientist found an outlet for their rational intelligence, madness or maniacal tendencies. With only minimal investment in the reflection of scientific reality and primarily focused on entertainment and commercial success, fiction films were free to dramatize and sensationalize scientific endeavour. On one hand, representations of male scientists as dangerous geniuses working outside the moral compass of ordinary society became a mainstay of science fiction and horror (for instance, *Dr Renault's Secret*, 1942; *The Ape Man*, 1943) whilst, on the other hand, their emotionally remote and socially inept counterpart reoccurred throughout the comedy genre (*Bedtime for Bonzo*, 1951; *Monkey Business*, 1952). In terms of what scientists 'did', what happened within the laboratory space was open to speculation, and, in the case of animal experimentation where scientific procedures and methods were particularly poorly understood, fiction films were left to construct representations that fed into the popular imagination.[2] The point to be made in this regard is that although animal imagery pervaded popular culture the day-to-day realities of animal experimentation were rarely brought into the public domain, a point which is unsurprising given that such practices remained highly contentious and largely unavailable to public scrutiny. In this sense, fiction film representations of experimental animals were the images most readily available to the public consciousness.

Imagery of experimental animals has continued to proliferate throughout popular culture. For instance, in the 2006 animated feature *Flushed Away*, the inept henchman is an albino ex-laboratory rat who, the film's official web site claims, 'has had one too many "shampoos" up in the laboratory which left him completely unfocussed on doing bad deeds' (Dreamworks, 2006). A key element in the plot of the 1980 horror film *Alligator* is the dogs that have been used as test subjects by a scientist developing a synthetic growth hormone. The film reflected public anxieties about pet dogs being sold to research laboratories, and in the film the experimental subjects all die and are dumped into the sewer system where they are consumed by an alligator which grows to horrific proportions. In *Beethoven* (1992) the eponymous canine hero is taken, under false pretences, to be used in a ballistics experiment to test the effects of a new type of bullet when fired into the test subject's skull. *Night of the Lepus* is another film to feature huge experimental animals, this time killer rabbits, inadvertently released from a research laboratory, and the monsters in *Piranha* (1978) and *Frankenfish* (2004) are the results of genetic engineering experiments. In the remake of the 1963 film *The Nutty Professor*, the chemistry professor Julius Kelp is rewritten for the 1996 version as the overweight Professor Sherman Klump who spends much of his time experimenting on guinea pigs to find a cure for obesity. In the opening scenes of the remake, hundreds of Klump's test subjects are accidentally released and invade the college campus. The 2007 blockbuster *I Am Legend* is the post-apocalyptic story of a scientist trying to find a cure for a mutated retrovirus that transforms humans and other species into monsters. Rows of glass-fronted cages in his basement laboratory contain test subjects, rats that have been infected with the virus. What these and other similar examples demonstrate is that, across various genres, fiction films have been responsible for providing much of the popular imagery of experimental animals since the 1940s.

The focus here is on one film which is identified as part of a larger group of films that include representations of apes and monkeys as experimental subjects. Such films constitute an identifiable corpus of texts which spans the twentieth and twenty-first centuries and illustrates an ongoing human fascination with non-human primates in popular culture. The continued material and symbolic importance of monkeys and apes is, as Donna Haraway (1989) has remarked, because they have 'a privileged relation to nature and culture for western people: simians occupy the border zones between those potent mythic poles' (Haraway, 1989, p. 1). Such privilege results in a complicated set of human–ape relations where the non-human primate body and mind occupy problematic zones of indeterminacy. In short, 'they' are human-like yet not human, and because of their likeness to humans, monkeys and apes in popular narratives offer both comedic and horrific possibilities, the dualism arising from the comedy spectacle of the humanized animal, on one hand, and the unsettling vision of animalized humanness, on the other. As a result, many such films fall broadly within two genre classifications: comedy (*Bedtime for Bonzo*; *Monkey Business*; *The Road to Hong Kong*, 1962) and horror (*Dr Renault's Secret*; *The Ape Man*; *Link* (1986); *Monkey Shines*, 1988; *Twelve Monkeys*, 1995; *28 Days Later*, 2002).[3]

*Bedtime for Bonzo*, released in 1951, was produced at a time when there had been a dramatic increase in the numbers of non-human primates being used in experimental research. It is also around this time that the scientist emerged as a recurring character type in popular films, as the film studios sought to reflect the attitudes and concerns of the time. The film's main premise (that of raising a chimpanzee as a child) and one of the key moments of narrative tension (when Bonzo is sold to a biomedical research laboratory) were based upon the realities of psychological and biomedical experiments being undertaken at the time. The film is explicit in raising questions about how Bonzo should be treated, although the responses to such questions reveal the film's inability to challenge the moral orthodoxy. The film utilizes gendered positions that inevitably oppose an emotional female 'voice' with a masculinized discourse of scientific rationality. As discussed in chapter 2, these gendered distinctions emerged in the late nineteenth century and they continued to resonate as meaningful within films of the twentieth century. The aim here is to explore how twentieth-century Hollywood dealt with and integrated animal experimentation into a mainstream feature film.

## Peter, Gua and Viki

*Bedtime for Bonzo* was initially conceived by screenwriter Raphael Blau who, as a graduate student, had studied with the educational psychologist Edward Thorndike. Blau's screenwriting career revealed an ongoing interest in psychology, and prior to writing *Bedtime for Bonzo* he had become familiar with various psychologists' attempts to raise chimpanzees within a domestic human environment, an idea that had been first proposed in 1909 by child psychologist Lightner Witmer in an article entitled 'A Monkey with a Mind'. Witmer carried out a series of tests on a young chimpanzee named Peter, a performer in a vaudeville act, to determine whether his seemingly humanlike intellectual capabilities were indicative of intelligence or merely stage tricks. Although initially reticent about testing a chimpanzee in a child psychology clinic and concerned that critics might assume he was making direct comparisons between human and chimpanzee intelligence, Witmer eventually reversed his judgement and became convinced that the young chimp's abilities were comparable with those of a human child. Furthermore, Witmer asserted that Peter was the 'missing link' between human and non-human primates as suggested by Darwin's theory of evolution by modified descent. To these ends Witmer wrote: 'The chasm between the mind of the highest anthropoids and the mind of man has been held to be not less than the chasm between their structures. This chasm Peter's mind practically bridges' (Witmer, 1910, p. SM7). In conclusion to his study, Witmer suggested that further experiments on chimpanzees had the potential to reveal important information about the significance of education and environment on psychological development: 'I venture to predict that within a few years chimpanzees will be taken early in life and subjected for purposes of scientific investigation to a course of procedure more closely resembling that which is accorded the human child' (Witmer, 1910, p. SM7).

Witmer's prediction was correct and in 1933 psychologist Dr W.N. Kellogg co-wrote, with L.A. Kellogg, *The Ape and the Child*, a book-length report that detailed the findings of a nine-month-long experiment in which his ten-month-old son, Donald, and a seven-and-a-half-month-old chimpanzee, named Gua, were raised together as siblings. Born in a captive colony in Cuba on 15 November, 1930, Gua was moved to the Anthropoid Experiment Station at Yale University where she was forcibly separated from her mother on 26 June 1931. Gua was then taken to the Kellogg household where, according to Kellogg, 'her humanizing was begun' (Kellogg & Kellogg, 1933, p. 16). Kellogg intended that the experiment with Gua and Donald would demonstrate the extent to which environment influenced early development and, in doing so, would shed light on the reasons why so-called 'wild children' – children who had been brought up by wild animals – were unable to adapt to human society or respond to teaching. As scientists were prevented legally and morally from attempting to replicate the upbringing of a 'wild child' as a psychological experiment, Kellogg proposed the following solution: 'Instead of placing a child in a typical animal environment, why not place an animal in a typical human environment? Why not give one of the higher primates exactly the environmental advantage which a young child enjoys and then study the development of the resulting organism?' (Kellogg & Kellogg, 1933, p. 11). Such ideas were not unique to Kellogg, and similar notions underpinned the growing scientific fascination with the utility of chimpanzees as 'experimental objects' that could reveal knowledge about humans without the ethical complications of experimenting on human subjects. As Robert Yerkes, the founder of the Anthropoid Experiment Station, wrote, 'study of the other primates may prove the most direct and economical route to profitable knowledge of ourselves' (Yerkes cited in Haraway, 1989, p. 62).

The questions that Kellogg's experiment sought to answer were summarized by psychology writer Marjorie Van de Water in a report for *Science News Letter* in 1933. She asked, 'If the human being's humanity is the result of his training and his human association and environment, not his heredity, would not the young ape respond to these things by becoming "humanized?"'. To answer this question, Gua was dressed and treated as a human child throughout the term of the experiment, and her physical, sensory, behavioural, emotional, learning and language development was monitored and compared to that of Donald. In many of the tests, the experimenters were surprised to find that Gua

performed better than her human counterpart, leading Kellogg to conclude, 'It is clearly in defense of the capacities of the animal that the
results of the present research are most significant' (Kellogg & Kellogg,
1933, p. 322). Kellogg's account argued that environment influenced
development[4] and Gua's results led him to propose that it was probable that other higher mammals – specifically, chimpanzees, dogs and
cats – were as sensitive to certain stimuli as humans (Kellogg & Kellogg,
1933, p. 321). He questioned what these findings meant for laboratory
animals subjected to 'the extreme forms of punishment and deprivation employed in many of the ordinary types of experiments performed
upon them' and the results obtained from such experiments (p. 322).
Despite asking 'Who, indeed, has thoroughly considered the point of
view of the animal?' (p. 322), Kellogg's intention was not to raise moral
objections to animal experimentation on the grounds of suffering but
instead to question the reliability of the results gained from experiments performed under laboratory conditions.[5] He wrote:

> To test a captive anthropoid seized by force in the jungle, kept later
> in a cage, and motivated by hunger in some experiment is one thing.
> To test a human child who is kindly and gently talked to and who
> is never under any circumstances caged or starved is certainly a dif-
> ferent thing. We treat one organism in ways we should never think
> of treating the other and, in so doing, we often tacitly assume that
> this treatment – sometimes years of it – has little or no effect upon
> any particular segment of behaviour which we may later choose to
> measure (Kellogg & Kellogg, 1933, p. 323).

Kellogg's study was not without its critics. To address the shortcomings of previous studies, in 1947, psychologists Keith J. Hayes and
Catherine Hayes adopted a chimpanzee named Viki with the intention
of studying the impact that environment had on her intellectual development and with the specific aim of teaching Viki to speak.[6] Taken
from her mother when she was just a few days old, Viki was raised as
a human child in the Hayes' home and underwent a series of tests, the
results of which were measured against the existing information held
about human children and laboratory chimpanzees. At three years of
age Viki's development was reported to have 'closely paralleled that of
a normal human child, her interests and abilities having appeared in
roughly the same sequence, and at about the same rate' (Hayes & Hayes,
1951, p. 106). Viki's acquisition of language proved to be less successful, however, although Hayes and Hayes reported that she was able to

vocalize three words: 'mama', 'papa' and 'cup'. Viki did not consistently deploy the words appropriately, but her mental development was such that the experimenters were led to conclude that 'our results strongly suggest that the two species [chimpanzee and human] are much more alike, psychologically, than has heretofore been supposed. They suggest, in fact, that man's superior ability to use language may be his only important genetic advantage' (Hayes & Hayes, 1951, p. 108).[7]

## Bedtime for Bonzo

Although sources are unclear about which particular psychologist's account[8] was the inspiration for *Bedtime for Bonzo*, the film bears close parallels with the Kelloggs' and Hayes's studies. For writer Blau, the experiments provided an opportunity for on-screen humour whereby the academic investigation of heredity versus environment functioned as a plot premise that could be used to exploit the comedic potential of a chimpanzee being treated as a human.[9] In the film, Ronald Reagan plays the role of a college psychology professor, Peter Boyd, who is engaged to Valerie Tillinghast, the daughter of the Dean. When it comes to light that Peter's deceased father was a convicted felon, Dean Tillinghast is immediately concerned that any future grandchildren will inherit criminal tendencies and demands that Peter break off the engagement. To keep his fiancée, Peter must prove that criminality is a product of environment and not genetics. As he feeds a chimpanzee in a colleague's laboratory, Peter develops an idea for an experiment which will demonstrate that nurture can succeed over nature. Peter explains to his colleague, Hans, that he will teach Bonzo the chimpanzee moral reasoning by raising him as a human child. When Hans remarks that Bonzo will also need a mother figure, Peter responds by hiring a young woman, Jane, to take on the maternal role. Together, Peter and Jane raise Bonzo as their son and attempt to teach him right from wrong, but Valerie becomes jealous and calls off the engagement. Peter decides to continue with the experiment in the hope that he can eventually win her back. The experiment goes well until Dean Tillinghast decides to sell Bonzo to Yale University for medical research purposes. Following an argument between Jane and Peter, Bonzo runs away, finds his way into a jewellery shop and steals an expensive necklace. Peter is arrested for the theft but is eventually freed when Jane asks Bonzo to return the necklace, which convinces the police that Bonzo and not Peter has committed the crime. Bonzo returns the jewels and, in doing so, proves that he has acquired moral reasoning. Hans buys Bonzo from the university, and instead of being sent to the medical research laboratory Bonzo goes to live with the newly married Peter and Jane.

In terms of popular entertainment of the time, the screenplay had a number of components which suggested that the film would have good commercial possibilities. Animal films were popular with audiences and, by the time *Bedtime for Bonzo* was released in 1951, chimpanzee characters were a staple of Hollywood films in no small part due to Cheeta, a role played by many individual chimpanzees and which had appeared in a string of highly successful Tarzan movies, preceded by two Tarzan serials: *Tarzan the Fearless* in 1933 and *The New Adventures of Tarzan* in 1935. The commercial potential of the character Bonzo can also be set in context given that Universal-International (U-I), the company that produced the film, had had success the previous year with *Francis* (1950), a film about a talking mule, and *Harvey* (1950), the story of a man whose best friend is a spirit which takes the form of a six-foot rabbit (see discussion of U-I gimmick films in chapter 3).[10] As the *New York Times* review of *Bedtime for Bonzo* wryly commented, 'Considering the fact that the people at Universal-International seem to have had a fine time with a rabbit in *"Harvey"* and a mule in *"Francis,"* it is hardly surprising that they are still casting in Hollywood's zoos' (*New York Times*, 6 April 1951).[11] The trade press also commented on U-I's increasingly animal-focused slate of films: 'Pictures about animals are, of course, no novelty – but horses and dogs have, in the past, been in the limelight as concerns such offerings. A new and somewhat exotic trend is reflected in U-I's employment of simians and linguistic mules [...]' (Spear, 1950, p. 20). *Bedtime for Bonzo* played to the vogue for animal films with the added novelty of a chimpanzee character displaced from the customary jungle context into a suburban setting, whilst, thematically, the film reflected some of the key social concerns of the time.

*Bedtime for Bonzo* tackled the 1950s' American preoccupation with 'the family' and the role of parents in imparting moral values to children. The family was considered to be the bedrock of post-war American society, and the model of a working father, stay-at-home mother and at least two children was encouraged by a national political agenda and idealized within popular culture.[12] Women were discouraged from working and encouraged instead to aspire to the role of mother and homemaker. This social context gave the two female characters in *Bedtime for Bonzo* identities that the audience could easily understand: Dr Valerie Tillinghast, the cold-hearted career academic, and Jane, the warm-hearted mothering figure. The dominant ideology of the time thus made it easy for audiences to support the romance between Peter and Jane, even though it is responsible for the break-up of Peter and Valerie's relationship, as Jane represents the idealized mother, a point emphasized in the film. Her goal is to get married and, most importantly, to be a mother. As Jane dresses Bonzo in a romper suit, Peter says to her, 'you enjoy playing mother don't you', to which Jane replies, 'Someday I'm going to be a real one and I want a large family; ten at least'. With many families broken apart during wartime, the narrative trajectory of *Bedtime for Bonzo* reflected the broader social and political drive toward reconstructing the family unit. In this sense the film takes three individuals, each of whom has suffered the trauma of losing a parent, and configures them as an idealized family: Peter who chooses to be referred to as 'papa' and grew up without knowing his own father, a lifelong criminal; Jane, referred to as 'mama' and whose own mother died when she was young, forcing her to raise her five brothers; and Bonzo, a chimpanzee taken away from his mother to become an experimental subject and eventually Peter and Jane's adopted surrogate child. The gendered roles which are established early in the film then become crucial in determining the responses to questions regarding Bonzo's treatment.

From the outset, the audience is made aware that Bonzo is a laboratory chimpanzee purchased by the university for Professor Hans Neumann, for the purposes of an experiment that remains unspecified throughout the film. In the opening scenes, Hans suggests to Peter that Bonzo is suffering from some type of psychological problem, saying that he has found Bonzo with a surgical knife and then outside on a high ledge in what is constructed by the film as Bonzo's suicide attempt. Returned to a small barren cage in the laboratory and slumped in a corner, Bonzo refuses to eat, leading Hans to remark to Peter that the young chimpanzee is on a 'hunger strike'. Hans says, 'I'm afraid to force feed him, it might be dangerous'. Peter asks, 'What do you think is wrong with him?' to which Hans replies, 'I don't know. He's very young. Only a month ago he came from Africa. Maybe he's lonesome for his mama'. Although Gua and Viki, the young chimpanzees used in the Hayes' and Kellogg's experiments, were from captive breeding colonies, chimpanzees destined for experimental purposes were, as *Bedtime for Bonzo* suggested, captured and imported from Africa.[13] Bonzo's fictional situation was therefore not untypical of the route by which many chimpanzees found themselves in research laboratories and is remarkably similar to Kellogg's description in 1933 of the realities of such a life as 'a captive anthropoid seized by force in the jungle, kept later in a cage, and motivated by hunger in some experiment [...]' (Kellogg & Kellogg, 1933, p. 323).[14]

In *Bedtime for Bonzo*, Hans's reference to Bonzo's state of mind being affected by maternal deprivation – being 'lonesome for his mama' – tapped into a key theme of scientific interest in the 1950s, particularly after the publication of John Bowlby's *Maternal Care and Mental Health*, a report sponsored by the World Health Organization (WHO) which stated that 'the prolonged deprivation of the young child of maternal care may have grave and far-reaching effects on his character and so on the whole of his future life' (Bowlby, 1952, p. 46). For Bonzo his trauma manifests in depression and an inability to eat, and the effects of being caught and separated from a parent are used as Peter's motivation to try bottle-feeding the young chimp and singing a lullaby. The strategy works and Bonzo begins to eat, which gives Peter the idea of raising him as a child and teaching him right from wrong to prove to Dean Tillinghast that environment is more important than genetics.

Hans's assessment of Bonzo's emotional distress at being 'lonesome' and resulting in a 'hunger strike' was not without basis, and although fictionalized and used for comedic purposes, the film nonetheless reflected earlier scientific observations. In 1933 Kellogg had reported that Gua's social and psychological dependency were closely interlinked so that, 'To shut her up in a room by herself, or to walk away faster than she could run, and so leave her behind, proved, as well as we could judge, to be the most awful punishment that could possibly be inflicted. She could not be alone apparently without suffering [...]' (Kellogg & Kellogg, 1933, p. 157).The depiction of Bonzo's emotional state and refusal to eat due to being separated from his mother echoed Kellogg's observations, and the topic of maternal attachment was taken up by Harry Harlow in his psychological experiments in 1957.

Six years after the release of *Bedtime for Bonzo* and the publication of Bowlby's WHO report, psychologist Harlow began his maternal deprivation experiments on rhesus monkeys, which led a few years later, in the early 1960s, to partial and total social isolation experiments, some of which were adapted by other scientists using chimpanzees in place of monkeys. In the partial social isolation experiments, rhesus monkey infants were taken at birth and placed in bare wire cages. Harlow wrote, 'These monkeys suffer total maternal deprivation and, even more important, have no opportunity to form affectional ties with their peers' (Harlow et al., 1965, p. 90). In the total isolation experiments, infant monkeys were taken a few hours after birth and placed in a stainless steel chamber for either three, six or 12 months so that 'during the prescribed sentence in this apparatus, the monkey has no contact with any animal, human or subhuman' (Harlow et al., 1965, p. 90). One of the outcomes of total social isolation from birth that emerged from Harlow's experiments was that the young monkeys developed 'emotional anorexia'. Harlow wrote:

> No monkey has died during isolation. When initially removed from total social isolation, however, they usually go into a state of emotional shock, characterized by the autistic self-clutching and rocking [...]. One of six monkeys isolated for 3 months refused to eat after release and died 5 days later. The autopsy report attributed death to emotional anorexia. A second animal in the same group also refused to eat and would probably have died had we not been prepared to resort to forced feeding (Harlow et al., 1965, p. 92).

The rhesus monkey babies functioned as experimentally produced psychologically traumatized human infant models that contributed to knowledge of the emotional health and well-being of humans. Donna Haraway emphasizes that this knowledge was utilized in the 'public space of the economy' where it was deployed within debates about working human mothers (Haraway, 1989, p. 236). Harlow's experimental models were erased of their monkey-ness to produce the ideal psychologically damaged human child model. Similarly, for both the Kellogg experiment and the fictional experiment in *Bedtime for Bonzo* to be successful, all elements of chimpanzee-ness needed to be displaced in favour of constructing the chimps as 'human children'. In *Bedtime for Bonzo* the overriding tone is no less humanistic than in Harlow's experiment; Bonzo the chimpanzee must become humanized – the ideal morally conditioned son – in order for Peter to find an understanding of himself as a man and a father and for Jane to fulfil her desire to be a mother and so meet the societal norms of a 'good woman'. Accordingly, whilst Gua, Bonzo and the monkeys involved in Harlow's experiments shared the erasure of their non-humanness in the search for the ideal 'child', 'son' and 'traumatised infant', the anthropomorphic constructions of human–non-human primate relations in mainstream film provide potent images of apes and monkeys as pseudo-humans who, within the fictional patriarchal world, were able to attain a level of moral significance over and above that dictated by the moral orthodoxy that governed the lives of real experimental subjects.

## Laboratory spaces/domestic spaces

The setting for scientific investigation in films is often used to connote whether or not the research is ethical. As a general rule, the setting used for a scientist working on ethically problematic research will be outside the sphere of public and peer scrutiny or institutional control (Weingart, Muhl & Pansegrau, 2003). Illegitimate experimentation is usually undertaken in a laboratory sited, for instance, in a cave, the basement or a secret locked room in a house, in a dungeon or at some location isolated from the norms of moral policing. Ethical research, or experimentation that does not seek to trouble the moral limits of an audience, takes place within an institutional laboratory setting or 'in the field' where it is visible and open to scrutiny. In their wide-ranging study of the representation of science in 222 films, Weingart, Muhl and Pansegrau (2003) argue that 'the disciplines that are ethically problematic are most frequently medical research, followed by physics, chemistry, genetics, psychology, and biology' (p. 285). As a result, there is a corresponding frequency of 'mad' or 'bad' scientists represented in films as working within these fields. Additionally, the chief reason for medical research to figure so prominently as ethically problematic science within films is due to its being most frequently represented as experimenting on living subjects, methods of gaining knowledge that are most likely to challenge moral norms (p. 284).

In *Bedtime for Bonzo*, Bonzo is initially caged in an institutional laboratory that has natural light flooding in through open windows. As a result the laboratory setting is visually coded to suggest that whatever the research purpose Bonzo was destined to be part of, it is legitimate, ethical and does not trouble the presumed moral boundaries of the audience. Hans's experimental research is never explained by the film, thereby allowing him to remain a 'good' scientist. In the university laboratory, Bonzo's status as a research object is negotiated by the narration, which adopts two distinct positions: Bonzo is referred to as an expensive research commodity but also acknowledged as sentient and able to experience psychological trauma. When Peter tries to prevent Bonzo jumping from an upper ledge of the university building, Hans expresses his concern over the situation, pleading, 'Peter, try something else. Two thousand dollars he cost the college'. Once rescued, any suffering that Bonzo experiences from being confined in a small barren cage in Hans' lab remains unquestioned by the narration, which instead explains his dejection by suggesting that Bonzo is feeling the effects of maternal separation. Later, as Peter interviews Jane at his house for the job of 'Bonzo's mother', the two hear banging from the upstairs bedroom where Bonzo has overturned the slatted-side crib and become trapped beneath it. Seeing Bonzo for the first time Jane screams and tries to run away but stops when she hears Bonzo crying, saying 'why, he sounds just like a baby'. Keen that Jane should stay, Peter replies, 'well he isn't much different when you get to know him'. On re-entering the bedroom Peter remarks, 'oh he's turned it completely over. I guess that's why he's crying. He probably thinks he is back in a cage again'. Peter reinforces the comparison that Jane has made between Bonzo and a human baby and, in doing so, manipulates her into staying and assuming the role of Bonzo's 'mama'.

Although the narration does not problematize Bonzo's confinement in the laboratory cage, there is an implicit ethical question about caging Bonzo that is articulated through Peter's observation that Bonzo's distress is due to his thinking that he is 'in a cage again'. However, concern about Bonzo's suffering comes from Jane and, additionally, from a gendered discourse which aligns the female response to animals in emotional and anthropomorphic terms. The narration legitimizes this emotion to the extent that the audience is encouraged to sympathize with Bonzo as a humanized character. Peter's response to Bonzo, although anthropomorphic in its framing of his behaviour, remains matter-of-fact, typical of the character of the emotionally remote scientist. When asked by Hans how he would feel about giving Bonzo up, Peter replies, 'Be sensible, I expect to give up Bonzo just as soon as the experiment's finished. It isn't wise to get too attached to animals'. When Hans asks how Jane will feel, Peter emphasizes their differences, remarking, 'Well I expect she'll take it pretty hard. She's very emotional about him. It's a sublimation – a transference – at the moment. She hasn't anyone about whom to lavish her affections'. Hans's response to Bonzo is located between the polarized positions of Jane's emotion and Peter's objectivity. He is upset when told that Bonzo must go to the medical research department at Yale University but complies with Dean Tillinghast's request. It is the prospect of Bonzo's departure to Yale that deserves particular consideration here, as it is this aspect of the film which highlights the narration's ambivalence toward animal experimentation.

On the day of Bonzo's birthday party, Dean Tillinghast tells Hans that he has sold Bonzo for $2500 to Yale University for medical research purposes, saying: 'They've just lost a chimpanzee and they have to have another one in order to complete the project'. Hans tries to object and tells the Dean that Bonzo 'thinks he's a little boy'. He adds, 'Our Bonzo is no ordinary animal. He's good and he's kind'. The Dean responds with incredulity, surprised to hear such things from 'a man of science' and dismisses Hans with the demand that Bonzo be shipped immediately. At the birthday party Hans keeps Bonzo's fate from Peter and Jane, who makes a wish for Bonzo saying that she hopes he gets a chance to show that being loved as a human being has made Bonzo 'feel like a human being'. Making an inadvertent reference to Bonzo's impending and certain fate at Yale University, Hans remarks to Peter 'I only wish Bonzo should live to have another birthday', and he becomes uncomfortable when Peter uses the word 'post-mortem'. Later in the film Jane returns to discover that Peter is in jail and Bonzo is in a shipping crate. She immediately takes him out of 'the nasty little cage' and goes to Dean Tillinghast to convince him that Bonzo must not be sent away. Hans explains that their experiment involved teaching Bonzo 'human ethics', but the Dean is infuriated and asks for Hans's resignation for misuse of college property. Hans leaves with Jane and Bonzo saying that he will reimburse the college the sum of $2000. Bonzo then demonstrates that he has learnt human moral reasoning by returning the stolen necklace to the jewellery store, and Hans is allowed to keep his job. Peter declares that he has proved that Bonzo was motivated by love for those who loved and protected him, and Bonzo is saved from the medical research laboratory.

*Bedtime for Bonzo* does not take an explicit stance against animal experimentation. On the contrary, the setting for Hans's research – the brightly lit institutional laboratory – is coded as ethically unproblematic, and even the setting for Peter's psychological experiment, which takes place away from the college, is undertaken in the comfortable, bright, family home, which establishes its ethical legitimacy. By way of a contrast to Hans and Peter's research, however, medical research is structured through the narration as something dreadful for Bonzo. It is made clear that he will die if he ends up at Yale, although the detail of what faces Bonzo as an experimental research object is left to the imagination of the audience. For instance when Jane asks, 'why the department of medical research?' and Hans replies, 'why do you think?'. Jane considers Hans' response for a moment and then, appalled, declares, 'oh no!'. The realities of what happened to a chimpanzee destined for experimental purposes at Yale University in the early 1950s were various and included being used in research into poliomyelitis and psychosurgery or psychological research on forms of restricted movement. The numbers of chimpanzees used in poliomyelitis research increased following studies undertaken by David Bodian and Howard Howe at

John Hopkins University in the mid-1940s. Bodian and Howe offered the following explanation:

> The chimpanzee, although a cumbersome experimental animal, is the animal of choice for such experiments since it is perhaps the only animal which sufficiently resembles man with respect to poliomyelitis to be of any considerable value for direct analogy, as well as for suggesting leads for study of the human disease in its inapparent form. It not only exhibits a clinical and pathological picture resembling that in man but has also been shown to eliminate virus in its stools, and to be susceptible to spontaneous infection in the inapparent form, as well as in the paralytic form (Bodian & Howe, 1945, pp. 255–256).

In Bodian and Howe's experiments, human stool samples with the active polio virus were administered to 13 chimpanzees either orally, by inoculation or by means of a gastric tube directly into the stomach. After a period of time, ranging from one to seven months from the administration of the virus, each chimpanzee was killed and examined. All but one of the 13 chimpanzees was named, and seven of these – Rosebud, Curley, Tina, Toto, Caroline, Bobo and Rollo – came from animal dealers. Angel, a four-year-old female chimpanzee, was 'received from a showman', but the sources that provided Gene, O'Toole, Bozette and Cilly were not recorded (Bodian & Howe, 1945). The unnamed chimpanzee, described as 'an adult tuberculous male, with severe cage paralysis of all extremities', was given the polio virus on four occasions during October 1940 and died 5 days after the final administration (Bodian & Howe, 1945, p. 258). Each of the chimpanzees used in Bodian and Howe's polio experiments was between two and five years of age, the majority recorded as being in 'excellent health', 'robust' or, in the case of Gene, having a 'lively and inventive disposition' (p. 259).[15] In later experiments undertaken at Yale University, chimpanzees between the ages of two and four years, the majority of which were supplied by the Yerkes Laboratory of Primate Biology, were used in polio experiments designed by Dorothy M. Horstmann and Joseph Melnick. The polio virus was repeatedly administered to Flora, Webb, Jent, Falla, Hickory and Catawba although Melnick and Horstmann noted that 'Studying the immunological response in chimpanzees in this fashion is laborious and cumbersome, but yields data so far unobtainable in any other way' (Melnick & Horstmann, 1947, p. 302). Other experiments undertaken by scientists from Yale that involved chimpanzees included those designed to assess the effects of restricted movement. Published accounts of such an experiment described how Rob, a male chimpanzee born in March 1948, was separated from his mother 36 hours after being born and put into a straitjacket at four weeks of age. From the age of five to 14 weeks Rob's hands and feet were restricted by being fully bandaged and held in place by adhesive tape. From 15 weeks of age, cylinders were placed over his arms and legs and kept in place by adhesive tape until he was 31 months old to assess the effects of the restriction of tactual, kinaesthetic and manipulative experience (Nissen, Chow & Semmes, 1951). Research into psychosurgery was also being pioneered at Yale University at the time that *Bedtime for Bonzo* was written and released. This involved making experimental lesions in the brains of monkeys, baboons, chimpanzees and 'genetically pure thorough-bred dogs' to assess the effects of such damage on behaviour (Fulton, 1951, p. 538). Whilst the nature of the research that Bonzo was intended for at Yale is never fully disclosed by the narration, Jane's horrified reaction as she considers the possibilities and Hans's objection, on the grounds that Bonzo 'thinks he is a little boy', suggest, implicitly at least, that the narration regarded animal research as ethically problematic under certain circumstances.

Taking into account the fact that at the time *Bedtime for Bonzo* was made support for the antivivisection movement had diminished (see chapter 2), how does the film resolve Bonzo's fate at an ideological level? The question of whether Bonzo should be sent to the medical research unit does finally rest on the issue of his moral worth. Yet, the moral orthodoxy of the time justified animal experimentation, and whilst there was an acknowledgement that animals had some moral status, human interests were considered to always outweigh those of animals. If the film had been informed by the dominant ideology, then Bonzo would have been sent to contribute his life for the 'greater good of mankind'. Of course, this does not happen, and the argument against Bonzo being sent to Yale for medical research purposes is that he is 'too human', and the narration reinforces this as it succeeds in establishing that Bonzo has acquired moral reasoning and is intelligent enough to think himself, as Hans puts it, 'a little boy'. This excess of humanness is, however, rendered meaningful only within the particular ethico-socio-political norms that motivate the action and narrative closure of the film. As David Bordwell argues, particular norms are present in Hollywood cinema and these norms constitute the classical film style (Bordwell, [1985] 2006, pp. 4–5). Apart from material and technical norms, ethico-socio-political norms take on particular aesthetic functions. In *Bedtime for Bonzo*, Bonzo's status as a pseudo-human child is framed within the patriarchal norms of the 1950s family. The narrative is driven forward toward the final restitution of the family unit – father, mother and child – and in this case the socio-political norms that governed the idealized family also elevate Bonzo's status, symbolically at least, to that of a human child, thereby conferring the same moral privilege on him. Of the two heterosexual romances in the film, the one that is doomed to fail is that between Peter and Valerie, as this would have required Bonzo to remain an object of science and only of use to the narrative to prove Peter's theory and allow him to win Valerie back. If this romance had succeeded, Valerie and Peter would be 'childless' at the end of the film. From the romance between Peter and Jane, Bonzo is enabled to become a 'real boy', and thus a 'proper' family unit can be created between the three characters. It is in this way that the film negotiates a position from within the socio-political norms of the time that could claim ethical concern for Bonzo without subverting the dominant moral orthodoxy.

## Visibility

*Bedtime for Bonzo* employed a feminized position to challenge experimental practices. However, this challenge was used as a soft rebuke that is shown by the film's narration to lack the rational grounding of scientific reasoning and is instead positioned as a sentimental response to animals. Such gendered positions operate from within an ideological framework that dismisses a feminized empathetic response to animals and instead privileges a masculinized discourse of justice, rights and rules wherein emotional responses are not taken to be adequate grounds for an argument in favour of ethical treatment. It is not without note that, in *Bedtime for Bonzo*, when Hans asks Jane what she thinks will happen to Bonzo at Yale, her response is silence and the performance of emotion. In other words the feminized response to Bonzo's impending death is reduced to an emotional reaction, and Jane is not given any opportunity within the narrative to articulate a rational justification as to why Bonzo should not be sold to the research lab. Jane's protest is thus doubly subordinated by the patriarchal ideology that frames the film and steers the narrative.

On one level, *Bedtime for Bonzo* is problematic because it (eventually) offers images of a happy experimental animal much the same as *Monkey Business*, another comedy about a scientist and chimpanzees which was released the following year. In *Monkey Business*, the two chimps, Rudolph and Esther, turn the tables on the scientist, played by Cary Grant, when Esther escapes from her cage and creates a formula for everlasting youth.

Esther and Rudolph are bathed daily, wear clothes and are highly intelligent, a point that is emphasized early in the film when they manage to confuse Grant's character by switching outfits. Similar to *Bedtime for Bonzo* the on-screen humour in *Monkey Business* called for chimp antics, a reframing by the narrative of certain behaviours as clownish actions that drew on existing stereotypes of chimpanzees, which were also used by zoos and circuses to draw in audiences for chimp exhibits and shows that were often the main attractions. It is not the intention here to propose that either of these films represent animal experimentation in ways that could lead audiences to question whether experimental animals are morally considerable. Indeed this very question is obscured by the generic conventions of comedy and the systems of representation that portray experimental animals as pseudo-humans. The point here is that there are multiple connections to be made between these fictional subjects and their real analogues, particularly given that fictional animal characters give some measure of visibility to the absent referent: the animals used in experimental research.[16]

When Kellogg's experiment ended, Gua was sixteen-and-a-half months old. Unlike Bonzo, who drives off into a future as a child with his adoptive 'father' and 'mother', Gua was, according to Kellogg, 'returned by a gradual habituating process to the more restricted life of the Experiment Station' (Kellogg & Kellogg, 1933, p. 16). Unlike the fictional Bonzo, Gua was used in further experiments. However, Bonzo is not detached from the lived realities of Gua, Viki and the many thousands of monkeys and chimpanzees that were, and continue to be, used in experimental research. Granted, Bonzo is the Hollywood-manufactured version of those realities, but the film also offers one of the few popularly available representations of animal experimentation. The film is grounded in what Blau knew to be the realities of the life of an experimental chimpanzee, and whilst there is little to challenge the moral orthodoxy, and Bonzo is, without doubt, a popularly commodified and cleaned-up version of animal testing, the challenge here is not to disentangle Bonzo from Gua or Viki but to recognize that the systems of cultural production and knowledge production that situate them, respectively, as film character and experimental object are intricately entwined. *Bedtime for Bonzo* thus reflects how within a history of human–animal relations overlapping and mutually reinforcing systems of subordination, production and exploitation define and connect fictional and real animals.

# 6
# Farmed: Selling Animal Products

There was little change to British farming practices between 1914 and 1916. As war broke out, the government's main concern was that there should be a large enough labour force available to ensure that crops could be harvested. Official guidance offered to farmers by the Agricultural Consultative Committee was limited to recommendations that wheat production should be increased and the numbers of livestock maintained. In the first two years of the war, the number of dairy cows stayed reasonably consistent at around 2.2 million whilst the overall size of the national cattle population increased to 7.44 million and the sheep population during the same time remained at around 25 million.[1] Increases in the cattle population reflected the choices that farmers made to maintain the numbers of cows in preference to sheep or pigs when, in 1915, feed shortages began to affect livestock farming. Sheep and pigs represented a much smaller capital investment than cattle, and cows also offered the advantage of milk as a constant income stream. The costs of rebuilding a national cattle herd were considered too high; sheep and pigs were thus more 'expendable' and as a result, by 1916, the numbers of pigs had decreased by 7 per cent (Dewey, 1989, p. 82). By 1916, it was clear that some sort of interventionist agricultural policy was required, and one of the first decisions taken by the new administration under Prime Minister Lloyd George was to appoint a Food Controller. A campaign for increased food production got underway and one of the driving forces behind the interventionist strategy was the scientific evidence, presented in a 1915 report, that land could be better managed to produce food for human rather than livestock consumption. Estimates suggested that 100 acres turned over solely to wheat would produce enough bread to support 208 people. The same area used for pasture would support the production of enough beef and mutton for only 40 people (Dewey, 1989, p. 92). The discourse of food and land management constructed livestock as inefficient and a drain on national resources.

During World War II, scarcity of food and ongoing rationing led to new legislation introduced to encourage home food production, and in 1942 Government initiatives promoted 'backyard' rabbit- and poultry-keeping as a way to alleviate food shortages.[2] A popular rabbit 'fancy' had grown up by the end of the nineteenth century that encompassed breeding and exhibition practices. Although not as popular as dogs or cats, rabbits nonetheless were established as pets with all but two breeds being classified as 'fancy' rabbits. 'Fur' rabbit breeding increased in popularity in the interwar years and by 1928 the number of fur breeds had increased from two to 13. Between 1939 and 1941 research into rabbit breeding was undertaken by the Ministry of Food, which met with the British Rabbit Council between 1938 and 1947 to discuss how best to promote the breeding of rabbits as part of the national home food production initiative. As a result, the domestic rabbit was officially promoted as 'food' in 1942.[3] Domestic rabbit keepers were entitled to seven pounds of bran per female rabbit per quarter as the British Government attempted to emulate the breeding programmes already in place in Germany and Italy. Prices were fixed and a four-month-old rabbit was worth between four and five shillings in flesh and between one shilling and seven and sixpence in fur.[4] In support of the introduction of the new legislation, the *Picture Post* magazine published an article which advised readers on how to start a domestic rabbit business under the headline, 'Two boys buy a rabbit: Rabbits are no longer pets' (*Picture Post*, 23 May 1942, pp. 22–23).

To encourage people to participate in home food production, sentimental attachment to utility animals was constructed as opposed to the war effort. To avoid sentimentality, it was suggested that backyard breeders should keep more than one animal or join a co-operative.[5] With only a single pig, hen or rabbit, there was an increased chance that people would become emotionally involved and find that they were unable to slaughter and eat their 'home food production'. Pig-keeper Stanley Pearce wrote, 'there is a psychological factor which operates against efficient production on an individual basis. People keeping one animal are liable to become sentimentally attached to it, treat it as a pet, and shrink from the thought of killing it for food' (*Picture Post*, 17 February 1940, p. 51). Pearce's comments reflected the commonly held associations between pet-keeping and sentimentality and also emphasized that the distinction between the 'pet' and the farmed animal was potentially ambiguous. Individuated animals encouraged people to regard livestock as 'pet-like' and, consequently, the scientific or social categorization of animals (by specie or as livestock) was not enough to regulate human–animal relationships. Although institutional discourses categorized rabbits as 'not pets', their classification was vulnerable to emotional attachment, which was considered to be characteristic of the earlier Victorian period. Therefore, apart from recommendations to increase the numbers of animals being raised for food, another way in which sentimentality was managed was through a discourse of industrial efficiency which, when applied to sentient creatures, reconfigured them as units of production.

In the case of home food production, rabbit breeding appropriated a discourse of 'industrial production' which referred to the rabbit as 'the product' and the young rabbits as 'output'. Guidance advised that 'the backyard rabbit keeper is recommended to limit his production line to four breeding does and one buck, who, between them, ought to have an output of one hundred young rabbits per year' (*Picture Post*, 23 May 1942, p. 22). The photostory that accompanied the *Picture Post* article followed two young boys at a rabbit dealer's establishment as they selected from Flemish, Chinchilla and Sable breeds, the latter of which, it was noted, would also provide fur as an additional income stream. Readers were also advised that although many people claimed to dislike rabbit meat, this taste preference was due to them having eaten wild rabbit. The article offered an assurance that 'domestic rabbit really does taste like chicken' (p. 23). Details about the overheads involved in establishing a rabbit production line were compared to the costs of keeping chickens, which, it was noted, was a much less economical venture.

People were encouraged to adopt the language of efficient production in relation to backyard food animals and this echoed the shifts that occurred within the discourse of farming. Postwar food production in the UK changed markedly with the introduction of new farming methods and technologies which were geared around increasing cost-effective production and which ushered in the era of intensive farming practices. The scientific management of livestock was first encouraged through legislation with the introduction of the 1947 Agriculture Act, which guaranteed prices for farm products and was introduced to address the postwar lack of domestically produced food, establish Agricultural Land Tribunals, allow ministerial land acquisition and institute control of the way in which land was utilized. A review of the Agricultural Policy in 1952 set out new objectives that included raising the levels of meat produced for the domestic market. Efficiency became the watchword of the post-1952 programme, and later reviews in 1958 and 1960 pushed for ever greater productivity which was encouraged by the introduction of subsidies. The drive for greater productivity in the postwar years was reflected in agriculture manuals and guides such as *The Science and Practice of British Farming*, written in 1949 for agricultural students, which stated: 'The efficiency of the animal in converting food into meat can be expressed as a ratio between its weight increment and its food consumption' (Watson & More, 1949, p. 498). In another guide written in 1959 and intended for veterinary and agricultural students, the average life of a dairy cow was measured in lactations whilst beef cattle were differentiated from dairy varieties by their ability 'to convert food, whether grass or concentrates, into beef with maximum efficiency' (Miller & Robertson, 1959, p. 462). These guides for British agriculturalists emphasized efficiency of productivity in every aspect of farming and were keen to dismiss traditional views about animal husbandry that were not quantifiable or scientifically provable.

Although production and efficiency dominated the postwar agricultural discourse, traditional views on animal husbandry did not disappear. Written in 1959, a popular manual on practical shepherding described the shift from pre-war pastoral farming to the postwar scientific management of livestock as problematic, saying: 'many potential shepherds, whilst conversant with the application of scientific discoveries, lack [...] the experience of practical shepherding. But remarkable as these scientific discoveries are, they are only an aid and cannot replace the knowledge of sheep and land possessed by the good shepherd' (Clarke, 1959, p. vii). Such shepherding knowledge, it was argued, included the ability to 'read' the sheep through an understanding of their bodily movements and sounds. The writer mourned the loss of the relationship between shepherd and sheep that was conceived in aesthetic terms as the 'Art of shepherding' and which was quite apart from the 'Science of shepherding' (Clarke, 1959, p. viii). Although the manual looked back to the benefits of traditional rural living and attempted to negotiate the passage from pre-war to postwar shepherding, it in no way suggested that the animals benefited from older farming practices. For example, the guide described 'traditional' methods for castrating lambs, which had involved cutting open the scrotum with a knife, drawing down the testicles and then cutting, burning or biting through the cord. Such practices were described by the author as 'crude and disgusting' and it was noted that the older method, apart from the pain the lambs experienced, also put them at risk of death from haemorrhage or infection (Clarke, 1959, p. 64). Newer practices, which the manual argued were painless for the lamb, were 'bloodless' and involved crushing the cords in the scrotum or tying a rubber ring above the testicles. The new practices were not, however, introduced to reduce the suffering of lambs but instead for economic reasons, to limit losses of stock and increase the body weight of lambs before slaughter.

## Going to work on eggs

In the guidance manuals on farming practices, welfare standards were couched in terms of the effects that disease, housing, feeding and so forth would have on profits. The suffering of farmed animals was either obscured by the language of production or simply denied. For example, one manual stressed that 'there is no cruelty in fur farming, and many women now insist on farmed skins, when purchasing, instead of pelts from animals which have suffered agonies in traps' (Miller & Robertson, 1959, p. 621). The scientific management of farmed animals was celebrated as a success of innovation and efficiency and was regarded as vital to the rebuilding of the postwar economy. At the same time that rationing in Britain ended, in 1953, farming practices underwent a considerable change, most notably in poultry-keeping where there was a swing towards battery systems and intensive farming techniques. In fact, poultry-keeping after 1950 has been described by one author as 'the best example of factory farming in Britain', a view that reflected its fast expansion and economic success (Holderness, 1985, p. 67). In the 1950s, poultry-keeping became highly specialized and farmers invested in either breeding, egg or meat production. Prior to this, poultry-keeping had been a diverse activity and the majority of mixed farms had some investment in each aspect of egg and meat production. With the creation of the British Egg Marketing Board (BEMB) in 1957 and the guarantee of subsidies, intended to stabilize the market and encourage higher levels of production, farms moved towards battery housing and large-scale operations. Other systems, such as 'the deep-litter system' in which around 250 birds were kept in sheds fitted with pens on concrete floors covered with about six inches of 'short litter' and the 'fold system' in which between 20 and 40 birds were kept in small portable houses with attached wire-netted runs that were moved every day to fresh ground, were increasingly abandoned in favour of battery systems. Thirteen per cent of flocks had over 1,000 laying chickens in 1957, but by 1965 that number had increased to 50 per cent. Intensive systems with between 30,000 and 50,000 chickens began to replace operations with less than 500 birds, which had previously accounted for three-quarters of the egg-producing industry. Such was the expansion of the industry that by 1965 plans for factory farms housing up to twelve-million chickens were proposed by J.B. Eastwood Ltd. which, at the time, produced 10 per cent of all eggs in the UK.[6] Whilst Eastwood's plans for such large-scale egg production did not come to fruition, it was nonetheless indicative of the trend towards ever larger-scale battery systems. Intensive farming of chickens for eggs and for meat was encouraged by the government, which was concerned to provide cheap sources of protein for the domestic market, and the BEMB was charged with the task of expanding the domestic market for eggs and standardizing the product. Soon after being established, the BEMB launched the 'Go to work on an egg' advertising campaign (Holderness, 1985, p. 86).

The BEMB wanted to copy the success that the Milk Marketing Board (MMB) had had with its campaign to 'drinka pinta milka day'. To emulate the MMB's achievement, the BEMB first used the radio and television star Tony Hancock in 'Go to work on an egg' television advertisements. Later, print advertisements for the campaign continued to stress the protein value of eggs, their versatility as a cooking ingredient, their utility as an aid to losing weight and their cheapness. A discourse of efficiency that constructed the chicken as a unit of production within farming also informed the marketing of eggs, which were promoted as standardized units of protein. Eggs were also intrinsically connected to the national identity through advertisements which stressed their importance within a classless taste culture. At its most obvious, this national ideology was expressed through the 'lion-brand' mark, a single rampant lion derived from the three lions symbol of the Royal Arms of England, which was stamped on every egg (Figure 6.1). The lion symbol functioned as a signifier of Britishness, but in appropriating it as a brand the aim was to create associations with notions of quality through processes of standardization. To reinforce the concept of eggs as a national, and therefore classless, food, one 1964 BEMB print advert used an image of a butler serving a boiled egg on a silver tray and a photograph of a housewife buying a box of eggs with the strap line 'Rich man's ritual – housewife's choice!' (BEMB print advertisement, June 1964). Eggs were for everybody, and elsewhere they were endorsed by celebrities and promoted as the food of working Britain primarily through the slogan, 'go to work on an egg' and by photographs and cartoon images of the nation's workers, who were depicted as standing on or straddling eggs. 'Work' in this sense encompassed children's schoolwork, 'women's work' in the home as well as the more traditional notions of men's employment. A discourse of health and well-being was aligned with the concept of human efficiency

*Figure 6.1*   British Egg Marketing Board advertisement. Image courtesy of the Advertising Archives

in the workplace, and adverts incorporated information about the positive effects gained from eating protein derived from eggs. With recommendations that housewives feed their children at least one egg every day, have two themselves and prepare at least three for their husbands, the advertisements promised 'Better temper all morning. Improved efficiency. A nicer nature' (BEMB advert, April 1966). The campaign did not shy away from sexualizing egg consumption, and the imagery used to promote eggs for 'slimming' changed during the 1960s from a picture of an egg with a belt around it to an image of a woman pulling out the sides of her dress to indicate how much weight she had lost, accompanied by the slogan 'If you want to be slim and delightful', to a bikini-clad female torso with the strap line, 'how you should be!' (BEMB advert, August 1965). In later promotions such as 'Breakfast fortnight', which encouraged the nation to eat an egg for breakfast every day for two weeks, young women were employed as 'Egg Chicks' to visit random homes and give £1 to anyone found eating an egg for breakfast.

The campaigns were incredibly successful in shaping the national taste culture and provided reassurances to the domestic market about the high standards of the product. All eggs were sold to the BEMB at a fixed price and were graded and stamped with the 'lion-brand mark', which was used not only to indicate quality to the consumer but also as a method for the BEMB to track each egg and ensure that it did not over-pay subsidies. As a consequence of the BEMB's campaign, consumption of eggs in Britain increased by 20 per cent between 1957 and 1970, rising in 1968 to an average national consumption of 13,676,000,000 eggs per year.[7] The high production and consumption rates came at great cost to the lives of chickens, and the introduction of intensive systems also brought with them a new set of behaviours that included 'feather picking', 'vent picking', cannibalism, 'toe-picking' and egg eating (Miller & Robertson, 1959, p. 557). *Practical Animal Husbandry* advised, 'many methods have been adopted to attempt to control these vices, without any real success, until debeaking was adopted' (p. 557). Using a portable debeaking apparatus, between 300 and 400 birds could be debeaked in one hour. The manual described how the electrically heated blade was used to sear through the beak to remove '½ of the distal extremity of the upper mandible, or in some cases of both upper and lower mandibles' (Miller & Robertson, 1959, p. 557).

The introduction of subsidies instituted through postwar agricultural policies was designed to bring stability to the market and to provide food for the population. Production at such levels was, however, dependent on the large-scale exploitation and suffering of chickens, and the outcome of this initiative was a grotesque superabundance of eggs and a surplus of egg products which were costly to dispose of (Holderness, 1985, p. 86). To tackle the surpluses, the BEMB responded in 1964 with an intensification of its marketing campaign, the aim of which was to increase demand for eggs and thereby tackle the problem of overproduction. And whilst the strategy worked in terms of raising national egg consumption, the surpluses remained. There was little in the way of public resistance to factory farming and although, by 1968, the relationship between salmonella and intensive poultry farming practices had been established, it was the better publicized concerns about a link between cholesterol and the risk of heart disease that caused a drop in egg consumption in the 1970s. The success of the BEMB advertising campaign was weakened on a political level by the economic controversy over the excesses of production, and the marketing messages about eggs and their benefits were undermined by the media reports on cholesterol. As a result, the BEMB was disbanded in 1971, but the commercial farming practices that had been established during the Board's management of national poultry production remained.

## Chickens

It is notable that chickens were absent in the advertising of eggs during the 1960s. The same was true for the advertising of chicken meat products in the 1970s, which used images of cooked broiler chickens or, in the case of a national campaign for chicken stock, a cartoon bird. On the whole, marketing campaigns avoided images of real chickens, thereby disconnecting the bird from their reconfigured form, part of a process that Carol J. Adams refers to as the thingification of beings. Adams argues:

> We do not want to experience uncomfortable feelings about violence, butchering, suffering and fear. This is the function of the *absent referent* – to keep our 'meat' separated from any idea that she or he was once an animal who was butchered, to keep some*thing* (like hamburger) from being seen as having been some*one* (a cow, a lamb, a once-living being, a subject.) (Adams, 2004, p. 23).

Inasmuch as the language of efficient production was effective in reconfiguring farmed animals as units of production and denying them any subject status, the marketing campaign for the commodities produced by such systems forced a further separation of the animal subject from the animal-as-product. In both senses, the entitlement of an animal to life and questions about their suffering were easily set aside through the processes of 'thingification'. Implicit, within much of the literature that referred to farmed animals as technological-industrial commodities, was the notion that the language of production was somehow neutral. In this way, the suffering caused through confinement under intensive systems was renegotiated through the discourse of industrial production as an efficiency issue, the mutilation of confined birds was promoted as industrial problem-solving, and the products of these systems – eggs and meat – relied upon and sustained the ideology of a cohesive national identity structured through eating practices and a classless taste culture. The various systems of state regulation, industrial production and cultural consumption were thus mutually sustaining not just at an economic level but also, crucially, at an ideological level.

One reason for the absence of chickens from the sphere of advertising is suggested by a survey undertaken in 2002, the results of which showed that the public perception of birds was poor, particularly when compared to pigs, horses and cows. The advertising agency that conducted the year-long research used focus groups with more than 600 people to determine that, for advertising purposes, the most effective animals were dogs, followed by cats, pigs, horses, lions, chimpanzees, dolphins, cows, penguins and, in tenth position, elephants (Born, 2002). Birds have been an unpopular choice for marketing and advertising purposes and thus chicken imagery has predominantly been restricted to pictures of 'eggs' and 'meat', and for this reason the stop-motion animation feature *Chicken Run* did function as a counter, albeit a limited one, to the paucity of chicken imagery.

As one of the few opportunities where humans have engaged with representations of the chicken as a whole being, *Chicken Run* situates chickens within socially constituted spaces of production and so reconnects them to an ethical discourse. The setting, an enclosed outdoor yard with rows of chicken houses, is a pastiche of the prisoner of war camp setting in the film *The Great Escape*. The narrative continues the parody as Ginger, the lead character, is repeatedly caught during escape attempts and thrown into a coal store, a reference to the captures of Steve McQueen's character, 'The Cooler King'. And whilst the setting does little to reflect the suffering incurred by chickens in battery operations, the subtle reference to prisoner of war camps maintains parallels between chicken and human suffering that do not allow the adult viewer to entirely dismiss the material conditions of egg production. A turning point in the narrative occurs when the farmer and his wife buy a machine which converts chickens into pies, and this shifts the focus of the film from egg laying to meat production. Given that images of broiler hens are so few, the connection between chickens and meat production in the film is significant, even if only for its rarity. An over-riding desire to experience grass and not to be confined drives the nar-rative, and whilst it is true that the film relies on anthropomorphic depictions of animals, which are far from realistic, the film does not shy away from dealing with the issue of slaughter and the production of animals as commodities.

The film segued, as an intertextual reference, into a television series made in 2008 for Channel 4, *Hugh's Chicken Run*, in which celebrity chef and smallholder Hugh Fearnely-Whittingstall presented three pro-grammes about intensively reared chickens. The programmes formed part of *The Great British Food Fight*, a series of factual programmes that dealt with the realities of intensive chicken farming, looking at both broiler farming and egg production and which also included a one-off programme, *Jamie's Fowl Dinners*, hosted by another celebrity chef, Jamie Oliver. The overriding theme of the programmes was that consumers were unaware of how animal products arrived in their supermarkets and on their plates and that the poor welfare standards of intensively reared animals resulted in poor quality products. *Hugh's Chicken Run* and *Jamie's Fowl Dinners* both advocated 'free-range' chickens on the grounds that better welfare standards equated to a better-tasting prod-uct. The ethical position with regard to chickens in these factual televi-sion programmes was somewhat different to that of *Chicken Run* in that the film representation attributed chickens with a right to life whilst the television series maintained a general welfarist position. In this sense, the television programmes argued that chickens were deserving of some measure of moral consideration but this was conditional on them functioning as better mechanisms of taste delivery. The confla-tion of taste with welfare opposed a previous ideology that the BEMB had promoted for eggs, that the quality of product came from stand-ardization and value. Whereas eggs in the 1960s had been celebrated for their low price and high worth as a protein source, the argument for free-range chickens, promoted by celebrity chefs, asked consumers to pay more for better quality and taste.

The programmes had an immediate effect and supermarkets reported increased sales of free-range chickens.[8] However, reposition-ing the debate within a discourse of taste polarized public opinion on the grounds of wealth and class difference. With celebrity chefs as the spokespersons for 'free-range', the issue of chicken welfare was associ-ated with the promotion of middle-class values and 'foodie' culture, which was conceived of as a form of cultural capital. Cheap chicken, a product of postwar state regulation of the farming industry, had become a mainstay of British working-class food culture, and thus the free-range debate became embroiled with issues of class and social identity. In an article published in the week following the broadcast of the television programmes, the restaurant critic and food writer for the *Observer* newspaper summarized the debate in the following way:

> The truth is that we live on a small, overpopulated island and if we are going to feed ourselves – and, in particular, those who struggle with the weekly budget – we are going to have to face up to what that really means, which is the unglamorous, unsexy business of mass food production...
>
> Fearnley-Whittingstall will doubtless argue that all this is missing the point, that his campaign is actually about animal welfare. No surprise there. Sentimentality always has been the British vice, be it over children, our history or the saintly chicken. But like a wonderfully, organically reared poulet de bresse, sentimentality is not something everybody can afford. You may be able to. But for a large number of people, people who do not have the luxury of being able to engage with the vivid middle-class foodie culture encouraged by Jamie, Gordon and Hugh, it is too high a price to pay (Rayner, 2008).

The position adopted by Rayner reflected one facet of public opposition to the debate and compartmentalized animal welfare as a middle-class issue. Polarized in this way, critique of the free-range discourse was bound up with a critique of class distinction and animal welfare, constructed as a 'taste' preference, and conceived of as a luxury afforded by the privilege of class identity. Pierre Bourdieu has argued that taste, and by taste he is referring to cultural habits, which include food choices, is invested with meanings that define class difference. He writes, 'Taste classifies, and it classifies the classifier. Social subjects, classified by their classifications, distinguish themselves by the distinctions they make, between the beautiful and the ugly, the distinguished and the vulgar, in which their position in the objective classifications is expressed or betrayed' (Bourdieu, 1984, p. 6). In this sense the chicken is symbolic capital, and framed in this way the relations between working-class and middle-class preferences were expressed through the bodies of free-range and broiler chickens. In this regard, animal ethics became a matter of class politics, and whilst the television programmes worked as interventions, in the sense that they did effect some change in cultural habits, these were limited to what could be accommodated from a welfare position that was framed by a discourse of 'taste' and which simultaneously promoted the consumption of chickens as a cultural norm.

## Farmed spaces: dairy

A discourse of animal welfare has impacted upon aspects of dairy produce advertising where the concept of 'free-range' has been used as a key marketing message. At the same time, concern about the impact of livestock on the environment has generated debates about how best to manage dairy farming practices. Soil erosion and compaction, loss of biodiversity from grazing and silage production, ammonia and methane emissions as well as high levels of water consumption have all been identified as direct effects on the environment from dairy farming activity.[9] Whilst the issues have been well reported in the press, there has been little in the way of imagery to accompany the environmental critique of milk production. Instead, much of the popularly available imagery of dairy farming has been generated by the dairy industry, where advertising in the UK and US has continued to deploy culturally specific visions of contented cows in rural landscapes. As a result, the publicly available meanings of dairy farming and cows have been refracted through readings of nature as 'environment' and 'landscape'. With little actual access to farmed-animal spaces, the majority of western urban-dwellers' experiences of livestock and farming practices are heavily mediated, often through food advertising. In such cases, the discourse of farming and the spaces in which animals are farmed are, of course, constructed to appeal to the consumer and both implicitly and explicitly offer reassurance that farmed animals are healthy and emotionally satisfied. Advertising of dairy produce, in particular, offers imagery of farmed animals that relies on associations between cows and green fields to sustain meanings, such as 'natural' and 'healthy', which are then assigned to dairy products. In turn, the imagery has reinforced associations between cows and the freedom to roam in natural surroundings, maintaining connections between dairy cows' lack of confinement and their willing productivity. Audiences are clearly savvy enough to negotiate the meanings of advertisements; nevertheless, the use of stereotypes and intertextual references has worked to sustain particular cultural tropes. Dairy farming thus maintains strong cultural associations in the UK and US with natural landscapes and rural tranquillity, and such practices occupy a zone in the cultural imagination that is markedly removed from the urban industrial experience.

Estimates suggest that the extent of farming in the UK is so great that 80 per cent of the landscape has been shaped by farming practices.[10] As a result, the industry has a major impact on both the management of land and the development of the landscape. In 2006, agriculture accounted for 77 per cent of land use in the UK, amounting to 18.5 million hectares, of which, around 38 per cent was grass and 30 per cent was land given over to rough grazing for domestic livestock. Employing over half a million people, the value of farming to the UK economy is substantial, generating around £5.6 billion per year, of which the livestock industry accounts for £7,351 million of output.[11] The combined UK cow population numbers around 3.8 million, and of these the larger proportion, slightly over 2 million, are dairy cows. Decreases in the dairy cow population over 50 years, from 2.6 million in 1956,[12] reflect changes in livestock management, policy, regulation and farming practices. In short, fewer cows are now producing more milk, and this increased efficiency of production has meant that the dairy industry has remained highly significant in economic terms. Dairy cows deliver the greatest proportion of output generated by livestock farming in the UK, which, in 2006, for example, accounted for £2,501 million worth of product. By way of comparison, the output from cattle meat accounted for £1,568 million of output, eggs and wool represented £357 million and £16 million, respectively, whilst meat from pigs, sheep and poultry generated £687 million, £702 million and £1,315 million, respectively.[13] In terms of land management, UK dairy farms continue to use hedges and dry stone walls to divide fields and, consequently, milk is not only economically significant but its production is also linked in very direct ways to the shaping of the rural landscape. Traditions within fine art and photography have, since the eighteenth and nineteenth century, respectively, idealized British pastoral landscapes and in doing so have constructed a range of cultural meanings around farmed land and the animals within it.[14] It is through this industrial and cultural organization of the land that cows have become an integral aspect of the material and symbolic meanings assigned to the countryside.

Although it is a New Zealand brand, Anchor Butter advertising in the UK has utilized a range of meanings derived from the symbolic relationships between cows and the landscape. Throughout the campaigns of the 1990s, the television advertisements featured Jersey dairy cows despite the fact that the majority of New Zealand's four million dairy cows were black and white Holstein-Freisans.[15] With a 'softer' and more appealing 'look', Jersey cows were referred to as 'lucky cows' depicted in lush green fields dancing, singing and proclaiming their good fortune at being able to 'chew the cud and browse'. An emphasis was placed on the consumption of 'green green grass' as the relationship between cows and spaces reworked the production cycle of milk so that the quality of the final product, butter, was entirely dependent on the consumption of high quality pasture. Such imagery short-circuited the realities of the processes by which cows are farmed and bovine lactation is managed, and instead it reduced the cycle to a simplified, and less ethically problematic, process of 'grass in – butter out'.

Each advertisement in the 'lucky cow' campaign included some manner of enclosure which ranged from white picket fencing, to wooden ranch-style fencing and traditional British hedgerows. This changed in the next campaign which sought to reflect the company's awareness of consumer concerns about welfare standards (Figure 6.2). As a result, the meanings of green spaces and landscape were reworked to operate within a discourse of welfare. Repositioned as the 'free-range butter company', Anchor advertisements replaced live-action commercials with animated cows that appeared to be made from 'Fuzzy Felt', soft fabric shapes that were popularly recognizable and sold as a children's toy in the UK. No longer restricted to representations of Jersey cows, the advertisements also depicted black and white and brown cows, references to Holstein-Freisans and Ayshire breeds. In the television advertisements, an animated cow kicked its way out of a shed, with an accompanying voice-over that stated 'There's no such thing as the great indoors. Only our cows are free to roam all year round'. In other ads, two cows studied a map of their extensive available space and another kicked off human footwear whilst a voice-over declared, 'If cows were meant to be kept indoors they'd be born with slippers'. Intertextual references to the film *The Great Escape* were used in a further advertisement that depicted a cow on a motorcycle trying to jump a fence to escape from farmers armed with pitchforks. The advert used the film's title music and the setting, although visually stripped back to incorporate impressions of snow-topped peaks, reminiscent of the familiar alpine setting used for the original motorcycle chase scene with Steve McQueen. Print advertisements that accompanied the free-range campaign used Polaroid pictures of cows in front of well-known landmarks such as the Eiffel Tower and a pyramid, with the strap line, 'Our cows are free to roam'.

Concerns were raised about the company's depiction of 'happy cows' and the free-range campaign received public criticism in 1997 when an advert that depicted a calf 'hatching' from an egg and then relaxing with its mother amongst other contented Jersey cows attracted 54

*Figure 6.2*   Anchor Butter advertisements. Image courtesy of the Advertising Archives

viewer complaints to the Independent Television Commission. Public objections to the advertisement were reported by the ITC as follows:

> a) that the use of the term "free-range" implied the cows used to produce Anchor are allowed to keep their calves with them, are in pasture all year round or are more humanely treated than usual. (Some farmers amongst the complainants pointed out that cattle in New Zealand traditionally have their tails docked); b) that Anchor butter is no more natural or pure than other brands (ITC, 1997, 'Anchor Butter').

None of the complaints were upheld by the ITC which, in its assessment of the objections, stated that the advertiser had confirmed that 'the New Zealand cows used to produce Anchor Butter were kept in pasture all year round which justified the use of the term "free-range"' (ITC, 1997). The complaints regarding the implication that calves stayed with their mothers received no response from the ITC, although the issue of tail-docking was accounted for in the following way: 'The animals shown in the commercial had not had their tails docked but the ITC did not think that inaccuracy was significant enough to make the advertising misleading' (ITC, 1997). Furthermore, the report noted that 'The ITC did not think the commercial implied that Anchor is better than other brands, rather that being in pasture all year is a more "natural" existence' (ITC, 1997). Although consumer objections to Anchor Butter advertising were directed towards the misrepresentation of farming practices and demonstrated tensions between interpretations of the advertisement and concerns over the implied meanings about cow welfare, the ITC's response made it clear that what was at issue was the representation of the product and not the misrepresentation of the realities of the lives of dairy cows.

In an attempt to recover butter-making within the discourse of tradition, a 2010 Anchor Butter commercial returned to live action and depicted cows leaving the fields to work in a factory with the strap line 'Made by cows since 1886'. The aim of the £10 million campaign was to position the company as the 'Original Butter Co.'.[16] A country music version of the Guns N' Roses song *Paradise City*, with the lyrics 'Take me down to a paradise city, where the grass is green and the girls are pretty, oh won't you please take me home', accompanied images of cows 'clocking-on', operating production machinery, performing quality checks and packaging the butter for delivery in a nineteenth-century factory setting housing contemporary industrial technologies. In the simulation of nineteenth-century factory production, the advert reimagined the relationship between cows and milk by excluding the process of milking. Rather than 'producing milk', cows 'make butter'. In constructing new associations between the company and tradition, Anchor Butter also shed its 'free-range' identity. And although the advertisement placed cows within the confines of the factory setting, taking on the humanized roles of operatives, the concept of the advertisement suggested that butter-making retained links with traditional agricultural and industrial practices. The opening and closing images still drew directly on the aesthetic traditions of nineteenth-century British landscape painting with large romanticized landscapes at daybreak and sunset. In this way, a nostalgia discourse framed butter-making as traditional and the company as authentic through the rather surreal imagery of cows being happily complicit in their own exploitation.

A challenge to the Anchor campaign came in the form of a counter-campaign by Country Life Butter which used the former member of the 1970s punk band The Sex Pistols, John Lydon, to front its advertising. The central message of the campaign was that Country Life Butter is British and Anchor Butter is from New Zealand. The Country Life campaign underscored how robust the associations were between the Anchor Butter brand and national identity and the counter-campaign sought to dismantle those meanings and reclaim the imagery of 'British' cows and the countryside. The television advertisement showed John Lydon experiencing various aspects of British rural life: the British countryside was depicted as sheep on a country lane and the concept of 'British milk' was represented by black and white cows chasing Lydon through an expanse of green fields. The pack shot at the end of the advertisement returned to the image of open green fields. The print adverts that were placed in broadsheets and the popular press used an image of Lydon bursting through the page of the newspaper under the 'headlines', 'Revealed: Anchor Butter is from New Zealand' (broadsheet advertisement, July 2010) and 'Anchor's from New Zealand' (tabloid advertisement, July 2010). The campaigns mounted by Anchor and Country Life revealed the high investment of meaning in cows and the landscape and, by extension, the commercial value of both.

Macnaughten and Urry argue that representations of natural space are socially and symbolically produced and that 'different features of the landscape are celebrated within different societies' (Macnaughten & Urry, 1998, p. 182). The spaces appropriated in advertising by Anchor Butter for the UK market and Country Life have borrowed from established conventions of representing 'the countryside' as peaceful, green and fertile and symbolically opposed to the industrialization of towns and cities. In this way, the production of meanings around cows and landscape are mutually reinforcing. Landscape can operate through a multiplicity of discourses as a form of nostalgia that recalls an idealized past and as a symbol of freedom, of 'naturalness', and in opposition to industrialization. Each of these meanings translates into context for the bovine body which is then understood as part of a cultural and social heritage and which, in turn, reproduces the sense that cows have always had freedom to roam and have always been apart from industrialization. Locating cows within the idealized landscapes of a particular country or region thus reinforces symbolic associations between a sense of place, conceived through the highly organized imagery of the natural world, and the 'naturalness' of the life of a dairy cow. In doing this, the connections allude to milk production as a wholesome process that takes place in only the most ideal of locations. As a result, in advertising for dairy-related products, agricultural spaces overlap with the meanings and values that are assigned to nature and 'the countryside', and these in turn close down the opportunities for questions about welfare standards and reduce dairy farming practices to an extremely narrow range of representations.

## Happy cows

A relationship between the traditions of dairy farming and the landscape has also evolved within American advertising where the organization of the industry has changed substantially to include large-scale Concentrated Animal Feed Operations (CAFOs). Milk was traditionally produced on diversified crop and livestock farms, where in 1954 the average number of cows per farm was seven.[17] Previous to this, at the turn of the century, dairy cows had been kept in even smaller numbers to provide milk for individual families or small communities until the rail infrastructure made it possible to transport large quantities of dairy produce across land. Dairy farming expanded westwards and during World War II food shortages prompted a drive for an increase in productivity. The focus on food production during wartime was reflected in the imagery of dairy farming, which was typically depicted as a few black and white cows, areas of ploughed land and well-kept barns and outbuildings. Barns used to house cows, and particularly the red-sided barn, became a symbol of the American homestead and part of the envisioning of the American rural landscape. Dairy cows were doubly integrated into this landscape, not only through their physical presence but also within the very fabric of the barns, as the red pigment that covered the exteriors was made from skimmed milk mixed with lime and red oxide.

From 2.9 million dairy farms in 1954, the number declined over the next four decades to 155,339 by 1992.[18] However, during the same time the average number of cows per farm had increased to 61. Farms became specialized, and in the case of milk production, which expanded rapidly in the southwest and west of the US, the trend was for fewer but much larger farms with more than 1,000 cows.[19] Alongside a decrease in the number of farms, the overall national cow population also reduced, but at the same time US milk production increased. For instance, between 1991 and 1996 there was a 4 per cent decrease in the US dairy cow population but a 5 per cent increase in milk production, which represented an overall increase in production of 9 per cent per cow.[20] With some fluctuations in numbers in the intervening years, the population decreased from 9.99 million in 1990 to 9.2 million in 2009 whilst milk production increased steadily at an average of 1.8 per cent per year.[21] By 2007, the number of specialized dairy farms was reported to be 57,318 and the sales of milk and dairy products totalled $31.8 billion.[22] California became the top dairy-producing state in the US and, with Wisconsin, New York, Pennsylvania and Idaho, accounted for more than 50 per cent of the total value of milk and dairy products in 2007.[23]

The domestic consumption of dairy products in the US increased at a rate of 0.4 per cent per year from 1990 to 2008,[24] a shift in consumer habits that reflected the outcome of investment into research, marketing and the promotion of milk and milk products by The National Fluid Milk Processor Promotion Board (Fluid Milk Board)[25] and The Dairy Board.[26] Created in 1994 and charged with the task of driving increased sales and demand for US dairy products and ingredients, Dairy Management Inc. (DMI) was made responsible for funding research projects that supported the marketing efforts of the Fluid Milk and Dairy Boards. From 2002, the Fluid Milk Board advertising and promotional programmes focused on the health benefits of milk and used celebrities to target women and teenagers as well as focused campaigns targeted at the Hispanic community. A sponsorship deal between the Fluid Milk Board and the Walt Disney Corporation was also utilized to promote milk to teens and young adults, milk being named ' "the official training fuel" of the Disney's Wide World of Sports' (USDA, 2008, p. 15). The increase in domestic sales of milk and dairy products reflected the success of the campaigns, which can be quantified in terms of the estimated 2 billion media impressions garnered in 2008 from the integrated programme of advertising and promotion (USDA, 2008, p. 18)

In North America, advertisements for Real California Milk and Real California Cheese employed a range of landscape imagery that maintained connections with earlier depictions of rural farmlands from the 1940s and 1950s and with the aesthetic conventions of American landscape painting. Wide shots depicted vast open unfenced areas of green land dotted with trees and traditional American barns. Each television advertisement depicted a small group of 'happy Californian cows' in this setting with the slogan 'Great milk comes from happy cows. Happy cows come from California'. The rhetoric of place was constantly reinforced through the narratives of the adverts, each of which stressed the cows' desire to live in California. For example, in an advertisement titled 'Blizzard', two calves cause their grandmother to recall, unhappily, that she used to live somewhere other than California; in 'Dream', a pig attempts to pass for a cow, implying that California cows have happier lives than pigs; and a series of adverts depicted cows from around the world auditioning for the role of the new 'happy cow'.

Consumer concern for animal welfare was reflected in the public reception of the advertisements, and criticisms, in the case of the Real California Cheese and Milk commercials, focused on their portrayal of 'happy cows'. In 2002, People for the Ethical Treatment of Animals (PETA) filed an unsuccessful suit against the California Milk Advisory Board (CMAB) for false advertising, arguing that the adverts were misleading for consumers and that they promoted the idea that California dairy cows were grass fed and free roaming.[27] The 'Happy cow' marketing campaign continued after 2002 with new television advertisements and expansion into the sale of ancillary merchandize, such as clothing, watches and DVDs, from the Real California Milk web site and online shop. DVDs of 'audition tapes' from the 'Vote for the next California happy cow' promotion offered another discrete point of entry into the happy cow world. In response to welfare concerns, the web site also included a short documentary-style film, produced by the CMAB, titled *Are California dairy cows really happy?*. The film was composed of images from various areas of California and interviews with dairy farmers who were asked to describe the conditions and facilities in which dairy cows were kept as well as their personal relationship to the cattle they farmed.[28] The film focused on the fact that the majority of milk production facilities were family-owned, reinforcing the rhetoric of dairy farming as a non-corporate endeavour.

## Marketing messages

Studies of human–animal interaction suggest that childhood experiences of animals and particularly animal narratives contribute to the formation of attitudes towards animals in adulthood.[29] Whilst it is certainly vital to consider childhood stories, Disney films, nursery rhymes and so forth as central to the formation of attitudes, it is equally important that advertising is taken into account as well, as exposure to marketing messages makes up a substantial proportion of our daily access to farmed-animal imagery. In contrast to the paucity of chicken imagery, the proliferation of cow imagery in both UK and US advertising suggests that at a symbolic level some animals are more economically significant than others. This concurs with the 2002 advertising survey in which cows appeared as the eighth most effective advertising animal. Their place within the commercial landscape finds its legacy in nineteenth-century landscape painting where benign bovine bodies have long been associated with the calm and tranquillity of British rural life – a culturally imagined antidote to industrialization and urbanization – and as part of the imagery that idealized the family-oriented American homestead. These landscapes have taken on new meanings in the light of welfare discourses. In short, the open spaces that signalled nonindustrialization have been transformed by marketing messages which have reconfigured landscapes as ethical spaces through associations with 'free-range' and 'free-to-roam'.

# 7
# Hunted: Recreational Killing

| | |
|---|---|
| *Fleischman*: | This is awful O'Connell. How could you do something like this? |
| *O'Connell*: | You eat meat don't you Fleischman? Well, say hello to meat. |
| *Fleischman*: | This isn't meat. This is a majestic animal living by its wits in the wild. |
| *O'Connell*: | *Was* a majestic animal living by its wits in the wild. What do you know about majestic or wild or even animals for that matter? Oh, unless of course we're talking about thoroughly demoralised animals living huddled behind bars in an urban zoo. |
| *Fleischman*: | There's a moral imperative involved here O'Connell. |
| *O'Connell*: | Oh really, what is it? |
| *Fleischman*: | For a person to derive pleasure out of causing the death of a vibrant living thing – that is ethically wrong. Not to mention morally repugnant and personally reprehensible. |
| *O'Connell*: | What do you know about it Fleischman? You know nothing. You think life is an intellectual construct: A set of deeply held personal beliefs that has absolutely nothing to do with reality as we know it out here in morally reprehensible Alaska. |
| *Fleischman*: | Okay, explain this to me. Really, I want to know. What gives you the right to be a murderer of animals for your own pleasure? |
| *O'Connell*: | My hunting license. |

This is the exchange that takes place between two characters, Maggie O'Connell and Joel Fleischman, at the beginning of an episode entitled

'A Hunting We Will Go', from series 3 of the highly successful 1990s television comedy drama *Northern Exposure*. Maggie has returned from a hunting trip with a 'ten point buck' strapped to the back of her station wagon and is challenged by the town doctor, Joel, a New Yorker who has been sent to the small isolated Alaskan town of Cicely to fulfil a four-year placement obligation.[1] Joel's struggle to fit-in with the lifestyle, customs and traditions of the townspeople forms the main premise of the series, and 'A Hunting We Will Go' follows his experiences as he attempts to understand the motivation to hunt. The programme explores some of the established positions within the hunting debate, but in fulfilling the generic conventions of a closed structure and rein-stated equilibrium demanded by a comedy drama series narrative, it has to arrive at a negotiated position by the end of the episode. The programme was targeted at an audience who, based on demographic profiles, would have been unlikely to support hunting, and the episode steers a course through the various arguments that continue to inform current debates. Attitudinal surveys on hunting during the 1990s indicated that 'there is no such thing as a general public. Opinions on consumptive wildlife-related activities vary dramatically among segments of the American public' (Duda & Young, 1998, p. 600). What is interesting about this episode is the way in which it traverses these varying opinions, and in doing so the narration reframes Joel's objections to hunting by the end of the programme. This chapter unpicks the arguments about hunting that are presented in *Northern Exposure* and other media texts. The aim here is to examine how the discourse of pleasure and a 'good death' is negotiated, normalized and reinforced.

## Making the case

The *Northern Exposure* episode, 'A Hunting We Will Go', mirrored public debates about hunting in the US in the 1990s. A decline in the hunter population from the 1980s onwards was, at the time the series was broadcast, being blamed on social shifts, an aging population, increased urbanization, increased costs associated with hunting, over-regulation, the influence of animal welfare and rights organizations and negative media stereotypes of hunters.[2] Attitudinal surveys suggested that whilst a majority of the American public strongly approved of legal hunting, more than a fifth of the population disapproved (Duda & Young, 1998, pp. 590–591). The reasons for their disapproval varied, but studies showed that certain social groups were more likely to oppose hunting than others. There was, for instance, a correlation between education and attitudes towards hunting, which suggested that as the level of educational attainment increased, the likelihood to approve of hunting decreased. Gender, geography and age were also identified as key factors. Men were more likely to support hunting than women, and it came as little surprise that urban residents were identified as being less likely to advocate hunting practices when compared with people from rural communities. Insofar as age was concerned, surveys revealed that those in younger age groups were more inclined to disagree with hunting but that attitudes shifted in favour of hunting as people got older.[3] Many of these attitudinal indicators were reflected in the character of Joel Fleischman who, as a young, educated urbanite, fitted the profile of someone who would be likely to oppose hunting.[4] Moreover, Joel's social identity mirrored that of the target audience for the programme, and therefore *Northern Exposure* viewers were likely to sympathize with his position.

During their exchange and as she unloads the dead buck from her station wagon, Maggie responds to Joel's objection to her killing the stag by pointing out that Joel eats meat and, gesturing towards the body, remarks, 'say hello to meat'. For the majority of the viewing public this point had resonance, as eight out of ten Americans, at that time, approved of using animals for food and only 3 per cent claimed that they did not eat meat (Duda & Young, 1998, p. 600).[5] For this reason, Brian Luke maintains that it is understandable that most Americans have supported hunting for meat, and he argues that hunters typically use meat-eating as common ground from which to deflect criticism of their activities. Luke writes, 'to oppose those who purportedly hunt for meat would put them in the awkward position of opposing fellow meat-eaters who at least do their own killing' (Luke, 2007a, p. 140). This highlights an obvious, although far from rare, inconsistency in human–animal relations and reflects the complex yet highly organized structuring of social attitudes towards killing animals. Peter Singer regards such inconsistencies as indicative of contemporary speciesism which he argues 'is so pervasive and widespread an attitude that those who attack one or two of its manifestations – like the slaughter of wild animals by hunters [...] – often participate in other speciesist practices' (Singer, 1995, p. 230). Singer's assessment is an accurate description of Joel's position in *Northern Exposure*, and Maggie's definition of the buck as 'meat' calls on their common identities as meat-eaters. However, Joel continues in his attempts to disentangle meat-eating from hunting and maintains that his key objection is made on other grounds. Instead, he moves the discussion away from the definition of the stag as 'meat' and reframes the dead body as that of a 'majestic animal', implying a strategic difference between food animals and non-food animals. Joel's manoeuvre holds little sway with Maggie whose argument – that Joel's city existence has disconnected him from the natural world and any disagreement he has is based on a misunderstanding of animals – is premised on the notion that those living a rural existence are 'closer to nature' and therefore have authentic knowledge of animals. Maggie deals with the issue of animal classification by raising a distinction between the wild animals of rural Alaska and those who are confined to an existence in a city zoo. Urban zoo animals have miserable lives, she argues, and therefore wrongly populate Joel's understanding of what an animal's life should be.

Putting aside the issue of animal classification for a moment, the assertion that a distinction persists between urban and rural knowledge of animals is a point that has continued to inform debates about hunting in the US and the UK. In the US, pro-hunt spokesperson Frank Miniter argues that hunters have an authentic knowledge of animals which non-hunters, environmentalists, biologists and animal-rights advocates do not possess (Miniter, 2007, pp 18–19). He proposes that because of this expert understanding the hunting fraternity is the rightful custodian of wild animals, and he maintains that hunters 'can tell when something is not right in the ecosystem. Hunters are our environmental watchdogs. They scream at state game agencies when they perceive that deer, quail or waterfowl aren't being managed properly. They actively watch over wildlife and lobby for them' (Miniter, 2007, p. 18). This view appeals to what Tom Regan regards as a 'perverse distortion' of 'humane concern' (Regan, 2004, p. 355). From a rights perspective, the identity of hunter-as-conservationist is wholly self-serving, and Regan argues that it has the explicit goal of ensuring 'that there will be a larger, rather than a smaller, number of animals to kill!'. He adds, 'With "humane friends" like that, wild animals certainly do not need any enemies' (Regan, 2004, p. 355). As such, a special interest in preserving certain animal populations reframes the hunter's interests as practices of species protection, and this relationship has been deeply embedded within hunting discourses. The point is made explicit in a report for the National Shooting Sports Federation which proposes that:

> Sportsmen [*sic*] are essential to species protection and species management as well. Game management programs, which are funded by sportsmen's [*sic*] dollars, have brought back numerous wildlife species from unhealthy population levels such as wild turkey, wood duck,

white-tailed deer, beaver, pronghorn antelope, and Canada goose (Responsive Management/National Shooting Sports Foundation, 2008, p. 2).

The report also states that 'sportsmen' are 'integral to habitat conservation' and more likely to support conservation organizations than 'non-sportsmen'. At a rhetorical level, the discourse identifies the hunter as being centrally concerned with animal protection, stating that 'sportsmen' have been the driving force behind species protection and 'essential' to the future of wildlife management. The way in which the discourse is constructed, however, appears to validate Regan's argument that humane concern has been distorted inasmuch as the term 'protection' is employed to describe the management of particular species populations for the purposes of killing them. In addition, the concept of population management also suggests that value is accorded only to certain species and on the basis of their utility as 'game'. In accord with this, Luke (2007b) suggests that population and wildlife management programmes contrive to regulate populations and habitats in ways that are beneficial to hunters rather than animals. He argues, 'Wildlife managers manipulate flora, exterminate natural predators, regulate hunting permits, and even at times breed and release deer, all in order to maintain herd sizes large enough to insure what they call a "harvestable surplus" of the animals men most like to kill' (p. 140). There is a wider economic context in which these practices can be located and, as such, wildlife management and conservation are part of a multi-billion-dollar hunting industry in the US that is geared primarily around profit. Reports do not dispute this point and in fact mobilize the economic worth of the hunting industry in its defence, pointing out that hunters spend $22.7 billion on hunting per year, support 593,000 jobs, and hunting produces $5 billion in Federal tax revenue and $4.2 billion in state and local tax revenue per year.[6]

In the UK, a well-reported crisis in Scottish deer populations brought the relationships between deer hunting (referred to as 'deer stalking'), deer population management and economics into focus as newspapers reported that the £105 million deer industry faced disaster as poaching and harsh weather conditions had reduced herd numbers.[7] The main concern was that stags, who were most at risk of starvation, had to be culled 'to prevent them suffering' (Johnson, 2010) and that this, alongside the loss of numbers to poaching, would have a substantial impact on the stalking economy which relies on 'trophy heads' (Tait, 2010). One news report summarized the relationship in the following terms:

Herd management is a careful balancing act. There must be enough hinds to attract the stags who may be shot during the rut but not so many that they eat all the grass and push the stags in search of fertile pastures elsewhere. Keeping enough stags on the estate for stalking guests supplies vital funding to keep the estates running. It's a delicate balance of economy and ecology (Tait, 2010).

By 2007, deer stalking in the UK was regarded as a growth industry reported to be worth £200 million, with stalkers paying up to £1000 for the right to hunt trophy roebucks (Copping, 2007). To widen the market, and in an attempt to shed the identity of being an upper-class pursuit, low-priced outings were offered by estate owners, the effect of which was to popularize deer stalking and grow the industry to service around 86,000 deer stalkers and upwards of 200,000 days of stalking in 2007 in the UK.[8] Supporters of the industry argue that deer stalking is one of the best ways to control wild deer populations which have flourished since the 1960s and if left unchecked will harm the environment. In this sense, they offer a rationale to underpin the burgeoning commercialization of deer population management. From a rights perspective, Tom Regan contends that the process of population management for the purposes of hunting treats animals 'as if they were a naturally occurring renewable resource, the value of which is to be measured by, and managed by reference to, human recreational, gustatory, aesthetic, social and other interests' (Regan, 2004, p356). UK animal advocates have argued that it has served the industry to emphasize damage done by deer as part of a strategy to maintain the deer stalking economy (Fowler-Reeves, 2007, p. 19). Such a position therefore makes the case that economic interests have become a central organizing principle of contemporary hunting practices.

## Pleasure

Compared to the wider industry discourse, few hunters propose that economics informs their choice to hunt and instead individuals tend to focus on the perceived personal benefits. There is a long history of justifying hunting as a means by which humans gain access to a different and more satisfying relationship with nature. It is not uncommon for hunters to regard themselves as more in tune with nature and possessing of an understanding about animals that can only be acquired by hunting and killing them. Trends in motivations for hunting would appear to corroborate the suggestion that increasingly hunters use hunting as a way to get close to nature. As the number of people hunting for meat reportedly decreased from 43 per cent to 16 per cent, those who hunted to be 'close to nature' doubled between 1980 and 2006.[9] Associations between hunters and nature are claimed to validate a relationship between hunting and conservation, and public anti-hunting sentiment tends to be blamed, in no small part, on media representations of hunting that exclude the hunter as a conservationist.[10]

Representations of hunters and hunting populate contemporary culture, and of these the death of Bambi's mother from the animated Disney feature *Bambi* (1942) is probably the best-known example. In fact, such is the cultural significance of *Bambi* that terms such as 'bambicide', 'bambi-killer', bambi-lover and the 'Bambi effect' or 'Bambi complex' have entered popular discourse as disparaging expressions for hunters, non-hunters and to describe the trauma experienced when confronted by the death of an animal. 'Bambi' has, in many ways, become interchangeable with the word deer, and according to Ralph Lutts *Bambi* has been largely responsible for mobilizing a substantial proportion of anti-hunting sentiment. Lutts asserts:

> It may be that more people have, consciously or unconsciously, based their understanding of deer and woodland life on Walt Disney's *Bambi* than on any other single source. Its images and concept of nature have been impressed on the American psyche and reinforced through decades of exposure to the film, its multitude of spin-offs, and Disney's marketing magic (Lutts, 1992, p. 169).

Given its significance as an anti-hunting statement, what is interesting, and often remarked upon, is that no human is ever depicted in the film (Lutts, 1992, p. 161). Bambi's mother is killed offscreen and the hunter is never visible. As one film reviewer wrote in 1942, 'Man makes no appearance in the picture because Disney wants to keep attention focused on the animals [...] However, they do see his dog and hear his gun [...] and other evidences' (Gill, 1942, p.4).

Concerned that popular representations have some degree of influence on the public understanding of hunting, and typical of complaints about attitudes towards hunters, one writer remarks, 'Militant antihunters view all hunters as knuckle-dragging, beer-swilling, blood-lusting, nature-raping cretins' (Petersen & Williams, 2000, p.61). Indeed, one does not need to look far to find popular representations which employ stereotypes such as the misogynistic 'great white hunter' in the horror films *Frankenfish* (2004) and *Alligator* (1980), the inept hunter epitomized by the cartoon character Elmer Fudd, and the 'redneck' hunter such as 'Shaw' in the animated feature *Open Season* (2006), a film about a domesticated grizzly bear and a deer forced to survive in a forest as hunting season begins. Shaw, referred to by the bear as 'the nastiest hunter in town' and the main antagonist in the film, appears in the second scene, driving precariously with a buck, who seems at first to be dead, strapped across the front of his truck. It transpires that Shaw has driven off the road at night to hit the deer and with three days to go before hunting season begins, and with a prior history of hunting illegally, the local ranger demands that Shaw be arrested. Shaw displays all the characteristics of the hunter stereotype: he claims that the natural order is 'Man on the top, animals on the bottom' and suggests that animals exist to be eaten. In reply to Shaw's comments, the ranger calls him a 'knuckle-dragger', a 'sick twisted puppy' and a 'six-toed gun monkey'. The film concludes with a final battle between the animals of the forest and the hunters, from which the animals emerge triumphant. Shaw bears a remarkable physical resemblance to Amos, the hunter in Disney's *The Fox and the Hound* (1981), a film in which hunting is foregrounded as a system that structures the relations of animals and forces the fox and hound to be enemies. As in *Open Season*, the hunter in the *Fox and the Hound* is willing to hunt and kill animals illegally and follows the fox, Todd, onto a game preserve which has a strict 'no hunting' rule. In this way, both *Open Season* and *The Fox and the Hound* share common points of reference with *Bambi* in their depictions of hunters engaged in illegal activity. It was this issue of illegal hunting which was central to the original hunter opposition to the 1942 film. The problem, Lutts notes, was that *Bambi* implied hunters shoot deer illegally in the spring; a point that led the editor of *Outdoor Life* to raise his objections with Walt Disney by telegram claiming that the film 'unfairly implied that the nation's law abiding hunters were "vicious destroyers of game and natural resources"' (Lutts, 1992, p. 162).

Concerns about media representations have also been raised by the pro-hunting lobby in the UK during media reporting on the story of the hunting rights to a rare white roe deer that were auctioned off to the highest bidder in 2009. The broadsheets that reported the story referred to the owner of the stalking business as a 'professional hunter, who is now taking bids' (Foggo, 2009) and 'keen to get the best possible price' (Johnson, 2009) whilst one tabloid described the auction as 'a bloodthirsty bidding war' (Angove, 2009). Deer stalkers argued that the papers misrepresented them and their activities, stating on deer stalking web sites, for instance, 'we sporting shooters do not kill everything that moves, contrary to popular belief', and maintained that deer stalkers 'are here not only to fulfil our hobby and passion, but to control the deer population' and also that the story led to 'coffee table conservationists [...] wanting to interfere with all aspects of country life which they have absolutely no idea as to what is what' (Deer Stalking Scotland, 2009). This notion of a rural/urban divide is significant as it also figured prominently in debates on hunting with dogs which have been constructed as a battle between 'town' and 'country', and it has been argued that due to media coverage the lives and practices of rural people are misunderstood by those living in urban areas. In the foreword to the *Rural Manifesto*, produced by the UK-based political campaign group The Countryside Alliance, Kate Hoey writes, 'Divisive politics, media misrepresentation and a lack of understanding can create a gap between rural and urban areas' (Hoey, 2009). Through claims to an authentic knowledge of wildlife, the pro-hunting discourse demonstrates that there is an ongoing epistemic struggle for credibility and legitimacy in a contest between different stakeholders to promote their own version of human–animal relations. At the core of this is the drive to acquire media coverage that legitimizes, what Andrew Linzey has described as 'the acceptance that cruelty is a "normal" or "natural" way of life in the countryside' (Linzey, 2009, p. 87).

Indeed, the normalization of hunting and killing as part of the rural way of life underscores Maggie's criticism of Joel's 'urban' view of animals in *Northern Exposure*. Joel's refusal to see the stag as meat brings him to restate his opposition to hunting on moral grounds and, in more specific terms, to argue that to hunt for pleasure is indefensible. In this sense, Joel articulated a view that reflected the attitudes of a substantial segment of the American public. Although meat-eaters made up the majority of the population, a proportion of these (19 per cent) still disapproved of hunting and more than half of these (56 per cent) maintained that they perceived hunting as being morally wrong (Duda & Jones, 2008, p. 5). Whilst those who disapproved of hunting were in the minority (a point that is echoed in the programme as Joel is the lone objector in Cicely) and overall there was widespread public approval of hunting in America, studies carried out in 1997 and 2006 revealed that public approval was conditional and based on perceptions of hunters' motivations. One report claimed, 'more Americans approve of hunting for food, hunting to manage game populations, hunting to protect humans from harm, and hunting for animal population control than approve of hunting strictly for recreation, for the challenge, or for a trophy' (Duda & Jones, 2008, p. 4). In fact, of those who supported legal hunting, only 28 per cent approved of hunting 'for a trophy' (RM 2006 in Duda & Young, 2008).[11] Sixty per cent disapproved of hunting 'for the challenge' and 47 per cent disagreed with hunting 'for the sport' (RM 2006 in Duda & Young, 2008, p. 4). In short, hunting for recreation or for personal profit were reasons that garnered the least support from the American public.

Studies such as these paint a highly compartmentalized set of attitudes towards hunting that the *Northern Exposure* episode demonstrated to be incompatible with the realities of hunters' motivations. Joel's accusation that Maggie hunted and killed for pleasure was able to tap into a much larger set of public objections, and, although she refers to the stag as 'meat', Maggie does not deny that she derives pleasure from killing. Instead she points out that recreational hunting, and any associated pleasure, is legitimized through state licensing. No matter what her motivations are – whether for the pleasure of killing, for profit or for meat – Maggie's actions are institutionally sanctioned. In this regard, the programme hinted at the moral messiness of hunting. Maggie's reasons do not fit in a tidy fashion into neatly acceptable or unacceptable categories of motivation. They are, instead, a mix of 'meat' and 'pleasure': reasons that were at opposite ends of the spectrum of acceptability according to public opinion but were more aligned with the realities of hunters' purposes. In the exchange between Maggie and Joel, the narrative thus opens up the questions of what circumstances justify the killing of animals, how animals should be classified and suggests that the reasons people use to validate hunting practices are multiple and morally ambiguous.

As the narrative unfolds, Joel questions various town residents about their feelings towards hunting. Ruth-Ann, the 75-year-old owner of the town grocery store, tells Joel that she used to hunt, derived the most enjoyment from skinning dead animals and only felt pangs of regret when she killed an animal that proved difficult to load onto her truck. When asked whether she hunts, Marilyn, an Alaska Native and the surgery receptionist, replies with only one word: 'fish'. Ed, a young man raised in the Alaska Native culture, dismisses the idea of hunting and claims that he would prefer to buy food in a store. Each town resident adopts a different position in relation to hunting, and although none claims to be recreational hunters, neither do they oppose hunting. One is a supporter who no longer hunts due to her age but is nostalgic about hunting traditions; another engages in traditional subsistence hunting; and finally there is a young man who, despite his cultural upbringing, is unconcerned about hunting tradition and instead favours modern convenience. When Joel finds himself in the local bar and restaurant, he speaks with the owner, Holling, and the local radio disc jockey, Chris. In a previous episode, it has been explained that Holling used to hunt until being confronted by all the animals he had killed, in a dream. In recounting the tale, Holling says, 'Every animal I'd ever killed; moose, elk, rabbits, deer, and hundreds of bears. All of them packing heat and aiming at me'. From that moment on, he puts away his shotgun and reasons that, 'until a wolverine could blow out my brains as easily as I could his, my gun [will] forever remain silent'.[12] In place of a gun, Holling uses a photographic stills camera instead. Yet, when Joel points this out to Holling, he replies, 'well that's personal choice. It in no way reflects a larger social agenda'. In this way, Holling distances himself from Joel's oppositional stance on hunting, claiming that his choice not to kill is based solely on personal guilt.

Mirroring Holling's fictional account of guilt, similar stories can be found narrated by real hunters in the many books that relate personal hunting tales. One such account describes a phase in a hunter's life when, being so keen to kill, he had to force himself to walk without pushing his friends out of the way in order to begin shooting (Carpenter, 2010, p. 165). He begins to have a recurring dream and explains that 'The pleasure in the hunt declined as my guilt about killing increased, and my recurrent dream was a measure of this guilty feeling' (p. 166). He describes how, in his dream, a frenzy overtook him as he lined up grouse and shot them 'until the last bird is gone' (p. 166). Part-way through the story, he ponders whether others have shared his guilt dreams and writes:

> But I wonder if, back in the days of the Wild West, those men who shot all those buffalo from sidecars and wagons and left them to rot – if they too have these remorseful dreams. I wonder if the men who shot thousands and thousands of great auks and passenger pigeons and whooping cranes for the so-called sport of it had dreams like mine.
>
> What is always missing from my dream of slaughter is the pleasure of the hunt (Carpenter, 2010, p. 166).

Both factual and fictional accounts suggest that guilt and pleasure over killing cannot coexist and one displaces the other. Diana Donald has, however, proposed that many hunters experience 'agonized sympathy, even self-identifications, with the sufferings of the prey', and this would seem to suggest that it is overly simplistic to construct hunters as emotionally remote from the animals that they kill (Donald, 2006, p. 50). Yet, when set alongside 'the pleasure' that many cite as being the primary reason to hunt, there is a resulting contradiction that appears impossible to resolve. According to Luke, pleasure in the hunt is often gendered and operates within a masculinized discourse. In this way, pleasure is derived from identifications with the 'challenging conquest', 'cooperative killing' and trophy collecting (Luke, 2007b, pp. 140–141). In *Northern Exposure*, Chris's reminiscences about hunting trips with his father and uncle and their male bonding illustrates Luke's point. Chris and Hollings's annual hunt is constructed in similar terms, as a time for male bonding, and this mirrors the findings of studies that have shown that over a third of hunters hunt with friends, a quarter with their father and 12 per cent with brothers (Responsive Management/ National Shooting Sports Foundation, 2008, p. 14).

In their conversation with Joel, Chris and Holling expand on their justification for hunting and maintain that animals 'expect' to be hunted by humans and contextualize this claim with reference to the natural order of things and the 'food chain': a similar justification to that given by Shaw in *Open Season*. Humans are designed to hunt and eat meat, they argue, having forward-facing eyes and large incisors. Chris continues to expound on the hunter-gatherer traditions of humans and suggests that hunting is an 'antidote for our current domestication'. He then adds, 'plus, bottom line, it's a gas'. 'Nothing like putting the breaks on something that's moving, I'm telling you now'. In this way, although Chris and Holling offer Joel a range of biologically deterministic arguments in support of hunting, in the end they come back to the 'indefensible' reason and claim that they hunt and, in Chris's case, kill for pleasure.

It is of little surprise that a general survey of the American public found that those who advocated hunting for pleasure were in the minority.[13] The notion of deriving pleasure from the act of killing an animal is equated by most people with cruelty. It seems self-evident that to take pleasure from the intentional death of another sentient being is indefensible; yet, in their explanation of hunting, Chris and Holling rely on constructing the activity as not only natural but also a practice that animals knowingly consent to be involved with ('they expect it of us'). In *Meditations on Hunting*, the philosopher José Ortega y Gasset (1995) defends the pleasure of hunting by suggesting that it is not directly derived from the death of an animal but that the death of an animal is necessary to authenticate the experience of the hunt. Ortega y Gasset argues that sport hunting reverses the purpose of subsistence hunting where the hunt is a means to an end: the death of an animal. In sport hunting, what interests the hunter is 'everything that he has to do to achieve that death' (Ortega y Gasset, 1995, p. 105). Pleasure, he proposes, is in the hunt, but to reach that pleasure the 'natural end' must be achieved: 'Death is essential because without it there is no authentic hunting' (p. 105). What the hunter wants, Ortega y Gasset argues, is 'having to win it, to conquer the surly brute though his own effort and skill with the extras that this carries with it: the immersion in the countryside, the healthfulness of the exercise, the distraction from his job and so on and so forth' (p. 105). This is a way of extricating hunting from 'the difficulties of its ethics', wherein Ortega y Gasset admits that 'hunting is counterposed to all that morphology of death as something without equal, since it is the only normal case in which the killing of one creature constitutes the delight of another' (p. 101). However, even with his lengthy justification of hunting, Ortega y Gasset is finally forced to admit that 'the moral problem of hunting is not resolved' (p. 105). In another analysis of hunting, Andrew Linzey looks at the major theories of normative ethics to conclude that 'all these theories, and their classical and modern exponents, would draw an absolute line at taking pleasure from cruelty' (Linzey, 2009, p. 86). In short, hunting struggles to find any convincing moral justification.

In spite of its apparent indefensibility, hunting has continued to be described in terms of pleasure, sometimes likened to the fulfilment of erotic or sexual desires and at other times compared to a form of spiritual bliss or aesthetic satisfaction.[14] Although Joel remains unconvinced by the various arguments presented to him in *Northern Exposure*, he asks to hunt with Holling and Chris so that he can judge from his own experience. Once armed with a gun, Joel begins to feel a rush of excitement and claims that he feels 'empowered'. When he and Chris shoot at two grouse and both are killed by Chris's gun, Joel insists that they all stay in the woods until he has killed something himself. That night, as they sit beside a fire, Joel declares that although he has never hunted before, it seems 'so familiar'. He likens their activities to man in the 'Paleolithic Age', howls at the moon and pronounces the experience to be 'so raw, so primal, so honest'. The following day Joel manages to shoot a grouse but discovers that he has not killed the bird. Chris and Holling pressure Joel to wring the grouse's neck, but he refuses, saying that the bird's eyes are open and looking at him. Suddenly, filled with remorse, Joel rushes the bird back to his surgery where he operates in an attempt to save the grouse's life. By way of explanation for Joel's guilt, Chris remarks that 'it appears that the shotgun blast delivered a psychic blast as well'. The bird dies and Joel, utterly dejected, explains to Maggie:

> The experience of hunting, it was great, it really was. Being out in the bush or whatever – the expectancy, the excitement, the total blood rush. And the killing, I mean, especially the killing: The killing was the best part. It was the dying I couldn't take.

Dying is a point of moral orientation between the pleasure of the hunt and the thrill of death for Joel. In the same way that Ortega y Gasset reduces hunting to a relationship between the hunt and the animal's death – each authenticating the other – Joel also realizes that he has detached hunting and death from the suffering. At one point, he remarks that the grouse has not 'followed protocol and died the way he was supposed to'. Seeing the bird in pain, suffering and eventually dying, Joel finds a parallel between human and animal existence. Whereas wild animals had seemed remote from his urban experience and he claims to have felt no connection to animals as a child, the visibility of suffering provides Joel with a bridge of familiarity between human and animal that brings animals into his framework of understanding. To make sense of the experience, Joel retreats to his home to cry and watch the films *Old Yeller* (1957), *The Black Stallion* (1979), *White Fang* (1936/1991) and *The Bear* (1988), each a depiction of nature and animal death in which he claims to discover a catharsis that was previously inaccessible to him. Watching the films again, he is struck by the tragedy and drama that is played out in nature and suggests that if humans and animals suffer then why should we presume that they do not love their mothers or feel distress at being alone in much the same way as humans do. Far from finding the films to be overly sentimentalized depictions of animal life, Joel finds a truth in them that he can relate to his own experience with the grouse.

## A clean kill

Hunting and the notion of a 'clean kill' plays a central role in the 2009 science fiction blockbuster *Avatar*, a film that constructs a fantasy of the hunter's authentic connection to nature. Unlike *Northern Exposure*, *Avatar's* politics are explicit, and director and writer James Cameron was very clear in interviews that the film deals with colonial imperialism and also has an environmental and spiritual message.[15] In *Avatar* Jake Sully, a paraplegic ex-Marine, arrives on the planet Pandora where a corporation from Earth is mining 'unobtanium', the richest deposits of which are located beneath the home of the Omaticaya clan of the Na'vi population. The Na'vi are blue humanoids, a hunter-gatherer species who live close to nature and without modern humanlike technologies. To gain a better understanding of the Na'vi, human scientists use avatar bodies – specially engineered human–Na'vi hybrid forms – which are connected to the host human through a mental link to interact with the tribe. Jake has to win the trust of the Na'vi and, after being taken to the leader of the Omaticaya Clan, he is given three months to learn their ways and become a hunter. Jake eventually sides with the indigenous Na'vi and against the RDA Corporation, and following a battle between the RDA's security forces and the Na'vi, which is finally won when the Pandoran animals attack the humans, he chooses to abandon his human form and exist in his avatar body instead. The story is, as one journalist described it, *'Dances With Wolves* in space' (Boucher, 2009).

Through *Avatar*, Cameron presents a fantasy of human and nature interconnectedness that is literally visualized by the Na'vi 'queues': long hair-like braids with tendrils at the end that can be connected to various flora and fauna of the planet, creating a neural link that allows the Na'vi to bond with other biological forms. In this way, the Na'vi can 'feel' and 'hear' the energy that flows through the planet. It allows them to bond with animals, listen to the voices of their dead ancestors and connect with Ewya, their deity and a goddess composed of all living things. In the process of 'going native' Jake must learn the Na'vi ways which include being able to ride a direhorse, described in Cameron's original script as 'six-legged, armor-skinned alien Clydesdales'. To do this he must connect his queue with the horse's antennae and create a bond which then gives the rider control. Neytiri, a female Na'vi, tells Jake that, once connected to the horse, he should 'feel her heartbeat, her breath. Feel her strong legs'. Jakes nods and closes his eyes and the camera tracks down and across the horse's body to visually describe the aspects of the horse's body that Neytiri describes. At this point the narration reveals that the bond is not an equal blending of Na'vi and horse but rather that it is a form of absolute control allowing the rider to pilot the horse using just the mind. The narration offers no sense of the feeling of being connected to another living being as the camera depicts only the external features of the horse and not the experience of 'being' the horse, which is suggested in the dialogue. Neytiri tells Jake that once connected to the horse 'you may tell her what to do', and Cameron's script makes it clear that the relationship between rider and horse is indeed one of domination when, in the description of an earlier scene, he writes, 'We see that the riders' QUEUES are connected to the horses' long moth-like antennae – a neural link with which they can command the horse, leaving hands free for weapons'. As such, the horse's body is taken over by the rider, in much the same way that Jake uses his avatar body and the RDA security forces use 'ampsuits' – human-operated, armoured walking machines. In this way the film describes relationships of control between armed forces and technologies, humans and biological avatar bodies and Na'vi and animals. This latter relationship of control and domination is further reinforced in a scene in which Jake must 'choose' capture and 'bond' with an ikran or mountain banshee, a pterodactyl-like creature, to finally become a hunter. The ikran must also 'choose' the hunter, according to Neytiri. Yet, the way in which the ikran indicates their choice of hunter is to try to kill them: an act that would suggest that the ikran does not enter into the relationship with the hunter willingly and, arguably, seems to be grossly misinterpreted by the Na'vi. To bond, Jake must throw a long strap, similar to a gaucho bolas, around the ikran's beak, then forcibly mount and connect with the creature. The whole act of bringing the ikran under the rider's control is purposefully likened to breaking a wild horse. Once 'broken', the ikran is completely under the control of the rider who has then completed their journey to become a Na'vi hunter.

During the film, Jake must hunt and prove that he can have a 'clean kill'. The deaths of animals are important turning points in the plotline and Jake's clean kill is contrasted with the wasteful kills that Neytiri makes to defend Jake in an earlier scene. Animal death is thus used to signal some key differences between Na'vi–animal and human–animal relationships. Na'vi hunt for food rather than for sport or recreation, and when Neytiri defends Jake from an attack by 'viperwolves' – wolf-like creatures with six legs and hands – she kills two of the animals. One that she shoots with an arrow does not die instantly and the animal lies, whimpering and crying, on the ground until Neytiri drives a knife into the creature's chest. Neytiri blames Jake for the deaths of the animals, suggesting that he attracted them to him with his torch and the noise he made in the forest. For Neytiri the deaths of the wolves are unnecessary and a cause for sadness. Jake, in a later scene, shoots a six-legged deer-like animal with his bow and arrow. The arrow hits the animal between the front two pair of legs. He then goes to the animal, who is still alive, and says a prayer of thanks before plunging the knife into the deer's chest as Neytiri had done in the earlier wolf attack scene. Neytiri regards this as a 'clean kill', and in completing this, Jake is ready to choose his ikran and complete his passage to being a fully-fledged Na'vi hunter. It is interesting to contrast the wasteful killing of the wolf with the clean kill of the deer in this film. One of the ways in which Cameron signals the worthiness and moral propriety of the killing is by the sounds that the animals make. In both scenes the animals are shot with arrows in the same place – behind the shoulder – in what is regarded by hunters as the ideal place on the body for the 'clean kill'.[16] Neither of the animals die from the arrow and both must be run through the chest with a knife to complete the kill. In the wasteful kill scene, the wolf's plaintive cries and pawing signify suffering and pain, whilst the deer emits one low cry before the sound of its voice is faded down so that the diegetic sound privileges Jake's voice whilst the non-diegetic mood music rises softly in the story space to accompany Jake's recitation of the prayer of thanks as he kneels over the dying animal. The death of the second animal is rendered more peaceful, even spiritual, through the manipulation of the aural realism.[17] Fading the deer's voice out of the soundscape literally removes the signifier of the animal's suffering, tidying up the kill and thereby implying a worthy death. In visual terms the deer occupies only the very bottom edge of the frame so that, for much of the scene, the dying animal is pushed out of visible space which is dominated by Jake as he prays. In much the same way that Joel detached dying and suffering from the hunt and the kill to experience pleasure in *Northern Exposure*, *Avatar* also disconnects the suffering animal from the act of hunting, by eliminating it visually and aurally from the frame, in order to venerate the symbolic 'clean kill'. To paraphrase Joel in *Northern* Exposure, by removing the signifiers of animal suffering from the story space, the animal dies 'according to protocol'.

## Defining hunting

*Avatar* employs subsistence hunting as an indicator of the Na'vi's closeness to nature. In his anthropological study, Gary Marvin writes that in hunting for food, rather than for recreation,

> the hunter does not seek out that contest for its own sake; it is simply a necessary, unavoidable and natural element of the relationship between predator and prey. Here the hunter does all in his or her power to minimize the nature of that contest in order to obtain meat in the most efficient and effective way possible (Marvin, 2006, p. 19).

For Marvin, hunting for food differs from hunting for recreation and pleasure, the latter of which is defined through the imposition of rules, regulations and restrictions which, for the sport hunter, establish the challenge as intrinsic to the hunt. Pleasure and satisfaction are attained, he argues, by overcoming the restrictions to create an encounter with an animal (p. 19). One of these 'rules' is that the animal must be able to escape, and Marvin offers the following as examples of activities which are 'not hunting': 'shooting a cow in a field', 'driv[ing] deer into an enclosure where they were shot' (p. 20). This definition of hunting has much in common with the traditions of 'fair chase' hunting which were defined by The Boone and Crockett Club, a hunting organization founded by Theodore Roosevelt as the 'ethical, sportsmanlike, and lawful pursuit and taking of any free-ranging wild, native North American big game animal in a manner that does not give the hunter an improper advantage over such animals' (Lautenberg, 2004, p. 17100). In *Northern Exposure*, Holling argues that whilst the hunter has a gun the hunt will always be weighted in his favour. However, 'fair chase' principles dismiss such suggestions and instead lay out a series of rules and obligations that the hunter must adhere to, which are thought to even up the odds for the hunted animals. By way of a comparison, 'canned hunting' ignores fair chase principles and represents, for many sport hunters, an example of unsportsmanlike hunting, where animals are placed in an enclosure, with little hope of escape. Such hunts often use tame or semi-tame animals, animals who are surplus to the requirements of zoos or circuses and old or infirm animals who are no longer of breeding age.[18] Participants in canned hunts pay for the guarantee of killing an animal whereas in sport hunting there are no such guarantees. In this way, the canned hunt is primarily about the kill, whereas sport hunting does not necessarily end in a kill. Marvin writes, 'a hunting event can only have occurred if the hunters set out to hunt, even if they failed to kill anything' (Marvin, 2006, p. 21).

The meaning of 'the kill' is at the core of hunting games in which the death of the animal is the goal. Hunting games have been commercially successful in North America where franchises such as *Deer Hunter* and the *Ultimate Hunt Challenge* games appeared in the '100 top-selling PC games of the 21st Century' in 2006, with unit sales of 250,000 and 210,000, respectively, generating revenues of $4.5 and $3.4 million (Edge, 2006).[19] Such figures begin to reveal the extent to which the hunting game genre in offline and later online gaming has been economically and culturally significant. For instance, in October 1998, the top-selling CD-ROM was *Deer Hunter II*, a hunting game developed to capitalize on the original *Deer Hunter* game which had been commissioned by Wal-Mart and was a surprise hit in 1997, selling over one million copies.[20] By 1999 *Deer Hunter* and *Deer Hunter II* had sold more than 2.3 million copies, making it one of the most popular games of any genre.[21] Hunting simulations began to dominate the software sales charts and by 2000 the Interactive Digital Software Association reported that software sales were booming thanks to hunting titles (Faulkner, 2000, p. 2). The same year, *Deer Hunter 4* was released with a first-person view giving the game a new sense of realism that other games sought to emulate. In 2006 *Big Buck Hunter Pro*, an arcade game, became the most commercially successful video game in bars and arcades in North America, and in 2008 *Deer Hunter* was reported to be the best-selling hunting game franchise of all time. When it made its debut on Xbox360, it became the first game to feature online multiplayer hunting tournament gameplay.

Miguel Sicart (2009) argues that computer games are 'ethical objects', and computer game players, 'ethical agents' (p. 4). In all computer games there are rules that guide behaviour and game worlds have values which give them the status of 'complex cultural objects' that 'relate to players who like to explore morals and actions forbidden in society' (Sicart, 2009, p. 4). The rules of the game world reveal a set of values that, in turn, govern the range of choices made available to the player. It is the choices that are offered and made during gameplay that constitute the ethical sphere of the game and the engagement of the player as an ethical subject. In the case of hunting games, the choices available to the player vary widely according to the individual game, although all have the death of animals as their goal. In a game such as *Cabela's Dangerous Hunts 2*, the player is an expert hunter who has to complete various missions in story mode guided by a companion, all the while being attacked by animals which the player must kill. The player's choices are limited to killing the animals or dying (and therefore ending the game), which led hunters to criticize *Cabela's Dangerous Hunts 2* as being mis-marketed as a hunting game. The predefined story was compared to adventure games which include cut-scenes to convey the game's backstory and give the gameplay context. Choices were limited as the story mode allowed the player little opportunity to 'hunt' but focused instead on killing animals as a means to survive each level. Players also complained that there was 'no realism' to the game, that it did not give the player 'trophies' and did not allow any choice of weapon or hunting paraphernalia.[22] In this sense the game inverted the idea that a hunt is defined by the activity that leads to the death of an animal rather than the killing itself, and the rules and principles of fair chase hunting were not respected within the gameworld.

Earlier hunting games such as *Deer Hunter II* carried a warning which stated, 'ADVISORY: VIOLENCE. Rewards injuring non-threatening creatures'.[23] This game was particularly popular with hunters who considered the gameplay realistic. Hunters made clear distinctions between games in which the gameplay was hunting and where the goal of the game was the slaughter of animals. One reviewer wrote about the game *Cabela's North American Trophy Bucks* that it 'violates the ethics of hunting to such a blatant degree. Instead of actually hunting, all the player does is kill as many animals as possible in two minutes'.[24] By contrast, *Hunting Unlimited 2009*, although having a 'kill-or-be-killed' series of confrontations also allowed players to stalk or ignore prey and included a range of different weapons and accessories as well as the opportunity to take a 'trophy photograph' after a kill. Critiques of games in which animals were slaughtered rather than hunted reinscribed the principles of the authentic hunt onto the game world and in so doing reflexively validated the principles of fair game hunting practices and the definitions of hunting. The choices that brought about the death of an animal in the game world were thus measured against the rules that governed the authenticity of killing in reality. The death of the animal was nonetheless still the goal of hunting simulation games, with success measured by the number of trophy heads and trophy photographs accumulated. Depending on where on the body they are hit, animals in *Hunting Unlimited*, for instance, may run away and bleed to death. The player must then track the animal to locate the dead body and claim the tag and then take a trophy photograph, at which point the game moves from first person to third person and depicts the player's hunter character kneeling beside the 'trophy' in typical trophy stance. None of the games have as their goal the accumulation of 'meat' and so are not framed in terms of subsistence hunting. In addition, conservation and the control of animal populations do not figure in the contextual framing of the gameplay, which is stripped down to the simple binary of hunter versus 'evil' animal (*Cabela's Dangerous Hunts 2*) or hunter as animal killer (rather than conservationist, for example). As there are no requirements to butcher dead animals when they have been shot and killed and although many games do give the player options to hunt, track, use decoys and scents, the goal of the games – to kill animals – reinforces the connection between pleasure and the death of the animal.

At the end of the *Northern Exposure* episode, the townspeople eat the grouse that Chris and Joel have killed. Although Joel has reconnected hunting to suffering and death, the narration ends by reintroducing the earlier contradiction of anti-hunt meat-eater and at the conclusion to the episode Joel attends the party where the grouse are being served. Joel pauses for a moment, seeks some clarification as to the source of the meat he is eating, and then remarks, 'it tastes good, kind of like an exotic chicken. I've never eaten a patient before'. By the end of the episode, the narration has negotiated a path through the various positions in relation to hunting but does not offer any definitive answers, and instead leaves the audience to unravel the multitude of contradictions that Joel embodies. Pleasure in killing remains an unsettling moral problem that the narration highlights rather than unravels, and at the crux of this is the issue of animal suffering. *Avatar* manipulates representations of animal death to inscribe a particular moral sensibility: A wasteful 'bad' death is contrasted to a good death, a clean kill. Yet, this distinction relies on visually and aurally silencing the animal. This refusal to acknowledge suffering resonates through the invitation to look at the dead animal in the trophy photograph, which marks the successful achievement of the goal in *Hunting Unlimited* and functions as a memento of a trophy hunt wherein the animal is fetishized as a dead body. In short, the death of a hunted animal is part of a process that has to negotiate or edit suffering in the pursuit of pleasure.

# 8
## Monsters: Horrors and Moral Panics

A quick glance at the roster of Hollywood horror films from any decade will reveal that filmmakers have had few problems in envisioning any species of animal as a monster. Insects, fish, birds and all manner of domestic and wild mammals have been marshalled by screenwriters, directors and studios in order that audiences should be terrified, horrified or, in the case of some of the more fantastical or ultra-low-budget horror depictions, amused. Horror films reflect social and cultural anxieties, and the circumstances that give rise to fictional monsters are often rooted in science-fact such that each new era of scientific discovery brings a new generation of monster forms into existence. Irrespective of the degree to which news media might celebrate scientific discoveries, horror films can cut through the abstraction of science and the hyperbole of human advancement to imagine the more sinister outcomes that such innovations might herald. In this sense, on-screen threats can imagine and amplify the offscreen risks to human and animal lives. Often the monstrous animal is not in itself the most terrible aspect of the narrative and is instead the outcome of a much greater hazard that has been wrought by humans interfering in some way in 'nature'. Risks posed by pollution, nuclear testing, genetic experimentation and so forth are the contexts from which monsters emerge, and many horror films eschew a closed narrative structure leaving the audience to ponder on what will happen next.[1] Thus, whilst it is true that open narrative structures leave the possibility of a franchised sequel on the cards, they also suggest that although the monster of *this* film may have been stopped the human science that created them still exists. This is one way in which fictional monsters can 'leak' into social reality.

According to Andrew Tudor, horror monsters can be subdivided into 'aliens' and 'anthropomorphs', differentiated by the extent to which the audience is invited to identify with them (Tudor, 1989, p. 115). In the latter case, 'our sympathy is invited precisely to the degree that such patently inhuman creations exhibit human inclinations, emotions and loyalties', whereas alien threats, Tudor contends, 'are not characters. They are, rather, narrative functions given physical form – necessary if there is a story to be told, but requiring of us no more than a belief in the immediate reality of their threat' (p. 115). Although Tudor is talking generally about monsters across the horror genre, his distinction holds true for monstrous animals. Where monstrous animals are attributed with humanized traits or motivations, the audience can find themselves cheering the creatures as they devour, dismember or mutilate the polluter, corporate villain or evil scientist who has, by dint of their greed, unethical behaviour or illegal experiment, brought about the monster's creation in the first place. In these cases, the line between evil human and animal monster is ambiguous and complicated by the emotional and moral structure of the film.[2] Monstrous animals can therefore shift from being a narrative function to an anthropomorph, particularly when the audience is given an insight into the creature's origin and the human actions that caused the mutation or monstrous behaviour to emerge. Indeed, if advertising, wildlife films and hunting narratives have given media consumers happy cows, huggable lions and Bambi, then part of the cultural work that monstrous animals do is to contradict such safe fantasies of human–animal relations.

By and large, horror films borrow widely from scientific fact and cultural myths to construct nightmare possibilities such as giant mutated insects, amphibians and fish; killer rabbits, dogs and sheep; and wild animals whose natural behaviour is magnified and contorted to horrific proportions. The mediation of science, via news reporting and myths, both ancient and urban, are mobilized through the animal monster and heightens the threat of the creature by giving it a foothold in the real world of science fact. In this way, representations of alligators in city sewers, ants the size of wolves, monstrous irradiated insects and rabid dogs are woven out of legend, myth and fact and play to wider concerns about the human manipulation of nature and its potential risks and failures. Film taglines summarize the threats to normality that such animals pose: 'FANTASTIC MONSTERS ATTACK EARTH' (*Them!*, 1954); 'It's the day that Nature strikes back!' (*Frogs*, 1972); 'For they shall inherit the earth…sooner than you think!' (*Empire of the Ants*, 1977); 'Last summer they were pets. Now they are predators' (*The Pack*, 1977). Ranging from the global to the local, animal threats somehow upturn or invert the anthropocentric 'natural order'. Pets become predators, small creatures grow to gigantic and powerful proportions and nature turns against humans.

Monstrous animals are abject in the sense that Julia Kristeva describes abjection: as that which 'disturbs identity, system, order. What does not respect borders, positions, rules. The in-between, the ambiguous, the composite' (Kristeva, 1982, p. 4). From an anthropological perspective, Mary Douglas has argued that rules about holiness, unity and perfection have been developed and extended to animals throughout history. Looking at evidence of this longevity by way of examples of uncleanness from the Old Testament, Douglas argues that 'Those species are unclean which are imperfect members of their class, or whose class itself confounds the general scheme of the world' (Douglas, 2002, p. 69). According to Douglas, 'uncleaness is matter out of place', and the way in which it is addressed is through 'order' (Douglas, 2002, p. 50). Order is re-established by labelling things as monstrous, reaffirming the rules that distinguish the proper from the improper, constructing anomalous things as dangerous, and through physical control, particularly killing (Douglas, 2002, pp. 48–50). It is not difficult to see that such methods of social re-ordering are inflected through the narrative trajectory of most horror narratives. In this way, monsters are understood as abject through systems of meaning which are socially prescribed and regulated and culturally reproduced. Furthermore, there are discursive intersections where fictional monsters and factual news reporting collide, inform and sustain one another. Animal monsters thus have a public significance that extends beyond fictional entertainment and has consequences for our understanding of human–animal encounters beyond the cinema screen.

## 1950s atomic monsters

A postwar boom in horror films introduced new monsters to the screen: giant arthropods and creatures created or mutated by radiation. It is not difficult to see why Hollywood would concentrate on themes of atomic power, radiation and nuclear threat in the 1950s. The bombing of Hiroshima and Nagasaki and the Bikini Atoll tests were still very much in the public memory and nuclear power was being promoted as both a technological wonder and a weapon of incomparable destruction. Perhaps less obvious is the focus on arthropods, but films such as *Them!* (1954), *Tarantula* (1955), *The Deadly Mantis* (1957), *Beginning of the End* (1957) and *The Black Scorpion* (1957), which in some cases brought the themes of insects and radiation together, reflected

Hollywood's obsession with such monsters. Yet, insects were, at the time, constructed by science as a major risk to human life and, coupled with the crucial role that they played in radiation testing, audiences were already culturally primed to regard insects as monstrous. It was easy to extend the alien threat motif to arthropods in general, and the combination of radiation and animal monster offered a potent narrative mix.

In 1946 the risks posed by radiation was a topic of interest for the press and the public. At the centre of the debate was the Nobel-winning geneticist Dr Herman Joseph Müller, nicknamed 'Mister Mutation' by his students, a moniker that the newspapers were quick to relate to their readership. With atomic testing at the forefront of public concerns, newspapers were keen to quote the Nobel prize-winner and an expert on the topic of radiation. Müller's claim quantified the level of threat in no uncertain terms when he stated, 'There is no dosage of X-rays so low as to be without risk of producing harmful mutations' (*Eugene Register-Guard*, 7 May 1947, p. 2). Results of his experiments in the late 1920s had shown that fruit flies exposed to radiation produced offspring with inheritable characteristics such as changed eye colour, three wings and a shortened life expectancy.[3] His results had been largely ignored by the press at the time but, in the wake of Hiroshima and Nagasaki and Bikini Atoll, Müller's views had much greater resonance with a public now keen for information from scientists and experts.[4] In the weeks prior to the Bikini Atoll tests, newspapers referred to the results of earlier radiation tests pointing out that when eggs of the vinegar fly were exposed to radiation in the laboratory, what emerged when they hatched were 'hardly vinegar flies at all'(*Sydney Morning Herald*, 4 June 1946, p. 2). The terms 'monstrosity', 'mutation' and 'monster' passed quickly into the popular discourse, and in describing mutated flies newspapers painted a vivid picture of the effects of radiation on living beings: 'Some have big eyes, some have one large and one small eye, some are blind, some are long-winged, and others are wingless. Furthermore when these monstrosities in turn breed, their progeny are also monstrosities' (*Sydney Morning Herald*, 4 June 1946, p. 2). Even more startling was the claim that the damage to biological life was hereditary, and although Müller dismissed the notion that women exposed to radiation would give birth to 'two-headed children', the greater danger he predicted was that mutations would appear in later generations. He cautioned that not only were the mutations permanent but also that 'the damage is permanent. It remains until the line dies out by reason of that disability' (*Eugene Register-Guard*, 7 May 1947, p. 2).

The 1946 tests at Bikini Atoll were given the name Operation Crossroads, and the world's press turned its focus towards the nuclear experiments being undertaken by US scientists and the military. Newsreels and newspapers reported on the preparations leading up to the first test on 1 July 1946. The tests were designed to investigate the effects of a nuclear blast on naval ships as well as the effects of radiation on living organisms, military hardware and a range of everyday items and foodstuffs. American propaganda newsreels, produced by Universal Newsreels in conjunction with the US Army and Navy, expressed an unrelenting patriotism and described Operation Crossroads in terms designed to reassure the public that the tests were safe and in world interest, and would allow scientists to gain greater understanding of the nuclear force that America controlled. In the newsreel, *First Pictures: Atomic Blast!* (1946), audiences saw images of the A-bomb test at Bikini. The iconic explosion and ensuing cloud were accompanied by rousing music and the well-known voice-over of Ed Herlihy describing Operation Crossroads as 'the motion picture spectacle of all time'. Newspaper coverage was mixed, however, and any enthusiasm about the contributions that the tests would make to scientific knowledge was tempered by concerns about the longer-term effects. Based on what was known about radiation from x-rays, one paper speculated that the Operation Crossroads tests might lead to 'the human race being doomed to breeding monstrosities and weaklings' and noted that the scientists who had studied the effects of radiation exposure on people at Hiroshima and Nagasaki expected that the progeny of those who had survived the blasts would be 'such monstrosities as science has produced low in the scale of living organisms in the laboratory' (*Sydney Morning Herald*, 4 June 1946, p. 2). In short, there was a widespread fear that the monstrous insects produced under laboratory conditions were a portent of what lay in wait for humans for generations to come.

There were 4,900 animals used as experimental models in Operation Crossroads. These animals – 4,000 white rats, 200 goats, 200 pigs as well as sheep, guinea pigs, mice and insects – were placed aboard 22 of the 73 test ships to be targeted by the nuclear blasts.[5] The British press and UK-based animal charities condemned the use of live animals, and significant concern was raised by the American public.[6] More than 5,000 letters of protest were received,[7] and in response the navy gave reassurances that the animals had their own veterinarian on-hand to look after their health, that the test animals were dining on specially prepared foods and that 'every effort has been made to see that they are kept comfy and cozy' (*Spokane Daily Chronicle*, 3 June 1946, p.

6). Newsreel imagery released in the week after the first blast was less comforting and showed pigs and goats being dragged across the deck of a ship, rats in small cages, goats in pens and sheep being partially shorn 'in the interests of science'; their fleece was removed in patches to enable scientists to study the effects of the blast on their skin. In the days prior to the tests, national and international protest grew, with the greatest opposition, outside of the US, to using live animals coming from Britain. Towards the end of June the British government was put under pressure by animal advocates who declared the experiments to be 'torture' and wanted officials to formally request that the US scientists anesthetize the animals.[8] In the days and weeks that followed the tests, the public were given updates on the progress of the animals. Figures varied, but most newspaper reports stated that around 10 per cent of the animals had died during the first bomb blast and a further 10 per cent died of radiation sickness soon after.[9] Within two weeks the remainder of the animals that had been subjected to testing were reported to be 'dying like flies', but this quote, from an unidentified naval officer, was quickly contradicted by an official statement from Vice Admiral William H.P. Blandy who claimed that only 15.3 per cent of animals had died and whilst he expected other deaths to occur during the next three months, mortality was proceeding at the 'expected rate' (*Miami News*, 16 July 1946, p. 8).[10]

Widespread public anxieties about nuclear risk continued to grow in the 1950s with the development of the H-bomb and the beginning of hostilities in Korea. At the same time, insects were especially newsworthy for a number of reasons. As US troops moved into Korea, newspapers reported that the main dangers they faced were from the fleas, flies, mosquitoes, lice and rats, which were responsible for the transmission of a range of potentially fatal diseases such as malaria, dysentery, typhus, filariasis, Japanese B encephalitis and dengue. Insects were regarded as 'enemies' of the troops and they became a crucial aspect of the rhetoric of the conflict. For instance, one newspaper stated that the Korean body louse was 'as tough and dangerous as any Communist enemy' and senior officials warned that if the US decided to use nuclear force against North Korea, insects were all that would remain (*Times-News*, 28 November 1951, p. 4). Insects were also at the centre of serious charges against the US when, in 1952, China and Korea claimed that America was engaged in biological warfare and that between 25 February and 5 March US planes had dropped 'germ bombs' containing insects carrying bubonic plague and cholera across Korea and Manchuria. The news coverage of the germ warfare accusation was vast and the issue became a major propaganda battleground.[11] Whilst the US strenuously denied the charges, the idea that insects were disease-ridden enemies and could be engineered as a deadly germ-carrying weapon was firmly planted in the public consciousness.

The discourse of insect threat had a parallel domestic dimension as well. Scientists had issued warnings in 1945 that polio was being transmitted by houseflies, and large-scale campaigns to eradicate infestations were undertaken in efforts to control the spread of the disease.[12] Newspaper reports provided graphic accounts of the means by which flies carried disease and left little room for public doubt that flies were a major threat. As one paper explained:

> When it is considered that the flies which are on the dinner table may have been feeding upon the discharges of tubercular patients or upon human excrement which possibly came from a typhoid or a poliomyelitis patient, it is then apparent that fly control is a matter of importance (*Eugene Register-Guard*, 19 June 1945, p. 5).

By 1952 it was estimated that insects cost America four billion dollars each year, largely through the destruction of crops; and in the foreword to the Department of Agriculture Yearbook 1952, the US Secretary of Agriculture Charles F. Brannan wrote, 'Although the science of entomology has made great progress in the past two decades, the problems caused by insects seem to be bigger than ever' (Brannan, 1952, p. vii). Dichloro-diphenyl-trichloroethane, which had been hailed as a huge leap forward in the control of 'enemy' insects, had become available to general consumers after the war. It had been used to control an outbreak of typhus in 1943 and 1944 and it was hoped that DDT would prove to be an effective weapon against all insect-borne diseases. Gypsy moth infestations across Pennsylvania in 1932 and 1948 were successfully treated with DDT and received significant press attention, but doubts began to emerge as to its safety, and by the early 1950s the public was being bombarded with messages concerning the potential risks that accompanied indiscriminate use of chemical controls. One newspaper drove home the message by making a chilling comparison: 'everyone is familiar with the fact that radiation burns – even death – can result from improper use of radiation devices. It is exactly the same with these two potent insecticides' (*Sunday Herald*, 1 June 1952, p. 112). But quite apart from the devastating effects that DDT was eventually found to have on humans, animals and the environment, it was clear by 1952 that DDT was also ineffectual against a large number of insects. It failed to eradicate the body louse in Korea in 1952 and in the same year it became apparent that some flies were developing resistance. By the mid-1950s the public had received information from scientists, government officials and the press about various threats posed by insects, but the efficacy of chemical control proved to be far from reassuring.

In 1957 an infestation of fire ants led to one of the largest programmes of chemical eradication in the US, with 60 planes readied to begin aerial insecticide spraying over 20,000, 000 acres of land. Newspapers gave chilling accounts of the advance of the insect invasion from Argentina into Mississippi, Alabama, Texas, Georgia, Florida, Louisiana, Tennessee and Carolina, and the eradication programme was described in combative terms as a 'war' against the 'menace'. Newspaper accounts of fire ants shared much in common with the on-screen fictional insect monsters that audiences were familiar with, as well as with the wider circulating factual discourse on insect threat. As one article explained:

> The South American killer-ant eats both plants and animals. It attacks newly-born calves and pigs and is particularly fond of quail and other young birds nesting in the fields [...] The hardy, strong-jawed insect clamps onto human beings and other forms of life with its jaws and injects stingers that feed poisonous fluids into the wound. In human beings the wound results in festering blisters that takes two to three weeks to heal (*Times-News*, 9 April 1957, p. 2).

As the programme rolled out, objections were raised by conservation department officials who were concerned about the effects of the insecticide on wildlife and claimed that up to three-quarters of wildlife may be at risk of dying due to the chemicals. Objections grew as more evidence was brought forward that wildlife, and particularly birds and fish, were being destroyed by the fire ant chemical treatments across the Southern states.[13] Claims from entomologists that the dangers of fire ants had been amplified and evidence that the chemical controls were not only ineffective against fire ant infestations but that it also had a fatal impact on wildlife did not halt the eradication programmes, although state support for them began to wane in 1960 (Tschinkel, 2006, p. 48).[14]

### Managing insect threat

By the latter half of the 1950s, it was becoming apparent that chemical controls developed by science – which had promised to deliver a world free from the ravages and diseases of insects – were proving hazardous to humans and animals and furthermore were failing to eradicate insects which were building immunity to pesticides. Further confirmation that insects were indestructible came with the official announcement from US army scientists that insects would be the only survivors of a full-scale atomic radiation attack. Able to withstand more than one hundred times the amount of radiation than humans or other animals, even the most feared threat to biological life, radiation, would prove ineffective against insect populations. An official spokesperson for the 4th Army medical laboratory stated: 'Should man destroy himself with awe-inspiring weapons and inventions, both man and animal could perish, leaving nothing but hardy insects to repopulate the world' (*Southeast Missourian*, 19 May 1958, p. 2).

The discourse on insect threat was indeed compelling. Newspaper reports seized on the 1952 Department of Agriculture Yearbook about insects and picked out some of the more terrifying points that the scientific experts had made. One newspaper article, which began with the headline 'Man Supreme? Insects May Be a Real Threat', proceeded to list the various insect descriptions that were mentioned in the book, which included ants the size of a wolf, enormous locusts whose legs could be used as saws, insects using gas warfare, moths with a wingspan of twelve inches and beetles so large that they sounded like B-52s (Figure 8.1). Although the article admitted further on that the first two were taken from accounts by the Roman naturalist Pliny and were generally agreed to be erroneous, the rest of the insect horrors were, it assured the reader, entirely factual (*Milwaukee Sentinel*, 13 September 1952, p. 24). Scientists' expert opinions on the threats posed by insects added to the general anxieties in 1952, and it is easy to see that their warnings could be assimilated into a horror narrative: the accounts needed very little dramatic intervention. For instance, one entomologist explained that whereas 6,500 species of insects in the United States had previously been considered injurious to people, that number had increased to 10,000 by 1952 (Sabrosky, 1952, p. 2). Moreover, insect numbers were so huge that they were estimated to account for around 80 per cent of all known creatures on the planet, a proposition which prompted concerns that insects had the reproductive potential to take over the earth.[15] One entomologist, Curtis Sabrosky, wrote, 'In one summer season from April to August, the descendents of one pair of house flies, if all lived and reproduced normally, would make a total of 191,000,000,000,000,000,000' and 'the descendents of one female aphid would amount to 1,560,000,000,000,000,000,000,000 by the

*Figure 8.1*    Cartoon by Frank Marasco used to illustrate a news article on the 1952
*Department of Agriculture Yearbook*

end of the season' (Sabrosky, 1952, pp. 2–3). The numbers were unfath-
omable to the general reader and the descriptions offered by scientists
seemed nightmarish:

> Every minute of the day and night billions of insects are chewing, suck-
> ing, biting, and boring away at our crops, livestock, timber, gardens,
> homes, mills, warehouses, and ourselves (Haeussler, 1952, p. 141).

> Some people have discovered that 'insects are getting harder and
> harder to kill.' They are partly right. A few of the hundreds of pests
> that farmers must control have developed resistance to insecticides.
> That means that an insect can survive and thrive in the presence of
> a chemical that is supposed to kill it (Porter, 1952, p. 317).

> As the number of homes in the United States becomes greater and
> greater, as our population becomes increasingly urban, and as industry
> and production continue to expand, the household-insect problems
> become more prevalent and more acute (Henderson, 1952, p. 469).

Insecticide companies were naturally keen to repeat and endorse the
official findings, and the language employed in advertising campaigns
sustained the notion of insect threat. Using a photograph of a baby and
an image of an enormous fly which appeared to be about to consume
the child, the makers of LURR insecticides, for example, asked: 'How
many bites can you count on your child's arms, legs and body? And how

many times have you had to brush a filthy, germ-carrying fly away from your food today?' (LURR with Gamma-Hex advertisement, July 1952). According to scientists and journalists, insects were voracious, mutated, destructive, disease-ridden, near-unstoppable threats against humanity; all Hollywood did was enlarge their physical proportions.

## Them!

In the film *Them!*, Hollywood brought together two of the major threats that were perceived to be facing human life in the 1950s: radiation and insects. The narrative incorporated factual information that was well-known to the American public and located a monster ant colony close to the site of the first atomic bomb test, which had taken place on 16 July 1945 in New Mexico in preparation for the attack on Hiroshima on 6 August. Two myrmecologists, a father and daughter team employed by the Department of Agriculture, quickly identify the radiation from atomic testing as the origin of a mutation which has caused ants to grow to gigantic proportions and they guide the military forces in their attempts to kill the monsters (Figure 8.2). The colony in New Mexico is set on fire, but two-winged queen ants escape. They are tracked and eventually killed before they can establish new colonies and wipe out all human life on earth. In the final scene, looking down at the burning bodies of the giant mutant ants, a soldier asks, 'If these monsters got started as a result of the first atomic bomb in 1945 what about all the others that have been exploded since then?' One of the US Department of Agriculture scientists responds, 'When man entered the atomic age, he opened a door into a new world. What we eventually find in that new world, nobody can predict'.

The closing lines of *Them!* were a sombre reminder of the nuclear threat that figured in general public anxieties about the postwar world. Yet, the film offered audiences an opportunity to see the immediate everyday threat – insects – defeated in the most spectacular way on-screen. It is difficult to argue that the enormous all-consuming ants in *Them!* which threatened to obliterate human life on earth were, as some scholars would have it, a metaphor for the Communist threat. Given the discourse of monstrous insects that had been constructed by science, government, the chemical industries and the press, the fictional monsters can be understood in a more literal sense. Audiences had been bombarded with information about the threats posed by all manner of insects since 1945, and the horrors of disease and their resistance to scientifically designed chemical controls gave the public access to a much more straightforward reading of the on-screen creatures.

*Figure 8.2  Them*, 1954. Dir. Douglas Gordon. Image courtesy of Warner Bros. The Kobal Collection

The film's characters included insect experts from the Department of Agriculture, a clear reference to those who had written the well pub-licized 1952 Yearbook whilst images of oversized insects were already present within the popular discourse being used as part of the strategy to market pesticides and ensure that consumers could see the insect threat magnified in their newspapers. Audiences would also have been quite familiar with the basic premise of the film: the ability of insects to mutate and survive chemical control and even radiation, both of which were proven to be deadly to humans.

By the time *Them!* was released in 1954, insects were already well-established as abject. Their associations with death, disease and dirt had been repeated through various authoritative channels, and whilst there was another ongoing debate in the scientific community about the benefits, if not absolute necessity, of insects,[16] the insect threat discourse was the one that gained the greater volume of press, public and government attention. Insects were largely undifferentiated in press reports, and so the 'enemy' was perceived to be immense in number. Furthermore, the lack of identification of particular species left Hollywood in the position that it could employ almost any insect, or arthropod for that matter, as the on-screen danger terrorizing earth. In short, the insect threat discourse that was already in wide circulation was easily transferred to any animal with an exoskeleton. Ants, scorpions, spiders, mantis, flies and grasshoppers were utilized as aliens, in the sense that the audience was not invited to identify with the monsters but instead found some reassurance in their demise: something that science appeared to be unable to deliver in reality. The failure of attempts to control insects by chemical means in the 1950s would go on to inform a later decade of horror narratives, and it is to this later construction of monstrous animals that this chapter now turns.

## Revenge of nature

In the 1970s there was another significant rise in the number of horror films produced and released,[17] although animal monsters were no longer the gigantic bugs of the 1950s.[18] During the 1970s, monstrous animals appeared in packs or as infestations and often demonstrated collective intelligence[19] (*Dogs*, 1976; *The Pack*; 1977; *Kingdom of the Spiders*, 1977; *Night of the Lepus*, 1972; *Willard*, 1971; *Ben*, 1972), although after the mid-decade blockbuster *Jaws* (1975) there was a notable shift towards individual animal monsters with films such as *Grizzly* (1976), *Orca* (1977), *Prophecy* (1979) and *Alligator* (1980). Many of the films during this decade also included references to pesticides, chemical poisoning, toxic waste or pollution (*Night of the Lepus*; *Frogs*, 1972; *Prophecy*; *Empire of the Ants*, 1977; *Day of the Animals*, 1977), synthetic hormones (*Alligator*) and genetic engineering (*Piranha*, 1978). In this way, these films were a cultural response to wider concerns about environmental pollution and the failures of science that had begun in the 1950s. Animals were a narrative mechanism by which filmmakers could express the idea of nature fighting back, but the monster representations of the 1970s, notably in the case of *Jaws*, and in much the same way that insects had been demonized, had repercussions for the way in which people perceived animals and animal threats.

In 1952 Robert Mobbs had testified to a House Interstate and Foreign Commerce Committee that pesticides and insecticides needed much stronger regulation. He argued that previous reports on insecticide toxicity had been 'largely ignored, minimised and suppressed' (*Tuscaloosa News*, 19 August 1953, p. 3). Experimental animals fed with insecticides containing benzene hexachloride convulsed and died, and the overuse of such chemicals had, it was argued, now contaminated foods and the milk supply, and DDT residue was traceable in human tissue. The controversy over fire ant control in 1957 and 1958 sparked a wider concern about insecticide poisoning, and by the early 1960s there was mounting evidence that chemical control was having a significant and devastating impact on the environment. One newspaper commentary attempted to summarize the state of various threats that were perceived to exist by the end of 1959, stating:

> [N]ow comes a scientist who voices fear that humanity may one day destroy itself through its own pollutants – chemical radiological, and other.
>
> The dangers are already present. A good deal of evidence suggests that people who breathe automobile fumes and similar city contaminants are more likely than others to develop lung cancer.
>
> No one needs to be reminded of the great fears surrounding nuclear fallout from countless experiments thus far conducted.
>
> Industrial wastes pollute our streams, our lakes and ocean shores, and add to the air pollution over cities. Alarm is rising over the spreading use of insecticides and weed killers that could harm the food supply (*Prescott Evening Courier*, 24 November 1959, p. 3).

What was of concern was not only that the problems were present but also that scientists and government officials did not have the answers. The public were given few reassurances and experts were candid in saying that they did not have the solutions. One water expert was quoted saying about water pollution, 'We do not have reliable methods for predicting their effect on man. We don't know how to remove viruses from treated water. We don't know the effects on the human system of the constant accumulation of small increments of present-day chemicals' (*Telegraph*, 30 December 1959, p. 4). Questions about the safety of chemical controls began to emerge with more force in the 1960s. In the UK, worries about an unprecedented number of dead wild birds found across the country forced a meeting of a special committee of the House of Commons in 1961 to investigate reports of pesticide poisonings.[20] In the US, the publication of *Silent Spring* (Carson, 1962) in 1962 raised public unease that the overuse of chemical controls, particularly DDT, was already producing profoundly negative effects in nature, humans and animals.[21] Rachael Carson anticipated later concerns when she questioned the motivating principles behind chemical control:

> Future historians may well be amazed by our distorted sense of proportion. How could intelligent beings seek to control a few unwanted species by a method that contaminated the entire environment and brought the threat of disease and death even to their own kind? Yet this is precisely what we have done... We are told that the enormous and expanding use of pesticides is necessary to maintain farm production. Yet is our real problem not one of *over-production*? (Carson, [1962] 1991, pp. 25–26, emphasis in original).

Central to Carson's account of the hazards of modern chemical usage was the concept of the environment. In *Silent Spring*, Carson inevitably reconnected humans to nature and animals. She argued that the dangers of chemical toxins were not localized geographically or within particular species; rather, all living beings were intrinsically connected to the environment, particularly through mechanisms such as the waterways and the food chain (Carson, [1962] 1991, p. 169). Carson recounted the results of studies which demonstrated that DDT residues of between 5.3 and 7.4 parts per million were commonly found in the American population between 1954 and 1956.[22] Taken in through the consumption of food, there was no escape from the build up of DDT residue in the human body: meat, fish, fruit and vegetables all harboured levels of the chemical. There was no doubt, in Carson's view, that the environment was being chemically poisoned and that poisoning was a consequence of modern 'civilisation'.

> To find a diet free from DDT and related chemicals, it seems one must go to a remote and primitive land, still lacking in the amenities of civilisation [...] Such a land appears to exist, at least marginally, on the far Arctic shores of Alaska – although even there one may see the approaching shadow [...] When some of the Eskimos themselves

were checked [...] small residues of DDT were found [...] The reason
for this was clear [...] For their brief stay in civilisation the Eskimos
were rewarded with a taint of poison (Carson, [1962] 1991, p. 163).

Carson suggested there was no escape from the combined effects of
Western science, industry and state, and environmental poisoning
emphasized the interconnectivity of all living beings. To these ends,
it became apparent that the environmental effects of chemical control
which had been widely advocated by scientists and governments could
not be locally contained.

Carson argued that important interrelationships and interdepend-
encies were, at best, misunderstood, at worst, ignored. The connection between humans and the natural world could only be appreciated
through an understanding of two ecologies: the ecology of the environment and the ecology of the body. Although connected, the two
ecologies differed in one significant way. Environmental ecology, or
'the web of life – or death' could be seen, witnessed, and transcribed;
the ecology of the body was an 'unseen world' where, she claimed,
'minute causes produce mighty effects; the effect, moreover, is often
unrelated to the cause, appearing in a part of the body remote from
the area where the original injury was sustained' (Carson, [1962] 1991,
p. 169). The human body, far from being resilient and under the protection of modern science, was vulnerable and constantly exposed
to risks that were not immediately perceived. The risks to humans
were, paradoxically, products of scientific, industrial, and ultimately
human, 'progress' and the nascent environmental discourse, implicitly at least, challenged the claims that science could make humans
invulnerable.

If attempts to control insects had been discussed in terms of a battle,
then the end of the 1960s brought with it a new reconciliatory discourse publicly expressed in Richard Nixon's first State of the Union
Address in January 1970:

> The great question of the seventies is, shall we surrender to our sur-
> roundings, or shall we make our peace with nature and begin to
> make reparations for the damage we have done to our air, to our
> land, and to our water?
> 
> Restoring nature to its natural state is a cause beyond party and
> beyond factions. It has become a common cause of all the people of
> this country. It is a cause of particular concern to young Americans,
> because they more than we will reap the grim consequences of our

failure to act on programs which are needed now if we are to prevent disaster later.

Clean air, clean water, open spaces – these should once again be the birthright of every American. If we act now, they can be.

We still think of air as free. But clean air is not free, and neither is clean water. The price tag on pollution control is high. Through our years of past carelessness we incurred a debt to nature, and now that debt is being called (Nixon, 1970, State of the Union Address).[23]

The first 'Earth Day' in 1970 firmly rooted the notion of 'making peace with nature' within the new public discourse of the environment and gave 'nature' an anthropomorphic presence that was envisioned in animal form by Hollywood. Monsters in the 1970s horror films exploited the metaphor of nature taking revenge on humans for the damage that had been incurred by decades of indiscriminate chemical use and industrialization. The waterways proved to be a popular setting for such narratives, and following on from the incredible success of *Jaws*, favoured settings for nature-revenge films included swamps, oceans, lakes and sewers.

Water is an alien environment, and writing about the ocean setting in *Jaws* Jonathan Lemkin points out that not only is the sea 'a place of the unknown' but that it is 'a place beyond the rule of man [*sic*], whose influence stops at the shoreline' (Lemkin, 2004, p. 323). In this sense, waterways offer a good narrative mechanism by which threats can travel and evade human capture or containment. Yet, inasmuch as the danger of the ocean was expressed throughout popular culture in terms of being beyond human control, wild and inhospitable, the sea also held a tangible risk for the public, in the form of pollution, which was embedded in the wider consciousness during the 1970s. Water pollution was an extremely well-publicized issue and had garnered a high degree of press interest from the 1960s. Throughout the 1970s, news media reported on the vast amounts of oil and raw sewage in the oceans that officials were finding difficult to quantify but were simply described by US scientists in 1973 as 'massive' (*Los Angeles Times*, 15 February 1973, p. D6). Beaches were closed due to pollution scares and people were warned not to fish or bathe along large stretches of coastline in the US and UK. Inland bodies of water were also devastated by pollution and across Europe the concerns were much the same. In 1972 Peter Ritchie-Calder sent out a dire warning in *Pollution of the Mediterranean Sea*:

The Mediterranean Sea is sick. It needs intensive care, day and night nursing. By nature it has always been delicate but its condition has grievously deteriorated in recent years. The short term prognosis is obvious: on present trends, things will get worse because the effects will be multiplied and magnified by the increase in industrial activity. Recreational beaches will be tarred and ordured. The sea will be out of bounds for bathers. Seafood will be a health hazard. In terms of epidemic diseases, the Mediterranean can become a biological time bomb. The trees will be dying around the coasts, suffocated or poisoned by polluted sea winds (Ritchie-Calder quoted in Haas, 1990, p. 66).

Although the discourse of the environment was, on one hand, drawing on the imagery of sickness which was coupled with the desire to 'make peace with nature', there was, on the other hand, an overwhelming sense of threat present in official and media discussion of water pollution. In this way, films such as *Jaws, Piranha* and *Alligator* were able to exploit public understanding of the dangers of the seas and connecting waterways that were writ large in press coverage, and risks from water pollution gave a specific context to the notion that the oceans were already hazardous places to be.

## *Jaws*

Unlike many other films of the decade that make specific references to environmental pollution, toxic waste, chemical testing and so forth, *Jaws* makes no such mention. Whereas the illegal testing of synthetic hormones on dogs and puppies is the reason that the eponymous monster in *Alligator* grows to such enormous and terrifying proportions, and the piranha in the film of the same name are the result of radiation and genetic mutation, *Jaws* gives no reason for the shark attacks in the film. Nonetheless, *Jaws* came along at a time when the hazards of swimming in polluted waters were well-publicized, and the notion that danger lurked in the oceans was thus already well established in the public mind. The great white shark in the film which preys on bathers in the waters around the fictional Amity coastal town is described as a lone rogue. If anything, it was the indiscriminate and motiveless killing that made the shark in *Jaws* so terrifying for audiences. In every sense, the on-screen shark was an alien and there was no attempt to encourage the audience to identify in any way with the monster. Director Steven Spielberg was successful in this regard, and at the test screenings audiences got out of their seats to shout, applaud and show their approval when the shark exploded at the end of the film.

*Jaws* was a phenomenon and broke all records at the time by taking more than $100 million at the US box office. An adaptation of the best-selling novel of the same name by Peter Benchley which had sold an estimated 3.5 million copies by June 1975,[24] the film was an immediate hit, and the effect of the film on attitudes towards sharks was significant. Given that one in every five American adults, and four in every ten young adults, saw *Jaws* at the cinema in the first three months of the film's release, the extent to which public perceptions were shaped was considerable.[25] The press described the public response to the film as 'shark mania', and one article explained that the film

> has resulted in thousands of unconfirmed sightings of sharks at resort beaches on the East and West coasts. It has veteran swimmers scared to go into deep water and novices and children afraid to stick their big toe in at all. It has caused hoaxes and it has officials fearing panic situations in which swimmers dash pell mell for the shore with resultant tramplings, drownings and heart attacks (*Milwaukee Journal*, 12 July 1975, p. 1).

The results of a survey of American filmgoers confirmed the newspapers' claims and reported that 35 per cent of people who had seen the film had said that the movie 'made them more fearful of swimming in the ocean' and that 47 per cent of women said it had 'increased their fear of venturing into the ocean' (*Lakeland Ledger*, 1 October 1975, p. 12). Within days of the film going into movie theatres, reports of shark sightings had increased, and the anxieties about going into the ocean that were reported by the later survey translated into a loss of trade for some coastal resorts which argued that a decline in hotel bookings during the summer of 1975 was directly due to the film.[26] The news media were keen to report shark attacks as well as sightings and 'near misses', and there were a number of articles which implied that town officials were attempting to cover up shark activity in their area for fear of losing tourist dollars.[27] In this way, news stories about sharks inevitably tried to find literal parallels with the narrative of *Jaws*.

The media attended to the public fascination and hostility towards sharks in equal measure. Articles on shark behaviour, advice on how to survive a shark attack and statistics on shark attacks, all focused attention towards the predatory nature of sharks as an undifferentiated group of killer fish. Shark-fishing suddenly grew in popularity and stories from 'real' shark hunters, now elevated to the status of experts, began to appear in papers which recounted the drama of the fight between human and shark in terms that reflected the general attitude of antipathy. For instance, one article on shark hunters described the death of a shark in the following way:

> The blue-gray beast wrenched across the deck, its jaws snapping together in a frenzied staccato. Its spine has been severed, but the blue shark was a long time dying. Once, it lunged forward and clamped its razor sharp teeth around a deckhand's boot. He leapt into the air to shake the jaws loose [...] The shark is gaffed when it is brought along side the boat. If small, it may be brought aboard and beaten to death with a hammer. If large, it is hung over the side by its tail and slit open to attract other sharks (Associated Press, *Nevada Daily Mail*, 20 August 1975, p. 6).

And another article described dead sharks as a public spectacle:

> On shore, everyone drives to the shark hanging post at the Bob Hall pier. Three sharks, including an 11-foot-long hammerhead, are already hanging and surrounded by onlookers. The sharks are photographed, then lowered to the ground for measuring their length and girth. Finally, surrounded by children, Tommy pulls out his knife and slices the jaws out of Jo Ann's bull shark. He throws them into his boat, as a trophy, then the group piles into his pick-up and drives home. Behind, the dead toothless bull shark lay in the sand. Later a tractor with a front-end loader will come along, scoop up the sharks and bury them somewhere down the beach (Sterba, 1975, p. 28).

The iconic image of open gaping jaws that appeared in the promotion for the film, as well as in the key scenes where the shark is first seen by the audience and later when it launches itself onto the deck of the sinking boat and consumes the shark-hunter, accompanied many of the newspaper articles, visually reinforcing the idea that sharks were nothing more than predatory killing machines. Any balance to the overwhelming demonization of sharks was limited to a few shark experts who critiqued the film's realism. The depth of public hostility towards sharks following the release of *Jaws* was profound and led in one instance to a group of 'weekend swimmers' pulling a baby whale from the water at Miami Beach, where the sick animal was attempting to beach itself. Although they were assured by lifeguards that the animal was not a shark, the group mauled and stabbed it in the belief that it was a '*Jaws*' (*Evening Independent*, 30 June 1975, p. 2).

## Monster panics

The case of *Jaws* suggests that media representations of monster animals can fuel a moral panic. Stanley Cohen originally asserted that the mass media were central to the creation of moral panics where news media, in particular, amplified the deviance of a particular group, establishing them as 'folk devils' (Cohen, [1972] 2002, p. 9). Although moral panics are thought of as typically affecting human social groups, the notion can be easily extended to animals. In this regard, animal deviance is closely allied with the idea of abjection and with 'matter out of place': each is subject to human processes of re-ordering, regulation and management to re-establish boundaries. In the case of deviant animals, all too often these processes result in the deaths of the demonized animals. There is a long list of animals that can be added to insects and sharks: dangerous dogs, mad cows and clones, for instance, have all been constructed as deviant and monstrous. Culture will always need fictional monsters on to which social anxieties can be projected, and these monsters are usually expendable. What the examples of *Jaws* and the bug movies of the 1950s suggest is that there is, all too often, a danger of slippage between the management of fictional monsters and real animals who are constructed as monstrous.

# 9
# Beginning at the End: Re-imagining Our Relations with Animals

Ridley Scott's *Blade Runner*, an adaptation of Philip K. Dick's *Do Androids Dream of Electric Sheep*, is set in a dystopian future where few animals remain. Rick Deckard, played by Harrison Ford, is assigned to hunt down and 'retire' escaped humanoids, known as 'replicants', who have made their way from an Off-World colony back to Earth. Suspected replicants are questioned using a 'Voigt-Kampf' test, which measures capillary dilation, blush reaction, pupil fluctuation and iris dilation, to assess the subjects' emotional response to a series of questions which are predominantly about animal products and practices. During one such test on Rachael, a highly advanced replicant created by the Tyrell Corporation, Deckard asks, 'One more question. You're watching a stage play, a banquet is in progress. The guests are enjoying an appetizer of raw oysters. The entrée consists of boiled dog'. Having responded quickly to the previous scenarios involving a butterfly-killing jar, a calfskin wallet and a wasp, on this occasion a close-up of Rachael suggests that she is unnerved and looks downwards without any comment. Deckard waits for a reply and watches as white noise appears on the screen that has been monitoring her iris and pupil response before shutting down. Deckard leans back in his seat, the test now complete, and Rachael leaves the room. Deckard declares to Tyrell that although she is unaware of the fact, Rachael is indeed a replicant. Rachael's inability to respond appropriately to the 'boiled dog' scenario has determined her ontology. As a result, after the test Rachael is, according to Deckard, no longer 'she' but an 'it', and he asks Tyrell, 'How can it not know what it is?'.

As Deckard's question implies, *Blade Runner* is concerned with what it is to be human, but in grappling with the topic the film relies on the spectre of 'the animal' for its social and moral logic. As a result, the narration reveals the fictional system of human–animal relations that is in operation in *Blade Runner* through Rachael's answers to Deckard's questions: A calfskin wallet given as a present should be returned and the giver reported to the police; a boy with a butterfly collection and a killing jar should be taken to a doctor; a wasp crawling on someone's arm can be killed, suggesting that only the threat of a sting renders the insect legitimately 'killable'. Set in a post-apocalyptic world, there are no 'real' animals in the narrative, and it is this absence that affords them status as fully moral patients. In other words, their scarcity has given animals a revised form of worth beyond that of being a commodity. Moreover, the presence of the animal, which is invoked during Deckard's questioning, is used to determine humanity. Vacillation between absence and presence in *Blade Runner* opens up a space where the spectre of the animal has effectivity within the social and ontological hierarchy portrayed, and that, in turn, gives meaning to the relationships between protagonist and antagonist. This notion of the animal as spectre is suggestive of what Derrida refers to as a *hauntology*, which overcomes the privilege afforded to being and presence, and leads him to ask instead, 'what is the *effectivity* or the *presence* of a specter'(Derrida, 1994, p. 10). Unlike Dick's original novel which explicitly centralizes the loss of animals, the film invokes the presence of the animal spectre as an effective force through oblique references. Deckard's final question about boiled dog is one such reference, and it draws the fictional film world and the audience's social reality together through a common understanding of the status of dogs as 'not-food'. As a result of these shared norms, the meaning of Rachel's hesitancy and Deckard's assessment are all the more understandable for the spectator.

In *Blade Runner,* there is an assumed universal response to animal questions that overrides any difference, cultural or otherwise, and implies that everyone, human and replicant alike, is subject to a common ideology of human–animal relations. The film's narration, following from Dick's novel, albeit less explicit in its articulation, takes the position that animals are morally significant, and each question in the Voigt-Kampf test locates the test subject within that dominant discourse. Moreover, the test measures empathy, and therefore to pass the test a subject must respond with not just the correct verbal answer but also the appropriate level of emotion. What is intriguing about Ridley Scott's post-apocalyptic dystopia is that the system of human–animal relations is unravelled to such an extent that empathy for animals is neatly polarized with lack of concern. The cultural ambivalence and cognitive dissonance that characterize contemporary human–animal practices and particularly those associated with eating animals are eradicated in favour of a narrative logic which is concerned instead with the complexities of human–technology relations. In *Blade Runner,* the emotional response to animals does not rely on resolving differences between humans and animals that have been typically invoked to justify their exploitation, for instance, on the grounds of species, lack of a soul, language or moral agency. Instead, animals automatically occupy a place of privilege and protection, a position which is taken further in *Do Androids Dream of Electric Sheep?* where animals are both sacred and fetishized commodities within a system of post-apocalyptic capitalism (Molloy, 2009, p. 113).[1] With the animal system disambiguated and animals effectively excluded from the narrative, the film is free to grapple with the thorny ontological questions raised by human–replicant difference. Indeed Stephen Mulhall argues that the film is not simply concerned with the question of what it is to be human but 'more precisely, it is obsessed with it' (Mulhall, 2008, p. 29).

Any text is polysemeous, however, and will always necessarily include what it seeks to exclude. In other words, eliminating something from a text will always reassert its presence, and in the case of *Blade Runner* the exclusion of animals from the narrative only serves to illuminate their presence in the socio-ethical logic of the Voigt-Kampf questions and also in the dynamics of interactions between replicants, who 'stand-in' for animals, and humans. In some cases, these moments of animal presence are more obviously foregrounded, such as towards the end of the film when Roy, the replicant leader, on finding one of his group dead, lifts his head, 'wolf-like', to emit a howl: a visceral expression of grief which launches the aural motif of animalistic sounds that accompany the rest of the scene. In other places the presence is more oblique, but even when dealing with the relationship between humans and technology, the film calls into question human–animal relations. Mulhall's analysis, which examines how *Blade Runner* deals with definitions of humanness, offers a useful route into considering how the film might simultaneously raise questions about animals. Mulhall maintains that violence against the replicants confronts 'the authorities' doctrine that such embodied beings are incapable of suffering' (Mulhall, 2008, p. 29). He goes on to explain that the audience's empathic response to the replicants is elicited by pain behaviour, which brings viewers to apply 'the full range of psychological concepts which constitute the logical space of the mental, and thereby demonstrates that our attribution of a mind to a given creature is a response to the behavioural repertoire with which their particular embodiment endows them' (Mulhall, 2008,

p. 30). Questions about whether moral consideration should be extended to beings whose behaviour is regarded as expressing pain and suffering have, of course, been at the crux of debates about animals. Thus, whilst the text excludes animals and simplifies human–animal relationships to such an extent that animals are unproblematically regarded as morally worthy, the questions that govern the reality of animal lives are raised in the spaces from which representations of animals are absent.

Deckard's questions are designed to measure emotional reactions in the test subjects, and the viewer is similarly asked by the film to reflect on the system of relations presented. Although the notion of a calf-skin wallet and dead butterflies may not trouble an audience's moral limits, the same cannot be said for the boiled dog scenario. Deckard does propose that the entrée is being eaten as part of a stage play, and this implies that it might be some sort of simulation. Yet, because eating dogs is considered taboo in Western culture, even the replication of such practices can elicit unease. In *Dog*, Susan McHugh maintains that eating dog is 'perhaps the most controversial animal practice today, because of the tremendous range of feelings stirred even by representations of dogs in Western industrialized cultures' (McHugh, 2004, p. 31). Certainly there is ample evidence to suggest that eating dog continues to be a practice that is used to define the bounds of humanity and which simultaneously asserts the norms of human–canine relations. For instance, in 2009, in New Zealand, SPCA officers were called to a house where a man had killed, skinned and gutted a dog and was in the process of cooking the carcase in a traditional umu pit. The man, of Tongan origin, had used a hammer to render his pitbull-terrier-cross unconscious before slitting the dog's throat. When interviewed, the man's wife explained, 'Dog, horse, we eat it in Tonga. It's good food for us' (ITN, 2009). The case was reported by the New Zealand media and subsequently picked up and later reported across Europe, Australia and North America when it transpired that the man could not be prosecuted. Under New Zealand's Animal Welfare Act, a dog could be slaughtered for food as long as the killing was humane, and authorities agreed that the pitbull-terrier-cross, named Ripper, had not suffered. The case made the tensions between legal prohibition and various cultural norms highly visible, and media discourses focused on four key issues: the gap between normalized animal practices and legislation, the handling of cultural difference by the authorities, the ethics of animal slaughter in general and the legitimacy of pitbull terriers as 'pets'.[2]

Glen Elder, Jennifer Wolch and Jody Emel argue that 'norms of legitimate animal practice are neither consistent nor universal. Instead, codes for harmful animal practices are heavily dependent on the immediate context of an event' (Elder et al., 1998, p. 73). Elder, Wolch and Emel make the case that the suffering of animals is interpreted in culturally specific and place-specific ways and that animal practices are legitimized over time within historically situated discourses that, in turn, are deployed in the construction of difference and the dehumanization of particular groups. In the New Zealand case, the question of differing cultural norms was complicated by statements from SPCA officers who claimed that their investigations revealed that eating dog was not typically part of Tongan cultural practices. Instead it was stated by the National Chief Executive of the Royal New Zealand SPCA that, 'Tongans say that this is actually quite rare. It's only poor people who eat their dogs and in fact they say, they don't eat their pet dogs, they'll eat a dog if it happens to be roaming around. So it isn't really a cultural issue at all. What we've found out is that most Tongans would not eat a dog and certainly the Korean community in New Zealand has come forward and said that they certainly don't eat dogs that are pets' (BBC, 2009).[3] Invoking distinctions between poor and wealthy Tongan practices bound social class into the issue, and a discourse emerged in the domestic media that legitimized eating of dogs in Korea and China on cultural grounds but maintained that such practices, despite the inability of legislation to prevent them, were socially taboo in New Zealand. Such fine-grained distinctions reflected sensitivity to the cultural make-up of New Zealand's population, and the public responses to the issue, posted on New Zealand media web sites, revealed a range of positions on the subject of eating dogs, from outrage at the killing of a pet dog for food to highlighting the hypocrisy of eating meat in Western culture. What emerged from these discussions was that the classification of animals was central to each set of debates where distinctions were made between 'pets' and 'animals for eating', differences which were then mapped onto other sets of animal practices, thereby exposing the ambivalence of such relations.

Within a couple of weeks, the incident had been appropriated as part of a marketing campaign for a New Zealand pizza company, Hell, which ran a billboard advertisement for gluten-free brownie bars that used the slogan 'At least our brownie won't eat your pet dog' (Hell billboard advertisement, August 2009). The advert received 62 complaints, the highest number that year, which the New Zealand Advertising Standards Authority (ASA) upheld on the grounds that the slogan was in breach of the advertising code by not adhering to the requirement for social responsibility and for its use of stereotypes in ways that would cause widespread offence. Central to the ASA's decision was the concern that the actions of one person had been used to generalize the behaviour of a wider group of individuals and that the term, 'brownie', used by the advertisement to describe that group, was clearly derogatory.[4] The concerns expressed by the ASA over the deployment of racial stereotypes in this way brings to mind what Elder, Wolch and Emel refer to as 'animal-linked racialization', a process by which animal practices are used as the basis for creating difference which then sustains power relations between dominant and subordinate groups (Elder et al., 1998, p. 72). As a result, the practice of eating dogs is used to articulate cultural boundaries and the borders of civilized behaviour, and the news media continues to play a central role in sustaining the discourse of difference.

In January 2010, a proposal was put forward to ban the sale and consumption of dog and cat meat in China. Developed through a process that included consultation with the Royal Society for the Prevention of Cruelty to Animals in the UK and the US-based International Fund for Animal Welfare, the proposal was intended for inclusion in a draft bill on animal welfare. It included penalties which would result in 15 days in prison for an individual or a 500,000 yuan fine for businesses. The details of the proposal were covered by the UK and US media where press reports suggested that the ban responded to the tastes of a burgeoning Chinese middle class, many of whom now kept dogs as pets and were critical of the traditional practices of eating dogs.[5] Reports marginalized the economic impact of a ban which, it was suggested by one newspaper, 'would be small because an increasingly affluent population was less dependent on dog and cat meat' (Watts, 2010, p. 1). In the UK, the *Guardian* newspaper maintained that the proposed ban had polarized the opinions of 'defenders of traditional values' and animal welfare groups (Watts, 2010, p. 2). The report did not include any quotes from 'defenders' of tradition but chose instead to cite public opposition to the ban, posted online, which claimed that the Chinese government was putting the welfare of animals before the welfare of people. The animal welfare discourse was presented by the newspaper through quotes from a law professor from the Chinese Academy of Social Sciences, and the founder of the Lucky Cats shelter in Beijing who warned that 'Beijing's dog restaurants get their meat mainly from vagrant and stolen dogs. In the suburbs, dogs are hung and slaughtered in front of buyers' (Watts, 2010, p. 2). The article thus linked the dog meat trade to social problems such as murder and theft and in doing so shifted the emphasis from cultural tradition to issues of social control.

Legal sources of dog and cat meat were presented by a CNN television news report on the issue, which used images of cats in wire cages and dogs in concrete and wire-fenced enclosures at a meat market and also images of a dog farm. Dog meat vendors and restaurant owners defended the practice of eating dogs on health grounds, citing the traditional view that dog meat acted as a tonic for the metabolism.[6] In the CNN report, the animal welfare position was located within a discourse which suggested that the ban on eating dogs and cats reflected the development of civilized behaviour and thereby positioned traditional practices as brutal and outdated. Despite the proposed ban including cat meat, the news discourse paid only scant attention to the practices involved in producing or consuming cat meat. Instead, media reports privileged the dog as a pet and used mainly images of dogs and dog meat.[7] At the core of this discourse was the classification of the dog as a pet, which functioned to align middle-class Chinese opinions with the Western construction of taboo animals. Moreover, within both the *Guardian* and CNN reports, the practices associated with eating dogs were used to distinguish between civilized and deviant behaviours.

Deploying the eating of dogs as a way to articulate difference and legitimize social power relations calls attention to the symbolic functions that are assigned to social traditions. As Klaus Eder argues, 'Because of the pastoral tradition in Europe, which did not exist in the Asian-Pacific countries, the dog became man's "friend", an attitude which is foreign in non-pastoral countries' (Eder, 1996, p. 82). Cultural traditions thus attribute social significance to animals, which is then bound to normative forms of symbolic logic that incorporate gastronomic practices. As a result, food taboos are functionally employed in the maintenance of difference and in cohering national identities. For example, a 1975 newspaper article which detailed the experiences of a group of American reporters in China stated, 'They presented with pride their accomplishments, many unimpressive by US standards', and later explained that Chinese people eat dogs and monkey brains and that their guide had proceeded to describe 'to the startled reporters how the brains were scooped out of the head with a spoon at the table' (Shirley, 1975, p. 20).[8] Reports about the cultural habits of China, as well as those of the Philippines, Korea and Nigeria where dog meat is also consumed as part of cultural tradition,[9] have continued to be deployed within a discourse that Stuart Hall has identified as 'The West and the rest', where 'the West' is a construction that is used to classify societies utilizing a system of representation that, in turn, provides a way of explaining difference and provides evaluative criteria against which otherness can be judged (Hall, 1992). Within this discourse, animal-linked racialization is one aspect of the system of representation which informs dominant modes of knowledge that, in turn, structures global power relations. Yet, inasmuch as these discursive processes are employed to dehumanize and construct subordinate human groups, they also function to obscure the suffering of animals in Western food production by normalizing Western practices and, through the binary of the West and the rest, legitimize Western modes of animal production and consumption.

The black comedy *Delicatessen* (1991) reflects on human practices of meat-eating. Set in a post-apocalyptic society where food has become scarce and humans have consumed almost every remaining animal, residents of an apartment building have, in their desperate need for meat, moved on to eating humans. The film is an ironic reflection on the relentless consumption of meat, and animals are largely present as iconic signifiers – sounds, photographs, video, poster art, fabric prints and so forth – within the film world. The only animals that appear in the film are spiders and, in the basement, frogs and snails which are raised by a man who lives partly submerged in water. Two apartment residents run a small business from a single room, making cow-in-a-can toys: cylindrical cans with holes drilled at one end which emit a 'moo' sound when they are turned upside down. The sound of the 'moo' is a reminder of the animal body that the residents crave in the form of meat. As the two men construct the toys, one comments, 'I like the smell of glue. It smells like fish. It brings back memories'. Sensory reminders of absent animals populate the residents' world as sounds, images and smells, and with most animals having already been consumed, only these iconic signifiers remain. A former clown arrives at the apartment building in answer to an advert placed by the butcher who owns the shop below the living accommodation. The clown, Louison, has no idea that he is about to become the residents' next meal. He explains to the butcher's daughter that his ex-partner in the circus, Dr Livingstone, had been killed and eaten. It transpires that Dr Livingstone was a chimpanzee, and Louison keeps mementos of Livingstone around his apartment, which include his band leader outfit, a poster for the circus act, and numerous photographs. The horror of Dr Livingstone's death is amplified by Louison's humanization of his chimpanzee companion. Indeed, Livingstone's death and consumption is presented by the film as more terrible than the slaughter of the apartment residents by the butcher. Livingstone is regarded as innocent whilst the residents are monstrous beings. In much the same way that *Blade Runner* mobilizes existing Western attitudes about eating dogs, *Delicatessen* draws on similar feelings about chimpanzees. The cultural traditions of eating non-human primates are thus naturalized and reinscribed by the narrative as inhumane and alien. Humans are divided into meat-eaters – who live above ground – and members of an underground vegan movement, Troglydism, who are socially marginalized and treated as terrorists. In this way, the eating practices which divide the below-ground Trogs from the above-ground 'meat-suckers' structure the binary between good and evil characters.

The classification of dogs as not-edible is so robust that it underlies the narrative trajectory of the film *Babe*, in which a pig learns to be a sheepdog and, in doing so, saves himself from being slaughtered and eaten by the farmer and his wife. By becoming a dog, Babe crosses over the boundary from farmed to non-killable and occupies a different order of being which is less concerned with species and more interested in utility. During the film it is explained to Babe that killable animals are those who do not provide any service to humans whilst non-killable animals such as cats, dogs, horses and cows provide some form of useful labour. Human–animal relations in the film are simply referred to as 'the way things are', yet the narration speaks from the position of the animals and in this way challenges the moral orthodoxy by assigning 'killable' animals with personhood. The narrative logic of the film does dictate that Babe must become something other than a pig to survive, and this is combined with the more traditional deployment of anthropomorphic conventions so that the animals in *Babe* appear to fulfil the requirements for what Tom Regan has termed subjects-of-a-life:

> Individuals are subjects-of-a-life if they have beliefs and desires; perception, memory, and a sense of the future, including their own future; an emotional life together with feelings of pleasure and pain; preference – and welfare – interests; the ability to initiate action in pursuit of their desires and goals; a psychophysical identity over time; and an individual welfare in the sense that their experiential life fares well or ill for them, logically independently of their utility for others and logically independently of their being the object of anyone else's interests (Regan, 2004, p. 243).

The anthropomorphic framing of the film was, to some extent, effective in calling on adult audiences to transfer the moral agency attributed to the character Babe into consideration for pigs as moral patients, and newspapers reported that sales of pork had decreased by 10 per cent and 20 per cent in the UK and US, respectively, in the months following the film's release.[10] Public reception of the film gave the press a number of interesting stories, amongst which were reports that in Thailand, Bangkok restaurant owners claimed that sales of roasted piglets had halved after the film's release.[11] People for the Ethical Treatment of Animals (PETA) capitalized on the public response to the film by using the slogan 'Please don't eat Babe for breakfast', and James Cromwell, the actor who played Farmer Hoggett, appeared in various advertisements for the organization. Critical reception of the film was overwhelmingly positive and praised the film's handling of the animals' viewpoint which avoided being overly sentimental or morally heavy-handed. A *Los Angeles Times* review stated that the film put 'prejudice in our laps with immediacy; for we are at the top of the chain. "Babe" doesn't let us feel sympathy for the animals' mortal condition without also feeling the tug of our own eating habits, of our attachment to "the way things are"' (Colburn, 1996, p. 3). Elsewhere the effects of the film were couched in even more direct terms, with reviewers stating that the animals 'display such character and emotion [...] that it's enough to turn you vegetarian', and also stating that 'this reviewer for one, hasn't been able to face a pork chop in the months since'(Film4, 1995; *Empire*, 1995).[12] Although rare, the same message was offered as a caution to parents by one reviewer who wrote, 'Be warned, seriously, that many kids may leave this movie wanting to become vegetarians' (Rhodes, 1995).[13] In economic terms, the film was a success and grossed over $66 million at the US box office and over $254 million worldwide, with the highest recorded non-US box office returns from Germany ($34 million), UK, Ireland and Malta ($30.6 million) and Australia ($27 million). *Babe* ended 1995 as the eleventh highest grossing film worldwide.[14]

*Babe* was an intervention in the normalized practices of eating pigs, although the film's effectiveness in raising public awareness about intensive farming practices was less apparent. Far from dealing with the realities of contemporary intensive techniques, *Babe* idealized farming practices. The setting for the film is an idyllic small-scale country sheep farm run by a farmer and his wife, and even though the film begins with images of large-scale pig farming, each sow and suckling piglet is depicted as living in a low-lit enclosure with clean straw on the floor and where each pig can stand up and move around. Death for the adult pigs, who are in robust health as they leave quietly and happily for the slaughterhouse, is renamed as the journey to 'pig paradise', and even when Babe discovers that there is no 'paradise', the film does not revise its representations of intensive farming. Like *Chicken Run*, *Babe* prompts questions about the ethics of killing and eating animals, most notably reconnecting the dead cooked body of a duck on the table with the real animal by asking '*who*' they had been. But again, the opportunities for a mainstream popular film to reflect the suffering of farmed animals in any way that approaches the reality of their experiences is always going to be limited. Consequently, boundaries are imposed on the extent to which popular film can engage with questions about the ethics of contemporary farming practices, and the film does not go beyond exploring the issue of whether pigs should be killable for human consumption.

*Babe* demonstrates nostalgia for an idealized pre-intensive vision of farming, and it is notable that the film was on general release in the UK during the BSE crisis of the mid-1990s when public anxiety about eating meat was particularly high. Fredric Jameson (1993) has argued that our fascination with nostalgia finds cultural form in films which appropriate a stylized version of the past to capture a desired aspect of history. Through pastiche, the 'nostalgia mode' recreates a sense of stability which is imagined to have existed but is deemed to have been lost in contemporary social reality. *Babe* was repeatedly regarded in both public and critical reviews as a film that 'worked' on two levels, that is, as a narrative for adults and also for children; one aspect of its pleasure for adult audiences was the representation of rural farming as an imagined lost relationship between humans and animals. The pastiche farm setting, described by one film-goer as an 'amalgam of all the rural cultures of the English-speaking world – Sometimes it seems like England, other times Kansas, Australia, New Zealand, it's really never anywhere particular,[15] – eschewed historical accuracy in favour of an 'approach to the present by way of the art language of the simulacrum, or of the pastiche of the stereotypical past' (Jameson, 1993, p. 76). The intrusion of the present into the sense of pastness created in *Babe* is most acutely felt when a bewildered Farmer and Mrs Hoggett receive a fax machine for Christmas, a piece of technology that is so clearly out of place and quite unnecessary within the world created by the film's idealization of rural farming of the 1940s and an imagined version of early twentieth-century livestock husbandry. The irony of the resistance to technology in the narrative is that the film itself relied on complex animatronics to convey the seamless drama of the animals' lives.

There is a decisive moment in Stanley Kubrick's *2001: A Space Odyssey* (1968) when the interspecies ape-like beings use tools for the first time. The 'Dawn of Man' segment of the film describes how, in the hands of apes, a rib-bone from an animal skeleton is transformed into technology. The first use this new technology is put to is to kill another animal, one of the tapirs that the apes have been depicted living along-side in previous scenes. This moment in the film signals a transition from animal to human, from nature to culture, from peace to violence, and from herbivore to carnivore.[16] Kubrick imagines the beginnings of humanness in terms of a technological evolution away from animal-ity, although the transition remains ambiguous in that it is neither venerated nor derided. Kubrick does not celebrate the casting aside of our animal being as a moment of transcendence, instead *2001: A Space Odyssey* asks the audience to contemplate what we have become. Has technology civilized us? Kubrick would seem to suggest not. In gaining technologies, *2001: A Space Odyssey* proposes that humans also acquire other characteristics: aggression, blood lust and a newfound predatory and dominant nature. In this way, *2001: A Space Odyssey* gives us pause to reflect on the beginnings of humanity and the development of a technological culture that has signalled our separation from animals and our own animal being. Like *Blade Runner, 2001: A Space Odyssey* suggests that the sense of our own humanity is perpetually structured through our relations with other animals.

# Notes

## 1 'Animals Sell Papers': The Value of Animal Stories

1. *Jurassic Park III* (2001) $181 million; *Planet of the Apes* (2001) $180 million; *Ice Age* (2002) $176 million; *Finding Nemo* (2003) $340 million; *A Shark Tale* (2004) $161 million; *King Kong* (2005) $218 million; *Madagascar* (2005) $193 million; *Happy Feet* (2006) $198 million; *Ice Age Two: The Meltdown* (2006) $195 million; *Ratatouille* (2007) $206 million; *Alvin and the Chipmunks* (2007) $217 million; *Kung Fu Panda* (2008) $215 million; *Madagascar 2* (2008) $180 million; *Horton Hears a Who!* (2008) $155 million; *Alvin and the Chipmunks: The Squekquel* (2009) $220 million.
2. I have elected here to use the terms 'tabloid' and 'broadsheet' to distinguish between types of journalism. However, as McNair notes, such distinctions have been redefined in relation to the UK market and there has been a shift in the way in which newspapers are classified, with new categories of 'heavy weight', 'mid-market' and 'red-top' (McNair, 2009, p. 5). For the purposes of this book I have elected to use the older terms.
3. For instance, the image of Phoenix played a key role in mobilizing public feeling against the contiguous culling policy in the UK.
4. See BBC (2001) 'Calf's Plight 'did not change policy'. BBC 26 April 2001, online at http://news.bbc.co.uk/1/hi/uk/1298362.stm.
5. Source: Dangerfield & Howell, 1975, p. 204.
6. See *The Alcade*, 'Valuable Reagan posters in HRC collection'. *The Alcade*, March/April 1981, p. 23.

## 2 Media and Animal Debates: Welfare, Rights, 'Animal Lovers' and Terrorists

1. Beers, 2006, p. 62.
2. Beers, 2006, p. 132.
3. Dr Frederick Banting won a Nobel Prize for the discovery of insulin as a treatment for diabetes. According to the Nobel Prize web site, Banting experimented on dogs using both canine and, later, bovine pancreases (http://nobelprize.org/educational/medicine/insulin/discovery-insulin. html). However, newspaper articles in 1922 variously mentioned the use of dogs, cows and pigs in the development of diabetes treatment. See, for example, *New York Times*, 6 December 1922.
4. In 1886 the ASPCA attempted to bring a case against chicken-butchers who plucked chickens whilst they were still alive. The case was dismissed by the judge. The *New York Times* covered the hearing and printed a follow-up editorial that urged the Society to continue in its work and then stated that the Society should go to the wharves to find the evidence that it needed to support its case (*New York Times*, 9 June 1866, p. 4).

5. Anticruelty laws in most of the other states were not enforced by any particular group or individual, and humane officers took it upon themselves to bring the prosecutions. Given the judicial resistance to anticruelty cases the results of these prosecutions were impressive with, for instance, the PSPCA securing 17,826 prosecutions between 1867 and 1921 and the MSPCA achieving 4,716 convictions by 1896 (Beers, 2006, p. 61). As the number of successful prosecutions grew states revised the laws to give particular humane groups the powers to investigate and prosecute and thereby established the welfare organizations as official agents within the regulation of human–animal relations in the US. Repeated calls from US advocates to extend anticruelty statutes to include the regulation of vivisection practices were not accommodated though, and opposition to such legislative change remained strong.

6. In 1824 the founding statement of the SPCA (Society for the Prevention of Cruelty to Animals) opposed vivisection in response to Magendie's work, stating "Providence cannot intend that the secrets of Nature should be discovered by means of cruelty" (SPCA, 1824 cited in Desmond, 1989, p. 189).

7. Published under the title, *The Shambles of Science*; the authors of the first-hand account, Lind-af-Hageby and Katherina Schartau, had attended the experimental procedures and then written about them in their own words.

8. For a full account of The Brown Dog Affair, see *The Old Brown Dog* (Lansbury, 1985).

9. Beers, 2006, p. 145.

10. Curnutt, 2001, p. 449.

11. Full details of the Draize testing procedure are included in Vogel et al., 2006, pp. 794–796.

12. Gull (1882).

13. It is also worth noting that the newspaper openly opposed stag hunting in the 1957. See *Daily Mirror*, 7 February 1957, p. 11 and 8 March 1957, p. 2 on the government's refusal to ban stag hunting.

14. *Daily Mirror*, 16 August 1958, p. 7.

15. Pet theft was a lucrative trade by the late 1950s, and prosecutions reported in the *Daily Mirror* revealed that the crime was well organized with thieves supplying dealers with stolen cats, which were purchased by universities and research laboratories. A single cat would command a price of 25 shillings in 1957. See *Daily Mirror*, 31 August 1957 p. 3.

16. *Daily Mirror*, 6 December 1958, p. 11.

17. *Daily Mirror*, 22 August 1962, p. 4.

18. A further shift in the discourse on animal lovers was evident by the late 1990s. The term 'animal lover' was seldom used to describe animal advocates but instead employed in articles about animal abuse to ask what had happened to a nation that professed to be animal lovers.

# 3   Stars: Animal Performers

1. *The Evening Independent*, 18 December 1980, p. 19.

2. The 'producer-unit' system was dominant from the early 1930s until the early 1940s when the 'package-unit' system began and which became

dominant by the mid-1950s. For a full account of the different systems and the corresponding division of labour, see Bordwell, Staiger and Thompson, 2005.

3. Source: Abbott, 1951.
4. A further clause was added to the MPPC, which banned the use of the 'Running-W', a wire device used to trip horses intentionally.
5. Until 1980, there was however no compulsory regulation, and with the Production Code abandoned in the late 1960s directors were entitled to have closed sets without any AHA presence. Incidents that occurred during 1979 and 1980 changed this when a water buffalo was hacked to death during the filming of *Apocalypse Now* and the same year a pig was shot in the head and its throat cut during the production of *Heartland*. In 1980 five horses died during the filming of *Heaven's Gate*, one of which had been blown up with explosives, and it was once again, the public outcry that prompted the industry into action which resulted in the tightening of regulation and a clause, negotiated between the AHA and the Screen Actors Guild, that called for directors to notify the association in advance of filming using animals (Wolfson, 1987, p. 51).
6. See *Life*, 15 June 1953, p. 103.
7. Although *Francis* (1950) was an adaptation of a novel by David Stern, the film is regarded here as a 'gimmick' film rather than a literary adaptation.
8. *Reading Eagle*, 8 July 1952, p. 14.
9. *Life*, 12 February 1951, pp. 30–31.
10. *Sarasota Herald-Tribune*, 30 March 1951, p. 2; *Sarasota Herald-Tribune*, 2 April 1951, p. 1; *Ottawa Citizen*, 29 March 1951, p. 56.
11. *Eugene Register-Guard*, 17 May 1951, p. 1; *Miami Sunday News*, 2 April 1951, p. 6.
12. *Eugene Register-Guard*, 17 May 1951, p. 1.
13. For instance, the *Reading Eagle* report of the press preview for *Fearless Fagan* stated 'The army had drafted Humeston and he insisted upon carting Fagan off to Ford Ord with him in direct violation of army regulations" (*Reading Eagle*, 8 July 1952, p. 14).
14. *Spokane Daily Chronicle*, 19 June 1953, p. 40.
15. Source: *Toledo Blade*, 21 April 1981, p. 13.
16. Source: *The Bulletin*, 10 July 1940, p. 2; *Sarasota Herald-Tribune*, 9 July 1940, p. 13.
17. *Sarasota Herald-Tribune*, 9 July 1940, p. 13.
18. The World Jungle Compound was renamed Jungleland in 1956. The farm changed hands a number of times but was repurchased by Goebels in 1961 and owned by him until 1969 when bankruptcy forced closure of the farm and all the remaining animals were auctioned (*Milwaukee Sentinel*, 8 October 1969, p. 1).
19. Source: *Toledo Blade*, 25 June 1950, p. 74.
20. Source: *Sarasota Herald-Tribune*, 14 March 1951, p. 11.
21. See Peninsula Telephone Company advertisements 1948 and 1949 in *St Petersburg Times*, 13 October 1948, p. 3 and 27 April 1949, p. 21. The subject of party lines continued to be a key pubic issue and formed the basis of the plot for the film *Pillow Talk* in 1959 starring Doris Day and Rock Hudson.

22. World Jungle Compound advertisement in *Billboard*, 22 July 1950, p. 61.
23. *Reading Eagle*, 1 February 1951, p. 12.
24. The pleasures for audiences and corresponding box office returns that are derived from onscreen animal performances continue to sustain the use of lions and chimps, as well as many other wild animals, in film production. In the case of chimpanzees destined for the entertainment business, baby chimps are still forcibly removed from their mothers and their 'careers' are usually over by nine years of age when they become too difficult to manage. Unable to be re-socialized with other chimpanzees many ex-entertainment chimps live out their remaining fifty or so year lifespan in solitary conditions. See Goodall & Peterson, 2000; *Oakland Tribune*, 24 August 2010, online at http://www.insidebayarea.com/news/ci_15892551

## 4  Wild: Authenticity and Getting Closer to Nature

1. Benjamin examines different technologies including lithography, the illustrated newspaper, photography and film.
2. *Evening Times*, 2007.
3. Online travel reviews and blogs bear out this point in visitor accounts to the Masai Mara, where *Big Cat Diary* was filmed, and describe their encounters with animal stars from the programme: 'Kike', 'Bella', Shadow' and 'the Ridge Pride'.
4. For instance, the weight of the lion cub varied from 110 lbs up to 400 lbs in different accounts of the incident. The higher weight was attributed in the tabloid coverage. See FoxNews, 2008; Drew, 2010; Moult, 2008; Borland, 2008; Troup, 2008; McGurran, 2008.
5. Comment posted 5 March 2007 at TripAdvisor online at http://www.tripadvisor.co.uk/ShowUserReviews-g294209-d563539-r6746206-Governor_s_Camp-Masai_Mara_National_Reserve.html#REVIEWS [accessed 18 March 2010].
6. To give some context to the audit of children's responses, news, current affairs and reality television shows were also rated and all were considered by some respondents, albeit a minority, to be 'never true'. Only nature and wildlife programmes were regarded as true at the very least 'sometimes' (Ofcom, 2006b, p. 23).
7. Seventeen per cent adults regarded current affairs as always accurate, 15 per cent documentaries, 14 per cent dramatized reconstructions and 19 per cent consumer advice programmes.
8. The term 'blue chip' refers to large-budget wildlife films with high production values which tend to depict mega-fauna, visual splendour, have dramatic story lines, an absence of science, politics, historical references and people (Bousé, 2000, pp. 14–15).
9. The 'diary' features were clearly not part of the main programme, which, when first broadcast on the BBC, concluded each episode with a final sweeping statement about 'nature' and a fade to black to signal the end of the programme to the audience. The 10-minute features were then easily excised so that a 48-minute-long episode could still occupy a one-hour time slot and allow for advertising when transmitted on commercial channels and were then resold as 'special features' on the DVD collection.

10. *Big Cat Live* (2008), episode one.
11. Comments posted 6 April 2009 and 16 November 2008 online at http://www.facebook.com/note.php?note_id=36452831237&comments [accessed 10 March 2010].
12. BBC One, *Big Cat Live* (2008) online at http://www.bbc.co.uk/bigcat/fieldreports/?category=&page=1 [accessed 18 March 2010].
13. Comment posted 6 October 2008 online at http://www.facebook.com/BBCBigCat [accessed 18 March 2010]. The 'kill' was also featured heavily on the web site and in the programme.
14. Comments posted to sites revealed that the perceived authenticity of the programme was part of its appeal. For instance, in response to the live web-cam lion kill footage, one viewer wrote 'excellent ... superb!!! a great natural video!!' Comment posted 9 October 2008 online at http://www.facebook.com/BBCBigCat [accessed March 2010].
15. For an account of *Simba*, see Mitman, 1999, pp. 31–35.
16. For instance, typical costs for True-Life Adventure film would be around $350,000 and films such as *The Living Desert* and *The Vanishing Prairie* took around $4 million at the box office. Compared to the production costs of the animated features, at around $2 to $6 million, the profit margins achieved by the Disney nature films were in excess of what was being realized by the animated features during the 1950s (See Mitman, 1999, p.114).
17. See Bousé, 2000, pp. 66–68; Barnouw, 1983, p. 210.

# 5   Experimental: The Visibility of Experimental Animals

1. For discussion of the influence of popular representations of scientists on public stereotypes, see Losh, 2010; Weingart, Muhl & Pansegrau, 2003; Haynes, 2003; Steinke, 2005.
2. Notably, films such as *The Island of Doctor Moreau*, released in 1933 and remade in 1977 and 1996 and based on the 1896 book by H.G. Wells, speculated on the dangers of allowing scientists and vivisectionists to manipulate nature.
3. *Project X* (1986) is notable, however, as an example that does not fit into the comedy or horror genres.
4. Some of Kellogg's conclusions were drawn from the unexpected influence of Gua on Donald. In particular, Kellogg notes Donald's development of 'climbing behaviour unusual for a child of his age' (p. 86); his 'attempting to bite or scrape the wall with his teeth' and 'picking up of a stick and transporting it to his mouth, just after Gua had done the same thing' (p. 145). Kellogg also concluded that 'neither subject really learned to talk during the interval of research', and although Donald reproduced the vocalizations made by Gua during the experiment, it was not until the end of the nine-month period that he made any advances in human language acquisition (pp. 280–282).
5. Kellogg did remark that Gua's psychological dependence and associated social behaviour meant that 'To shut her up in a room by herself, or to walk away faster than she could run, and so leave her behind, proved, as well as we could judge, to be the most awful punishment that could possibly be

inflicted. She could not be alone apparently without suffering [...]' (Kellogg, 1933, p. 157).

6. Referring to Witmer's and Kellogg's experiments, Hayes and Hayes wrote, 'We hope, in the present study, to avoid various shortcomings such as brief duration, unsystematic observation, insufficient reporting, and inadequate objective records, which have detracted from the value of earlier efforts' (Hayes & Hayes, 1951, p. 105).

7. In Kellogg's study he refers to Gua's vocalizations – *The Bark; The Food-Bark; The Screech or Scream; and The "Oo-oo" Cry* – as 'language responses' and claimed that although Gua did not 'talk' she was able to communicate with the experimenters (Kellogg, 1933, pp. 282–287). Kellogg's assertions that the mental performance of an infant chimpanzee was superior to that of an infant child in 1932 were countered by the findings of Louis W. Gellermann of Yale University who argued that it was the 'superior ability to "verbalize" [which] distinguishes the mentality of humans from that of apes' (*Science News Letter*, 17 September 1932, p. 175).

8. A number of other similar early psychological studies of chimpanzees indicated that their subjects displayed intelligence equal to that of humans. For instance, one such study carried out by Dr William T. Hornaday, a supporter of Witmer and Director of the Bronx Zoological Gardens, on a chimpanzee performer called Consul reported that 'Both Peter and Consul show evidence of minds highly developed for lower animals [...] There is the evidence of the existence of mind and intelligence there' (Hornaday, quoted in *The New York Times*, 18 December 1909, p. 7). Hornaday was responsible for helping Robert Yerkes acquire his first two non-human primates, Chim and Panzee, in 1923 (Yerkes, 1963, p. 207). For accounts of Robert Yerkes's establishment of the captive chimpanzee colony at Yale, see Yerkes, 1963; Haraway, 1989, pp. 59–83.

9. Reference to the acquisition of a human moral framework by chimpanzees was mentioned in Witmer (1910) where he stated that 'It would be hazardous to conclude from Peter's demonstration of affection of his general behaviour that he would be susceptible to moral training' (Witmer, 1910, p. SM7). Kellogg's study assumed that the ages of Donald and Gua would prevent both from having an understanding of right or wrong (Kellogg, 1933, p. 164). He wrote: 'Neither subject was ever observed, after commencing some form of forbidden activity, suddenly to inhibit the act "as if from memory" of previous directions, or from the ethical influence of a developing "conscience"' (Kellogg, 1933, p. 164).

10. In *Bedtime for Bonzo* a direct reference is made to *Harvey* when a policeman, convinced that Peter Boyd has been drinking, asks him if he has seen a six-foot rabbit.

11. Review available online at http://movies.nytimes.com/movie/review?res=95 03E2D71E3EEF3BBC4E53DFB266838A649EDE

12. Significantly, the realities of ape and monkey lives were thoroughly entangled with the ideology of family, a point illustrated by the infamous maternal deprivation experiments designed by Harry Harlow using rhesus monkeys to support the prevailing discourse about mothers. In Harlow's experiments rhesus monkeys were separated from their mothers and placed with a surrogate mother made of either wire or cloth. Harlow performed various tests on the baby monkeys to see which surrogate mother was preferred.

13. Until the CITES agreement in 1973 there was no legislation regulating the importation of chimpanzees to America. For a full account of the CITES agreement see Peterson and Goodall, 2000.
14. It is also the same route and method by which chimpanzees were acquired for use in the entertainment industries. See chapter 3.
15. Like many of the chimpanzees used in polio research, the fictional character Bonzo is, the narration states, between two and three years old and healthy. Being wild-caught, Bonzo would have, like many of the chimpanzees in Bodian and Howe's experiments, been sold to a research laboratory by an animal dealer.
16. I use the term 'absent referent' here to describe the separation of the culturally commodified animal from the real experimental animal in the sense that borrows from Carol J. Adams. Adams uses the term to describe the relation of humans to meat and states that the structure of the absent referent 'separates the meat eater from the other animal and that animal from the end product' (Adams, 2004, p. 23).

## 6   Farmed: Selling Animal Products

1. Source: Dewey, 1989, p. 81.
2. Source: Public Records Office MAF 54/98 and 54/99.
3. Sources: 'Tame rabbit keeping: meeting with the British Rabbit Council', Public Records Office document MAF 54/79; 'Agricultural Research Council: report of sub-committee appointed to review the position of rabbit breeding research in Great Britain', Public Records Office document MAF 54/80; and, 'Relaxing local authority rules on poultry and rabbit keeping', Public Records Office document MAF 54/90.
4. See *Rabbits: Policy and Prices 1939–1942*, MAF 54/76 and *Rabbits Policy and Prices 1942–1949*, MAF 54/77.
5. See *Picture Post*, 3 February 1940, p. 20
6. *Commons Hansard*, 3 March 1965, Vol. 707, cc 1482–92.
7. Source: *Ottawa Citizen*, 14 February 1968, p. 4.
8. Channel 4 web site (2008) 'Chickens, Hugh and Tesco Too' online at http://www.channel4.com/food/on-tv/river-cottage/chickens-hugh-and-tesco-too/chicken-hugh-and-tesco-too-08-12-15_p_1.html [accessed 3 January 2009].
9. Source: Defra (2008) *The Environmental Impact of Livestock Production*
10. Source: The National Trust (2001) *Farming Forward*
11. Source: Defra (2008) *The Environmental Impact of Livestock Production*.
12. Source: Miller and Robertson, 1959, p. 432.
13. Source: Defra (2008) *The Environmental Impact of Livestock Production*.
14. I use the term pastoral here to refer to the cultural idealization of cowherding as well as shepherding.
15. Source: NZ Government web site, 'Dairy cattle numbers 1895–2005' online at http://www.teara.govt.nz/en/dairying-and-dairy-products/10/1/1 [accessed 4 May 2010].
16. Source: *Marketing Week*, 26 February 2010 online at http://www.marketingweek.co.uk/news/anchor-launches-%C2%A310m-ad-push-to-support-brand-repositioning/3010501.article [accessed 3 March 2010].

17. Outlaw et al. (1996) *Structure of the U.S Dairy Farm Sector.*
18. Outlaw et al. (1996) *Structure of the U.S Dairy Farm Sector*
19. Source: Outlaw et al. (1996) *Structure of the U.S Dairy Farm Sector*
20. Source: United States Department of Agriculture (1996) *Changes in the US Dairy Industry: 1991–1996.*
21. Source: Cessna (2010) *Situation and Outlook for the US Dairy Industry.*
22. Source: USDA (2007) *2007 Census of Agriculture: Dairy Cattle and Milk Production.*
23. Source: USDA (2007) *2007 Census of Agriculture: Dairy Cattle and Milk Production.*
24. Source: Cessna (2010) *Situation and Outlook for the US Dairy Industry*
25. The Fluid Milk Board is authorized by the Fluid Milk Promotion Act of 1990 to develop advertising programmes aimed at market expansion.
26. The Dairy Board operates under the Dairy Production Stabilization Act of 1983 to promote milk consumption through research and nutrition education.
27. See Peta (2010) online at http://blog.peta.org/archives/2009/11/happy_cows.php
28. *Are California Dairy Cows Really Happy?* (CMAB, 2010).
29. See, for instance, Serpell, 1999; Serpell, 2002; Anderson & Henderson, 2005; Pallotta, 2008.

# 7   Hunted: Recreational Killing

1. Joel is sent to Cicely as a condition of the Alaskan State scholarship that has funded his Medical School education. Unfortunately, Joel has not read the conditions and so arrives in Cicely completely unaware of what awaits him.
2. See BC Wildlife Federation, 1993; Duda & Young, 1998; Duda & Jones, 2008; Georgia Department of Natural Resources and Responsive Management, 2008.
3. Duda & Young, 1998, p. 591.
4. It is useful to point out that the episode inverts the typical gendered responses to hunting, although it is also useful to note that, in this regard, a key feature of the programme was the quirky and eccentric characters. In this sense the programme often challenged gender stereotypes.
5. For the purposes of the survey, a non-meat-eater was a person who had not eaten meat for at least two years. Within the non-meat-eating population, 40 per cent stated that their choice was made on health grounds, 27 per cent because it was morally wrong to eat animals and 20 per cent because animals were treated inhumanely. According to these figures, only approximately 1.4 per cent of Americans objected to meat-eating primarily on ethical grounds (Duda & Young, 1998, p. 600).
6. Sources: USFWS/US Census 2007, Southwick Associates 2007 cited in Responsive Management/National Shooting Sports Foundation, 2008, p. 3.
7. Johnson, 2010.
8. Copping, 2007.

9. In a 1980 study, 10 per cent of people reported that they hunted to be close to nature, compared with 21 per cent in 2006 (Responsive Management/ National Shooting Sports Foundation, 2008, p. 48).
10. For example, Miniter, 2007, p18; BC Wildlife Federation, 1993.
11. Eighty-five per cent felt that it was appropriate to hunt for meat or to protect humans from harm (RM 2006 in Duda & Young, 1998).
12. *Northern Exposure,* Season One, 'A Kodiak Moment'.
13. Duda & Jones, 2008.
14. For an extensive discussion of eroticism in hunting, see Luke, 2007b.
15. James Cameron interview for *TribalLink* at the Ninth Session of the United Nations Permanent Forum on Indigenous Issues, April 2010, online at http://www.youtube.com/watch?v=1M1QoJCRtP0
16. It is described by one hunter in the following way: 'A quick, efficient death will produce better meat, period. This is where the thrilling marksmanship challenge must be taken to heart to become absolutely proficient with our chosen weapon. Hit em [*sic*] square behind the shoulder, forward into the heart and lungs of the inner chest, for an instant kill, whether with bow or firearm. Then track the animal and get to work' (Nugent & Nugent, 2002, p. 17)
17. Jake is the same distance from the 'camera' as the deer and his voice matches that proximity.
18. Lautenberg, 2004.
19. Figures refer to unit sales for *Deer Hunter 4*.
20. Quittner, 1998.
21. Source: Gordon, Jon (1999) 'Redneck Software?' feature on Minnesota Public Radio, 29 September 1999.
22. Source: 20 public reviews of *Cabela's Dangerous Hunts 2* posted at amazon.com between 2005 and 2010. Full reviews online at http://www.amazon.com/Cabelas-Dangerous-Hunts-2-playstation/product-reviews/B0008GJRRI/ref=cm_cr_pr_link_2?ie=UTF8&showViewpoints=0&pageNumber=2&sortBy=bySubmissionDateDescending [accessed 14 July 2010].
23. Source: Gordon, Jon (1999) 'Redneck Software?' feature on Minnesota Public Radio, 29 September 1999.
24. Review of *Cabela's North American Trophy Bucks* posted online 4 October 2007 at http://www.amazon.com/Cabelas-North-American-Trophy-Xbox-360/product-reviews/B000Q6ZLIY/ref=dp_top_cm_cr_acr_txt?ie=UTF8&showViewpoints=1 [accessed 14 July 2010].

# 8   Monsters: Horrors and Moral Panics

1. For example, *Rats, Alligator, The Birds, Them!* Also, for a discussion of open narrative structures in horror films, see Tudor, 1989, pp. 18–19.
2. Tudor expands on this point in relation to 'human monsters' who undergo a metamorphosis, wherein he argues, 'the conjunction of monstrous and human in one character can then become a central element in our already ambiguously motivated pleasure in the narrative collision between threat and normality' (Tudor, 1989, p. 116).
3. *Eugene Register-Guard,* 7 May 1947, p. 2; *Boyle,* 1947b.

4. Jon Turney (1998) gives a very good account of Müller's influence on public thinking and argues that Müller was 'the most prescient of geneticists active before the war, who did most to forge the link in public thought between radiation and mutation' (Turney, 1998, p. 128).

5. *Ellensburg Daily Record*, 1 June 1946, p. 1; *Spokane daily Chronicle* 3 June 1946, p. 6.

6. *The Daily Mirror*, 29 June 1946, p. 2.

7. *Eugene Register-Guard*, 19 June 1946, p. 4.

8. *St. Petersburg Times*, 29 June 1946, p. 77.

9. *Deseret News*, 5 September 1946, p. 3.

10. One pig who, it was thought, had managed to escape the bomb blast was heralded as a hero by the press and a symbol of hope for a public that needed some reassurance about the possibility of surviving a nuclear attack. 'Pig 311' was supposed to have escaped from close to the centre of the bomb blast and survived by swimming for up to 15 hours in the waters around the target ships before being rescued by navy crew members. Despite much speculation in the press that Pig 311 had not been at the site of the blast at all, as late as April 1949, some three years after the Bikini tests, the Navy stated that she was still alive but sterile (*Tri-City Herald*, 28 March 1949, p. 37; *Sunday Herald*, 3 April 1949, p. 23).

11. *Milwaukee Journal*, 3 March 1952, p. 13; *Pittsburgh Press*, 8 March 1952, p. 1; *Milwaukee Journal*, 23 March 1952, p. 56; *Schenectady Gazette*, 5 April 1952, p. 5; *Times-News*, 12 March 1952, p. 6; *Spokane Daily Chronicle*, 13 March 1952, p. 47; *Reading Eagle*, 26 March 1952, p. 21; *Herald-Journal*, 8 March 1952, p. 15; *Ottawa Citizen*, 28 June 1952, p. 6.

12. Dr L.P. Gebhardt, professor of bacteriology at the University of Utah medical school, proposed in his presentation at the Utah Public Health Association Conference in May 1945 that poliomyelitis was carried by flies. For press report, see *Deseret News*, 30 May 1945, p. 7. For a press account of the 'Fly Clean-Up Campaign' in Tuscaloosa, see *The Tuscaloosa News*, 22 June 1953, p. 3. For a report on the mosquito and fly control programme in Sarasota to combat polio, see *Sarasota Journal*, 21 July 1953, p. 16.

13. *Daytona Morning Journal*, 7 July 1958, p. 6; *Times-Daily*, 24 June 1958, p. 2; *Gadsden Times*, 20 April 1958, p. 7; *Gadsden Times*, 19 June 1958, p. 78; *Rome News-Tribune*, 25 June 1958, p. 2.

14. There was a loss of support from a number of states; however, the eradication programme did continue. For comprehensive accounts of fire ant control in the US, see Tschinkel, 2006; and Buhs, 2004.

15. *Milwaukee Sentinel*, 13 September 1952, p. 24.

16. See *Miami News*, 12 May 1948, p. 2.

17. Andrew Tudor notes that during the 1970s the average number of horror films released per year in Britain increased to 34 over the course of the decade. See Tudor, 1989, p. 56.

18. The notable exception here is *The Giant Spider Invasion* (1975) which referenced the giant bug movies of the 1950s.

19. The precursor for these films is considered to be Alfred Hitchcock's *The Birds* (1963).

20. Carson, [1962] 1991, pp. 117–118.

21. *Silent Spring* (1963) stayed on the bestseller list for 31 weeks and sold 500,000 copies (source: Macnaghten & Urry, 1998: 45).

22. See Carson, [1962] 1991, p. 162–163.
23. Transcript of Richard Nixon State of the Union Address (22 January 1970) available at Miller Center of Public Affairs online at http://millercenter.org/ scripps/archive/speeches/detail/3889 [accessed 20 July 2010].
24. Sales figures for *Jaws* cited in *Victorian Advocate*, 20 July 1975, p. 10.
25. Adult audience statistics for *Jaws* reported in *Lakeland Ledger*, 1 October 1975, p. 12.
26. East Coast communities reported a 15 per cent decline in weekend business (*Times News*, 2 August 1975, p. 21). Also, *Anchorage Daily News*, 5 July 1975, p. 7; *St. Petersburg Times*, 13 July 1975, p. 22. However, it should also be noted that there are accounts of record numbers of people visiting resorts in the hope of seeing sharks. See, for instance, *The Miami News*, 28 June 1975, p. 96.
27. *Modesto Bee*, 16 July 1975; *Sarasota Herald-Tribune*, 6 July 1975, p. 8.

## 9   Beginning at the End: Re-imagining Our Relations with Animals

1. There is a point to be made here regarding the differences between the book and the film which, being produced some 14 years apart, reflect the differing socio-cultural anxieties of their respective eras.
2. In support of Taufa's actions, one media commentator stated that 'They should be giving him a medal. If every pit bull owner in the land followed his lead, New Zealand would be a safer place to live', 24 August 2009, online at *BBC News* web site, http://news.bbc.co.uk/1/hi/world/asia-pacific/8218534. stm [accessed 22 September 2009].
3. BBC interview with Robyn Kippenberger of the New Zealand SPCA, 24 August 2009, online at *BBC News* web site, http://news.bbc.co.uk/1/hi/ world/asia-pacific/8218534.stm [accessed 22 September 2009].
4. New Zealand ASA complaint 09/536 decision 8 September 2009.
5. See *The Guardian*, 27 January 2010, p. 1.
6. See CNN report, 'Inside the dog and cat meat market in China', 9 March 2010, online at http://edition.cnn.com/2010/WORLD/asiapcf/03/09/china. animals/index.html [accessed 12 March 2010].
7. The *Guardian* report was accompanied by one image: a close-up of a dog's head behind rusted metal caging. The dog's gaze addresses the viewer from a subordinate position, looking slightly upwards and into the camera.
8. These distinctions have not, however, been confined to expressing difference between European and Asian-Pacific practices and have historically been deployed at more local levels. During the American Civil War, for example, newspapers reported that Confederate supporters accused Yankee soldiers of catching, cooking and eating dogs and that they were serving canine meat to starving Rebel prisoners. It was suggested that Confederate prisoners were thus doubly dehumanized by their captors who not only starved them but forced them to consume 'taboo' food. Utilizing the consumption of dog meat to reflect difference in moral attitudes and culinary practices during the Franco-Prussian War, in 1871, Prussian commentators maintained that French soldiers were eating abandoned dogs that 'may be heard howling piteously at night'(*The Globe*, 10 February 1864, p. 2).

9. For an excellent account of the various cultural traditions of dog-eating, see McHugh, 2004, pp. 29–40.
10. Sources: *Daily Mirror*, 26 December 1995, p. 3; *Guardian*, 5 July 2000 online at http://www.guardian.co.uk/film/2000/jul/05/news3 [accessed 12 February 2010].
11. *Herald-Journal*, 30 March 1996, p. 5.
12. For full reviews, see *Film4* (1995) review online at http://www.film4.com/reviews/1995/babe; and *Empire* (1995) review online at http://www.empire-online.com/reviews/reviewcomplete.asp?FID=231
13. For full review, see Rhodes (1995) online at http://www.imdb.com/reviews/39/3914.html [accessed 12 February 2010].
14. Source: *Box Office Mojo*
15. Public review of *Babe* posted 5 July 2005 online at *IMDb.com*.
16. I am grateful to Peter Kramer for talking about his interpretation of the sequence I have discussed here. A full analysis of this scene is included in *2001: A Space Odyssey* (Kramer, 2010).

# Bibliography

Abbott, Sam (1951) 'Animals, Too, Are Movie Stars'. *Billboard*, 7 April 1951, p.52.

Adams, Carol J. (2004) *The Pornography of Meat*. Continuum, New York and London.

AMO (2000) *Insights Into Bowhunters: Their Attitudes, Motivations, and Economics. Bowhunting in the U.S: A Market Study.* AMO Publication funded though Wildlife Restoration Grant Agreement No. 14–48-98210-98-G049.

*Anchorage Daily News* (1975) 'Shark Expert Sees No Cause for Alarm'. 5 July 1975, p.13.

Anderson, Maria V., & Henderson, Antonia J. Z., (2005) 'Pernicious Portrayals: The Impact of Children's Attachment of Fiction on Animals of Fact'. *Society and Animals*, vol. 13, no. 4, 2005, pp.297–314.

Angove, Kenny (2009) 'The Dear Hunter'. *The Scottish Sun*, 9 March 2009, online at http://www.thescottishsun.co.uk/scotsol/homepage/news/article 2306292.ece.

Arnold, Gary (1975) 'America Anxious To Be Terrified'. *Victoria Advocate*, 20 July 1975, p.10.

Ashton, John (2007) 'Never Mind the Terror, Will It Be Sunny?' *Birmingham Post*, 28 March 2007, online at http://www.thefreelibrary.com/Never+mind+the+te rror,+will+it+be+sunny%3F-a0161093664.

Associated Press (1958) 'Wildlife Suffers From Fire Ant Control Chemicals'. *Times Daily*, 24 June 1958, p.2.

—— (1970a) 'Attack Launched on Pollution of Air, Water, Environment'. *Daytona Beach Morning Journal*, 2 January 1970, p.3.

—— (1970b) 'Let's Make Peace With Nature: Nixon'. *Ocala Star-Banner*, 23 January 1970, p.6.

—— (1973) 'Sea Pollution Massive'. *Victorian Advocate*, 13 February 1973, p.9.

—— (1975a) 'Shark Sighting Reports Credited to Movie "Jaws"'. *Lawrence Journal-World*, 25 June 1975, p.20.

—— (1975b) '"Jaws" and Shark Sightings'. *Miami News*, 28 June 1975, p.18.

—— (1975c) 'Shark Hits Youth in Brevard Surf'. *Sarasota Herald-Tribune*, 6 July 1975, p.13.

—— (1975d) 'Skipper Kills "Real Jaws"'. *Pittsburgh Post-Gazette*, 30 July 1975, p.1.

—— (1975e) 'Shark Jaw Sales Boom With Movie'. *Kentucky New Era*, 8 August 1975, p.2.

—— (1975f) 'Shark Hunters in Limelight'. *Nevada Daily Mail*, 20 August 1975, p.6.

—— (1975g) '"Jaws" Makes Film History'. *The News and Courier*, 14 September 1975, p.4.

—— (1996a) 'Dalmatian Fad Feared'. *Lodi News Sentinel*, 13 November 1996, p.2.

—— (1996b) 'Not All Dalmatians Are Lovable'. *McCook Daily Gazette*, 2 December 1996, p.20.

—— (1997a) 'Popularity of 1996 Film Fills Shelters With Unwanted Dalmatians In 1997'. *Chicago Tribune*, 10 September 1997, p.11.

—— (1997b) 'True Dalmatian Story Lacking Happy Ending'. *Sarasota Herald-Tribune*, 10 September 1997, p. 7B.

Bacon, James (1952) 'Lion Is Signed as Answer to Talking Mule by MGM'. *Reading Eagle*, 8 July 1952, p.14.

Baker, Steve (2001) *Picturing the Beast Animals, Identity, and Representation.* University of Illinois Press, Urbana & Chicago.

Ballinger, Lucy (2009) 'Rare and Beautiful, the White Deer that is Just a Trophy for Hunters'. *Daily Mail*, 9 March 2009, online at http://www.dailymail.co.uk/news/article-1160395/Rare-beautiful-white-deer-just-trophy-hunters.html.

BBC (2001) 'BBC Defends Indoor Lobster Footage'. *BBC News*, 14 October 2001, online at http://news.bbc.co.uk/1/hi/entertainment/1598813.stm.

—— (2007) 'Survival Show Faces 'Fake' Claim'. *BBC News*, 23 July 2007, online at http://news.bbc.co.uk/1/hi/entertainment/6911748.stm.

—— (2008) 'Grylls Apologises for 'Fake' Show'. *BBC News*, 19 March 2008, online at http://news.bbc.co.uk/1/hi/entertainment/7304617.stm.

BCWF (1993) 'The North American Hunting Dilemma'. Online at http://www.peachlandsportsmen.com/bcwf100.html.

Beers, Diane L. (2006) *For the Prevention of Cruelty: The History and Legacy of Animal Rights Activism in the United States.* Swallow Press, Ohio.

Benjamin, Walter (2008) *The Work of Art in the Age of Its Technological Reproducibility, and Other Writings on Media.* Harvard University Press, Cambridge, Massachusetts.

Berg, Louis (1950) 'Monkey of the Year'. *Los Angeles Times*, 17 December 1950, p. G10.

*Berkeley Daily Gazette* (1946) 'Final Bikini Preparations Made Ready'. 20 July 1946, p.9.

Billboard (1950) 'World Jungle Compound "Wild Animal Acts" advertisement'. 22 July 1950, p.61.

—— (1951) 'Bonzo, Other Animals Lost in Calif. Fire'. 17 March 1951, p.37.

Bodian, D. & Howe, H.A. (1945) 'Non-paralytic Poliomyelitis in the Chimpanzee'. *Journal of Experimental Medicine*, 1 March 1945, vol. 81, no. 3, pp. 255–274.

Bordwell, David [1985] (2006) 'An Excessively Obvious Cinema' in Bordwell, D., Staiger, J. and Thompson, K. (2006) *The Classical Hollywood Cinema*. Routledge, London, pp. 3–11.

Bordwell, David, Staiger, Janet & Kristen Thompson (2005) *The Classical Hollywood Cinema: Film Style & Mode of Production to 1960.* Routledge, London.

Borland, Sophie (2008) 'British Teacher's Lion Attack Caught on Film'. *Telegraph*, 6 March 2008, online at http://www.telegraph.co.uk/news/uknews/1580999/British-teachers-lion-attack-caught-on-film.html.

Born, Matt (2002) 'Pigs Bringing Home Bacon, but Dogs Are an Ad Man's Best Friend'. *Daily Telegraph*, 13 May 2002, online at http://www.telegraph.co.uk/news/uknews/1394005/Pigs-bringing-home-bacon-but-dogs-are-an-ad-mans-best-friend.html.

Boucher, Geoff (2009) 'James Cameron: Yes, "Avatar is 'Dances with Wolves' in space...sorta"'. *Los Angles Times*, 14 August 2009, online at http://hero-complex.latimes.com/2009/08/14/james-cameron-the-new-trek-rocks-but-transformers-is-gimcrackery/

Bourdieu, Pierre [1984] (2010) *Distinction*. Routledge, London & New York.

Bousé, Derek (2000) *Wildlife Films*. University of Pennsylvania Press, Philadelphia.

Bowcott, Owen (2010) 'Illegal Slaughter that may Claim 50,000 Deer a Year'. *Guardian*, 22 March 2008, online at http://www.guardian.co.uk/environment/2008/mar/22/wildlife.conservation.

Bowlby, John (1952) *Maternal Care and Mental Health*. World Health Organization, Geneva.

Boyle, Hal (1947a) 'Race Being Weakened By X-Ray, Says Doctor'. *Sarasota Herald-Tribune*, 7 May 1947, p.7.

Boyle, Hal (1947b) 'Dangers in Use of X-Rays'. *The Evening Independent*, 9 May 1947, p.14.

Brannan, Charles F. (1952) 'Foreword'. In *Yearbook of Agriculture 1952: Insects*. US Department of Agriculture, Washington, p. vii.

Broomfield, Andrea and Sally Mitchell (eds) (1996) *Prose by Victorian Women*. Garland Publishing, New York and London.

Browne, Anthony (2001) 'Calf? I nearly died'. *The Observer*, 29 April 2001, online at http://www.guardian.co.uk/news/2001/apr/29/politics.footandmouth.

Brunton, T. Lauder (1882) 'Vivisection and the Use of Remedies'. *Nineteenth Century* 11, 1882, pp. 479–87.

Buettinger, C. (1993) 'Antivivisection and the Charge of Zoophilia-psychosis in the Early Twentieth Century'. *The Historian*, 55(2), pp. 277–88.

Carpenter, David (2010) *A Hunter's Confession*. Greystone Books, Vancouver.

Carson, Rachael [1962] (1991) *Silent Spring*. Penguin Books, London.

Cessna, Jerry (2010) *Situation and Outlook for the U.S. Dairy Industry*, online at http://www.usda.gov/oce/forum/2010_Speeches/Speeches/DairyOutlook2010.pdf.

Clarke, H.G. (1959) *Practical Shepherding*. Farmer & Stock-Breeder Publications Ltd., London.

Cohen, Stanley [1972] (2002) *Folk Devils and Moral Panics: The Creation of the Mods and Rockers: Third Edition*. Blackwell, Oxon.

Colburn, Jerry (1996) 'Lingering Over the Lessons of "Babe"'. *Los Angeles Times*, 26 February 1996, p.3.

Coleridge, Stephen (1900) 'Letter to the Editor'. *Daily News*, 6 June 1900, p.7.

Copping, Jasper (2007) 'Deer Stalking Is the New People's Sport'. *The Telegraph*, 11 March 2007, online at http://www.telegraph.co.uk/news/uknews/1545156/Deer-stalking-is-the-new-peoples-sport.html.

Countryside Alliance (2009) *Rural Manifesto*. Online at http://www.countryside-alliance.org.uk/blogcategory/rural-manifesto/.

Crickmer, Clive (1970) 'A "Pet Register" to Thwart the Thieves'. *Daily Mirror*, 7 August 1970, p.19.

Crosby, John (1951a) 'Radio and Television in Review: Wonder of Electronics'. *Pittsburgh Post-Gazette*, 26 February 1951, p.33.

—— (1951b) 'Radio and Television in Review: The Animal Kingdom'. *Pittsburgh Post-Gazette*, 6 April 1951, p.30.

Curnutt, Jordan (2001) *Animals and the Law: A Sourcebook*. ABC-CLIO, California.

Curran, James and Seaton, Jean (2003) *Power without Responsibility*. Routledge, London & New York.

*Daily Mail* (2007) 'Give Me a Kiss, You Big Softie'. *Daily Mail*, 16 January 2007, online at http://www.dailymail.co.uk/news/article-428490/Give-kiss-big-softie.html.

—— (2008) 'Honey, Star of Big Cat Diary, Killed by Vet's Blunder'. *Daily Mail*, 2 February 2008, online at http://www.dailymail.co.uk/news/article-511955/Honey-star-Big-Cat-Diary-killed-vets-blunder.html.

*Daily Mirror* (1946) 'The Last Chance'. 29 June 1946, p.2.
—— (1957a) 'National Club for Your Pets'. 4 November 1957, p.11.
—— (1957b) 'How Little Mrs. Rogers Beat the Cat Man'. 31 August 1957, p.3.
—— (1958a) 'Beware of Pet Pirates!'. 16 August 1958, p.7.
—— (1958b) 'Stop the Cat Thieves'. 6 December 1958, p.11.
—— (1959) 'Cat Snatchers Are on the Prowl Again'. 24 April 1959, p.11.
—— (1960) 'Don't Fall for This Cruel Trick'. 16 July 1960, p.9.
—— (1961a) 'Beware of Pet Pirates!'. 4 February 1961, p.7.
—— (1961b) 'Sink the Pet Pirates...'. 11 March 1961, p.9.
—— (1961c) 'Viewpoint'. 15 November 1961, p.10.
—— (1962a) 'Don't fear the pet-snatchers says Minister'. 7 July 1962, p.4.
—— (1962b) ' "Spare the Pets from Pain" Plea'. 22 August 1962, p.4.
—— (1963a) 'Cash-For-Cats Man Quits'. 9 March 1963, p.5.
—— (1963b) 'Viewpoint'. 28 November 1963, p.10.
—— (1964a) 'Dogs Die in Poison Test'. 6 January 1964, p.5.
—— (1964b) 'Night Raid to Free Dogs for "Prison" ', 14 April 1964, p.8.
—— (1967) 'New Fury Over Labs of Death'. 8 December 1978, p.11.
—— (1969) 'The Ten "Lab" Dogs that Were Seized'. 1 February 1969, p.3.
—— (1978a) 'Pets for Slaughter'. 14 November 1978, p.1.
—— (1978b) 'This Cruel Trade'. 14 November 1978, p.2.
—— (1978c) 'The rights of Animals'. 16 November 1978, p.15.
—— (1978d) 'Pet-lovers Was on "Snatchers" '. 23 November 1978, p.4.
—— (1981a) 'Pet Lovers' Paint Raid on Fur Shop'. 6 March 1981, p.11.
—— (1981b) 'Protestors Raid Chicken Factory'. 5 May 1981, p.5.
—— (1981c) 'Animal Lovers Threaten Lab's Staff'. 7 September 1981, p.13.
—— (1983) 'Where Do These Dogs Come From?'. 13 January 1983, p.14.
—— (1984) 'Animal Crackers'. 20 November 1984, p.2.
—— (1988) 'Guilty: But Do You Care?'. 19 November 1988, p.1.
—— (1997) 'Beagles Are Out'. 15 August 1997, p.7.
—— (1998a) 'Sty Freedom'. 16 January 1998, p.19.
—— (1998b) 'Found Hog Day'. 17 January 1998, p.19.
—— (1998c) 'What's Going on at Mr Brown's Cat Farm?'. 2 June 1998, p.8.
—— (1998d) 'Victory Over Cruelty'. 16 November 1998, p.4.
—— (2001a) 'Save Phoenix from Ashes'. 25 April 2001.
—— (2001b) 'Saved by the Nation'. 26 April 2001, pp. 1, 4 & 5.
—— (2004) 'The Tamworth Two'. 12 April 2004, pp. 26–27.
—— (2006) 'Saved from the Chop'. 17 March 2006, p.17.
—— (2007) 'This Little Piggy (Nearly) Went to Market'. 11 August 2007, p.3.
—— (2009) 'Traffic Ham'. 31 December 2009, p.31.
*Daily Telegraph* (2009) 'Tourist Tangles with Killer Lion'. 9 March 2008, online at http://www.dailytelegraph.com.au/news/world/tourist-tangles-with-killer-lion/story-e6frev00-1111115748188.
*Daily Times* (1851) 'A Word About Ourselves'. 18 September 1851, p.1.
Dallos, Robert E. (1975) 'Shark Wave: Americans Are in the Jaws of a Scare'. *Milwaukee Journal*, 12 July 1975, p.1.
Dangerfield, Stanley & Howell, Elsworth (eds) (1975) *The International Encyclopedia of Dogs*. Pelham Books, London.
*Daytona Beach Morning Journal* (1951) 'Bonzo Is Full of Monkeyshines'. 23 March 1951, p.9.

—— (1958) 'Sportsmen Fear Ant Poisons Will Endanger Wildlife'. 7 July 1958, p.6.

Deer Stalking Scotland (2009) 'Stalking, Hunting & Shooting News'. Online at http://www.deerstalkingscotland.co.uk/news.html.

Derrida, Jacques (1994) *Specters of Marx: The State of the Debt, the Work of Mourning, and the* New International. Routledge, London & New York.

*Deseret News* (1945) 'Fly Believed Carrier of Dread Polio'. 30 May 1945, p.7.

—— (1946a) 'A-Bomb Trigger Test Set Friday'. 15 July 1946, p.2.

—— (1946b) 'Deadly Rays Killing Bikini Test Animals'. 15 July 1946, p.2.

—— (1946c) 'Atom Bomb Kills Animals in Tightly-Closed Ship'. 5 September 1946, p.3.

—— (1947) 'Film Animals Happy: Humane Officer Sees That They Get "Rights" '. 14 June 1947, p.8.

—— (1950) 'Wanted—Some Girl Who Resembles Marie (Irma) Wilson'. 5 July 1950, p.13.

—— (1951) 'Music Hath Charms for Bonzo, New Star'. 9 January 1951, p.24.

Desmond, Adrian (1989) *The Politics of Evolution: Morphology, Medicine, and Reform in Radical London.* University of Chicago Press, Chicago and London.

Dewey, Peter (1989) *British Agriculture in the First World War.* Routledge, London & New York.

Donald, Diana (2006) 'Pangs Watched in Perpetuity: Sir Edwin Landseer's Pictures of Dying Deer and the Ethos of Victorian Sportsmanship'. In The Animal Studies Group (2009), *Killing Animals.* University of Illinois Press, Urbana & Chicago, pp. 50–68.

Douglas, Mary (2002) *Purity and Danger.* Routledge, London & New York.

Drew, Kate (2010) 'Experience: I was Mauled by a Lion'. *Guardian*, 23 January 2010, online at http://www.guardian.co.uk/lifeandstyle/2010/jan/23/mauled-by-lion-and-lived.

Duda, Mark Damian (2002) 'The Hunting Mind'. *North American Hunter*, October 2002, pp. 45–47.

Duda, Mark Damian & Kira Young (1998) *American Attitudes Toward Scientific Wildlife Management and Human Use of Fish and Wildlife: Implications for Effective Public Relations and Communications Strategies, 63rd North American Wildlife and Natural Resources Conference Proceedings.* pp. 589–603.

Duda, Mark Damian & Martin Jones (2008) *The North American Model of Wildlife Conservation: Affirming The Role, Strength and Relevance of Hunting in the 21st Century.* Responsive Management, Harrisonburg, Virginia.

Dyer, Richard (1998) *Stars.* BFI Publishing, London.

—— (2004) *Heavenly Bodies: Second Edition.* Routledge, Oxon. & New York.

Eder, Klaus (1996) *The Social Construction of Nature.* Sage, London.

Edge (2006) 'The Top 100 PC Games of the 21st Century'. *Edge*, 25 August 2006, online at http://www.next-gen.biz/features/the-top-100-pc-games-21st-century?page=0%2C1.

Elder, Glen, Wolch, Jennifer & Jody Emel (1998) '*La Pratique Sauvage*: Race, Place, and the Human-Animal Divide'. In Wolch, J. & Emel, J. (eds) (1998) *Animal Geographies: Place, Politics, and Identity in the Nature-Culture Borderlands.* Verso, London & New York, pp.72–90.

*Ellensburg Daily Record* (1946) ' "Noah's Ark" of Animals, Germs Off For Bikini'. 1 June 1946, p.1.

Epstein, Andrew (1980) 'Bonzomania: Marketing A Dead Chimp'. *Los Angeles Times*, 9 November 1980, p. N7.

*Eugene Register-Guard* (1945) 'War on House Fly Urged by Official to prevent Polio'. 19 June 1945, p.5.

—— (1946) 'Doomed Bikini Test Animals Getting Kindest Navy Care'. 19 June 1946, p.4.

—— (1947) ' "Mister Mutation" Tells Writer of X-Ray's Potential Harm'. 7 May 1947, p.2.

—— (1951) 'Fearless Fagan Kisses Master on Reunion in San Francisco'. 17 May 1951, p.32.

—— (1953) ' "Jackie" Lion Takes Movie "Patsy" Award'. *Eugene Register-Guard*, 24 March 1953, p.10.

—— (1940) 'Throwing Horses by Use of Wire Now Banned in Films'. *Evening Independent*, 12 December 1940, p.10.

*Evening Independent* (1975) 'They Mauled Baby Whale Because They Thought It Had "Jaws" '. 30 June 1975, p. 2A.

—— (2007) 'Forget Fears over Terror – What about the Weather?'. *Evening Times*, 27 March 2007, online at http://www.eveningtimes.co.uk/forget-fears-over-terror-what-about-the-weather-1.945947.

Faulkner, Robert (2000) 'It's Virtual Open Season; Computer Games Find Sales Gold in the Thrill of the Hunt'. *Toronto Star*, 6 November 2000, p.2.

Flicker, Eva (2003) 'Between Brains and Breasts – Women Scientists in Fiction Film: On the Marginalization and Sexualization of Sexual Competence'. *Public Understanding of Science*, vol. 12, pp. 307–318.

Foggo, Daniel (2009) 'How much to Kill this Deer?'. *The Sunday Times*, 8 March 2009, online at http://www.timesonline.co.uk/tol/news/uk/article5864850.ece.

Fowler-Reeves (2007) *With Extreme Prejudice: The culling of British wildlife*. Animal Aid, Kent.

Fox News (2008a) 'Teacher Survives Attack by 400 lbs Lion, Claiming "It Was Only Playing" '. Online at http://www.foxnews.com/story/0,2933,327825,00.html.

—— (2008b) 'Disney Unveils Disneynature Documentary Film Unit Following "March of the Penguins" Success'. *Fox News*, 22 April 2008, online at http://www.foxnews.com/story/0,2933,352101,00.html.

Fulton, John F. (1951) 'The Psychological Basis of Psychosurgery'. *Proceedings of the American Philosophical Society*, vol. 95, no. 5, 17 October 1951, pp. 538–541.

Gad, Shayne C. (ed.) (2006) *Animal Models in Toxicology*. Taylor & Francis, Boca Raton, London & New York.

*Gadsden Times* (1958) 'Chemical Control of Fire Ants Urged By Conservation Heads'. 20 April 1958, p.7.

—— (1959) 'Chemicals Used To Kill Fire Ants Killing Wildlife'. 19 June 1958, p.8.

Gasset, José Ortega (1995) *Meditations on Hunting*. Wilderness Adventures Press, MT.

George, Peter James (1982) *The Emergence of Industrial America: Strategic factors in American Economic Growth Since 1870*. State University of New York Press, Albany.

Georgia Department of Natural Resources/ Responsive Management (2008) *Increasing Hunting Participation by Investigating Factors Related to Hunting License*

*Sales Increases in 1992, 1999 and 2004 Against 13 Other Years of Hunting License Sales Decline.* Responsive Management, Harrisonburg, VA.

Gill, T, (1942) 'No Men Permitted in "Bambi" Picture'. *Milwaukee Journal,* 22 March 1942, p.4.

Goldman, Adam (2006) 'Deer Hunting Game is a Surprise Hit'. msnbc.com, 25 July 2006, online at http://www.msnbc.msn.com/id/14030610/

Goodwin, David (2009) 'I'm on Facebuck'. *Scottish Sun,* 12 March 2009, online at http://www.thescottishsun.co.uk/scotsol/homepage/news/2314278/Facebook-campaign-to-save-rare-white-dear-Pearl.html.

Graham, Sheilah (1951) 'Sheilah Graham Heralds Hollywood'. *Sunday Herald,* 18 March 1951, p.39.

Green, Lloyd (1975) 'Imitations Planned: Films Infected by Jaws' Bite'. *Montreal Gazette,* 20 August 1975, p.20.

Groves, Julian McAllister (2001) 'Animal Rights and the Politics of Emotion: Folk Constructs of Emotion in the Animal Rights Movement'. In Goodwin, Jeff, James M. Jasper and Francesca Polletta (eds), *Passionate Politics: Emotions and social movements.* University of Chicago Press, London.

Gull, W.W. (1882) 'The Ethics of Vivisection'. *Nineteenth Century,* 1882, pp. 456 – 467.

Haas, Peter (1990) *Saving the Mediterranean: The Politics of International Environmental Cooperation.* Columbia University Press, New York & Oxford.

Haeussler, G.B. (1952) 'Losses Caused by Insects'. *Yearbook of Agriculture 1952: Insects,* US Department of Agriculture, Washington, pp. 141–46.

Hall, Stuart (1992) 'The West and the Rest: Discourse and Power'. In Hall, S., & Gieben, B., (eds), *Formations of Modernity.* Polity, Cambridge.

—— (2005) 'Encoding/Decoding'. In Hall, S., Hobson, D., Lowe, A. & P. Willis *Culture, Media, Language.* Routledge, London, pp.117–127.

Hamilton, Susan (ed.) (2004) *Animal Welfare and Anti-vivisection 1870–1910: Francis Power Cobbe.* Routledge, London & New York.

Haraway, Donna (1989) *Primate Visions: Gender, Race and Nature in the World of Modern Science.* Routledge, New York & London.

Harlow, Harry F., Dodsworth, Robert O. & Margaret K. Harlow (1965) 'Total Isolation in Monkeys'. *Proceedings of the National Academy of Science of the United States of America,* vol. 54, no. 1, July 1965, pp. 90–97.

Harris, Thomas [1957] (1991) 'The Building of Popular Images: Grace Kelly and Marilyn Monroe'. In Gledhill, C. (ed.), *Stardom: Industry of Desire.* Routledge, London, pp. 40–44.

Hayes, Keith J. & Catherine Hayes (1951) 'The Intellectual Development of a Home-Raised Chimpanzee'. *Proceedings of the American Philosophical Society,* vol. 95, no. 2, pp. 105–109.

Haynes, Roslynn (2003) 'From Alchemy to Artificial Intelligence: Stereotypes of the Scientist in Western Literature'. *Popular Understanding of Science,* vol. 12, pp. 243–253.

Henderson, Damien (2007) ' "Babymoon" Is Part of New Trend for Holiday Companies'. *The Herald,* 27 March 2007, online at http://www.heraldscotland.com/babymoon-is-part-of-new-trend-for-holiday-companies-1.855075.

Henderson, L.F. (1952) 'Household Insects'. *Yearbook of Agriculture 1952: Insects,* US Department of Agriculture, Washington, pp. 469–75.

*Herald-Journal* (1952) 'Stalemate in Korea'. 8 March 1952, p.16.

Hoey, Kate (2009) *Countryside Alliance Rural Manifesto*, online at http://www.countryside-alliance.org.uk/blogcategory/rural-manifesto/.

Holderness, B.A. (1985) *British Agriculture Since 1945*. Manchester University Press, Manchester.

*The Independent* (1998) 'Fake Shots "Routine" in TV Wildlife Programmes'. *The Independent*, 10 August 1998, online at http://www.independent.co.uk/news/fake-shots-routine-in-tv-wildlife-programmes-1170749.html.

ITC (1997) 'Television Advertising Complaints Reports: "Anchor Cows"'. 1 November 1997, online at http://www.ofcom.org.uk/static/archive/itc/itc_publications/complaints_reports/advertising_complaints/show_complaint.asp-ad_complaint_id=25.html.

ITN (2009) 'Man Eats Dog' 16 August 2009, online at http://itn.co.uk/3eabe4c2 8224d5bbcb051053a24cb1f8.html.

Jameson, Fredric (1993) 'Postmodernism, or The Cultural Logic of Late Capitalism'. In Docherty, Thomas (ed.) *Postmodernism: A Reader*. Harvester Wheatsheaf, New York and London.

Jarboe, Greg (2009) *YouTube and Video Marketing*. Wiley Publishing, Indiana.

Jenson, Oliver (1947) 'Persecuted Lion'. *Life*, 3 March 1947, pp. 19–22.

Johnson, Erskine (1950) 'Chimp Bother Ronald Reagan'. *The Pittsburgh Press*, 1 October 1950, p.65.

Johnson, Simon (2009) ' "Rare White Deer" to Be Subject of "Hunting Auction". *Telegraph*, 8 March 2009, online at http://www.telegraph.co.uk/earth/earthnews/4957310/Rare-white-deer-to-be-subject-of-hunting-auction.html.

——(2010) 'Thousands of Deer Starving in Big Freeze'. *Telegraph*, 5 February 2010, online at http://www.telegraph.co.uk/earth/wildlife/7167488/Thousands-of-deer-starving-in-big-freeze.html.

Jorg, Daniele (2003) 'The Good, the Bad and the Ugly – Dr. Moreau Goes to Hollywood'. *Public Understanding of Science*, vol. 12, pp. 297–305.

Kean, Hilda (1998) *Animal Rights: Political and Social Change in Britain Since 1800*. Reaktion Books, London.

Kellogg, W.N. & Kellogg, L.A. (1933) *The Ape and the Child: A Study of Environmental Influence Upon Early Behavior*. McGraw-Hill Book Company Inc, New York & London.

Kete, Kathleen (1994) *The Beast in the Boudoir: Petkeeping in Nineteenth-Century Paris*. University of California Press, Los Angeles & London.

Kramer, Michael (1980) 'What President Reagan Would Mean for New York'. *New York Magazine*, 28 April 1980, pp. 27–29.

Kristeva, Julia (1982) *Powers of Horror: An Essay on Abjection*. Columbia University Press, New York.

Lansbury, Coral (1985) *The Old Brown Dog: Women, Workers, and Vivisection in Edwardian England*. The University of Wisconsin Press, London & Wisconsin.

LA *Times/Washington Post News Service* (1975) ' "Jaws" Is Shocking Reminder for Sea Tragedy Survivors'. *Sarasota Herald-Tribune*, 7 August 1975, p.30.

*Lakeland Ledger* (1975) 'Liking for Jaws Film Continues'. 1 October 1975, p.12.

Lane, Ralph (1951a) 'News in Review'. *Southeast Missourian*, 10 February 1951, p.6.

——(1951b) 'News in Review'. *Southeast Missourian*, 8 March 1951, p.6.

Lautenberg (2004) 'A Bill to Amend Title 18, United States Code, to Prohibit Certain Interstate Conduct Relating to Exotic Animals'. *Congressional Record*, 22 July 2004, p.17100.

Lemkin, Jonathan (2004) 'Archetypal Landscapes and *Jaws*'. In Grant, Barry Keith & Christopher Sharrett (eds), *Planks of Reason: Essays on the Horror Film*, Scarecrow Press, MD.

Lesch, John E. (2006) *The First Miracle Drugs: How the Sulfa Drugs Transformed Medicine*. Oxford University Press, Oxford and New York.

*Lewiston Daily Sun* (1939) 'What They Say'. 2 March 1939, p.4.

*Lewiston Daily Sun* (1946) 'Bikini Test Animals "Dying Like Flies"'. 15 July 1946, p.2.

—— (1951a) 'Fearless Fagan Finds A Home'. *Life*, vol. 30. no. 7, 12 February 1951, pp. 30–31.

—— (1951b) 'Fearless Fagan Goes To Hollywood'. *Life*, vol. 31, no. 4, 23 July 1951, p.107.

*Life* (1953) 'Universal Appeal'. *Life*, vol. 34, no. 24, 15 June 1953, pp. 103–109.

Lind af Hageby & Schartau (*sic*), Leisa (1903) *The Shambles of Science: Extracts from the Diary of Two Students of Physiology*. Ernest Bell, London.

Lindley, Donald (1975) ' "People are Entering the Domain of Other Creatures": Shark Menace Pales Beside Highway Slaughter'. *Daytona Beach Morning Journal*, 30 July 1975, p.9.

Linzey, Andrew (2009) *Why Animal Suffering Matters: Philosophy, Theology, and Practical Ethics*. Oxford University Press, Oxford.

*Lodi News-Sentinel* (1975) 'Daly City Man Feels Jaws of a Large Shark'. 11 August 1975, p.2.

*Los Angeles Times* (1973) 'Massive Pollution of the Sea'. 15 February 1973, p. D6.

Losh, Susan Carol (2010) 'Stereotypes about Scientists Over Time Among US Adults: 1983 and 2001'. *Public Understanding of Science*, vol. 19, no. 3, pp. 372–382.

Luke, Brian (2007a) 'Justice, Caring, and Animal Liberation'. In Donovan, Josephine & Carol J. Adams (eds), *The Feminist Care Tradition in Animal Ethics*. Columbia University Press, New York, pp. 125–152.

—— (2007b) *Brutal: Manhood and the Exploitation of Animals*. University of Illinois Press, IL.

Lutts, Ralph H. (1992) 'The Trouble with Bambi: Walt Disney's *Bambi* and the American Vision of Nature'. *Forest and Conservation History*, vol. 36, October 1992, pp.160–171.

Macnaghten, Phil & Urry, John (1998) *Contested Natures*. Sage, London.

Marvin, Gary (2006) 'Wild Killing: Contesting the Animal in Hunting'. In The Animal Studies Group, *Killing Animals*. University of Illinois Press, Urbana and Chicago, pp. 10–29.

Maxwell, Hugh (1886) 'Letter to the Editor'. *Weekly Dispatch*, 6 June, 1886, p.9.

McGurran, Aidan (2008) 'Essex-Girl Kate Drew Mauled by a "Tame" Lion While on Safari in Zimbabwe'. *Daily Mirror*, online at http://www.mirror.co.uk/news/top-stories/2008/02/02/essex-girl-kate-drew-mauled-by-a-tame-lion-while-on-safari-in-zimbabwe-115875–20306319/.

McHugh, Susan (2004) *Dog*. Reaktion Books, London.

McNair, Brian (2009) *News and Journalism in the UK*. Routledge, Oxon.

Melnick, J. & Horstmann, Dorothy M. (1947) 'Active Immunity to Poliomyelitis in Chimpanzees following Subclinical Infection'. *Journal of Experimental Medicine*, 28 February 1947, vol. 85, no. 3, pp. 287–303.

Mendelius, Maree (1975) 'Some Big Jaws Are Waiting Out There'. *Lodi News-Sentinel*, 24 July 1975, p.11.

*Miami News* (1946a) 'Bikini Animals Now Dying at "Expected Rate"'. 16 July 1946, p.8.

—— (1946b) 'Doctor Sees Peril in Relying Too Much on X-Ray Treatment'. 6 November 1946, p.17.

—— (1948) 'Control Has Its Hazards: Pollution Declared Danger in War on Mosquitoes'. 12 May 1948, p.2.

—— (1952a) 'New Films'. 1 October 1952, p.105.

—— (1952b) *Fearless Fagan* advertisement. 1 October 1952, p.29.

*Miami Sunday News* (1951) 'Lecturing Parent, Sleepy Soldiers and Balky Circus Mule'. 2 April 1951, p.6.

Miller, William & Robertson, E.D.S (1942) 'Humane Society O.K.s Treatment of Animals in the Horse Opera'. *Milwaukee Journal*, 26 August 1942, p.29.

Miller, William & Robertson, E.D.S (1946) 'Chimpanzee Tops the List of Ten Smartest Animals'. *Milwaukee Journal*, 5 October 1946, p.13.

—— (1959) *Practical Animal Husbandry*. Oliver & Boyd, Edinburgh & London.

*Milwaukee Journal* (1952a) 'Red Chorus of Propaganda Plays Germ Warfare Theme'. 3 March 1952, p.13.

—— (1952b) 'Potato Big Propaganda Breeds Chinese Sequel of Germ Warfare'. 23 March 1952, p.56.

—— (1955) 'A Korea "United for Insects"'. 12 August 1955, p.6.

*Milwaukee Sentinel* (1928) 'How Man Reached The Head of the Animal Class'. 8 December 1928, p.12.

—— (1952) 'Man Supreme? Insects May Be a Real Threat'. 13 September 1952, p.24.

Miniter, Frank (2007) *The Politically Incorrect Guide to Hunting*. Regnery Publishing Inc., Washington.

Mitchell, Sally (2004) *Frances Power Cobbe: Victorian Feminist, Journalist, Reformer*. University of Virginia Press, Virginia.

Mitman, Gregg (1953) 'Balky Lion Turns Back As He Wins Acting Award'. *Modesto Bee*, 21 March 1953, p.5.

—— (1999) *Reel Nature: America's Romance with Wildlife on Film*. University of Washington Press, Seattle and London.

*Modesto Bee* (1975) 'Shark Attacks Swimmer Day After Alert Ended'. 16 July 1975, p. D2.

Molloy, Claire (2009) 'Dreaming of Electric Sheep and Negotiating Animality'. In Batra, N. & Messier, V. (eds) *Of Mice and Men: Animals in Human Culture*. Cambridge Scholars Publishing, Newcastle upon Tyne, pp.106–120.

Moorhead, Jim (1980) 'Reagan's Election Boosts Chimps Notoriety'. *The Evening Independent*, 18 December 1980, p.19.

Moult, Julie (2008) 'Teacher Survives Attack by 400lb Lion, Claiming "It was Only Playing"'. *Daily Mail*, 2 February 2008, online at http://www.dailymail. co.uk/news/article-511673/Teacher-survives-attack-400lb-lion-claiming-playing.html.

Mulhall, Stephen (2008) *On Film: Second Edition*. Routledge, London & New York.

*New York Times* (1866a) 'The Rights of Animals'. 11 March 1866, p.4.

—— (1866b) 'American Society for the Prevention of Cruelty to Animals'. 22 May 1866, p.8.

—— (1866c) 'Chicken-Butchers and the Anti-Cruelty Society'. 9 June 1866, p.4.

*New York Times* (1867a) 'Which Are The Brutes?'. 3 February 1867, p.4.

—— (1867b) 'The Brute Creation'. 5 February 1867, p.4.

—— (1867c) 'Prevention of Cruelty to Animals: A Card form Mr. Bergh'. 24 February 1867, p.5.

—— (1875a) 'Vivisection'. 24 February 1875, p.4.

—— (1875b) 'Torturing in the Name of Science'. 30 April 1975, p.6.

—— (1885) 'Vivisection'. 17 March 1885, p.4.

—— (1909) 'Trick Chimpanzee Fulfills Mind Test'. 18 December 1909, p.7.

—— (1910) 'A Monkey with a Mind'. 30 January 1910, p. SM7.

—— (1980) 'Reagan Campaign Sparks Bonzo Boom'. 3 November 1980, vol. 13, no. 43, p.11.

Nichols, Bill (2001) *Introduction to Documentary*. Indiana University Press, Bloomington & Indianapolis.

Nissen, Henry W., Kao Liang Chow & Josephine Semmes (1951) 'Effects of Restricted Opportunity for Tactual, Kinesthetic and Manipulative Experience on the Behavior of a Chimpanzee'. *The American Journal of Psychology*, vol. 64, no. 4, October 1951, pp. 485–507.

Nugent, Ted & Shemane Nugent (2002) *Kill It and Grill It: A Guide to Preparing and Cooking Wild Game and Fish*. Regnery Publishing Inc., Washington.

Nunwood, (2007) *The Travel Foundation Consumer Research*. Nunwood, Leeds, online at http://www.thetravelfoundation.org.uk/assets/files/get_involved/learn_more/further_research/1.%20Consumer%20Research%20(nunwood)(1).pdf.

Ofcom (1951) 'Night Club Career Short-Lived for "Fearless Fagan"'. *Ottawa Citizen*, 29 March 1951.

—— (2004) *The Communications Market 2004 – Television*. August 2004.

—— (2006a) *Media Literacy Audit: Report on Adult Media Literacy*. 2 March 2006.

—— (2006b) *Media Literacy Audit: Report on Media Literacy Amongst Children*. 2 May 2006.

—— (2010) *Adults' Media Literacy in the Nation: Summary Report*. 17 May 2010.

*Ottawa Citizen* (1951a) 'Bedtime for Bonzo'. *Owossa Argus-Press*, 22 June 1951, p.14.

—— (1951b) 'You Can Still Hire a Lion for a Hundred Bucks a Day'. *Owossa Argus-Press*, 13 October 1951, p.7.

—— (1952) 'Scientific Report Disproves Endicott's Germ War Charge'. 28 June 1952, p.6.

Outlaw, Joe L., Jacobson, Robert E., Ronald D. Knutson & Robert B. Schwart, Jr. (1996) *Structure of the U.S. Dairy Farm Sector*, online at http://www.cpdmp.cornell.edu/CPDMP/Pages/Publications/Pubs/M4.pdf.

Palotta, Nicole R., (2008) 'Origin of Adult Animal Rights Lifestyle in Childhood Responsiveness to Animal Suffering'. *Society and Animals*, vol. 16, no. 2, 2008, pp.149–170.

Parsons, Christopher (1971) *Making Wildlife Movies*. David & Charles, Newton Abbot.

—— (1982) *True to Nature*. Patrick Stephens Limited, Cambridge.

Perry, P.J. (1973) *British Agriculture 1875–1914*. Routledge, Oxon.

Petersen, David, & Ted Williams (2000) *Heartsblood: Hunting, Spirituality, and Wilderness in America*. Johnson Book, Colarado.

Peterson, Dale & Jane Goodall (2000) *Visions of Caliban: On Chimpanzees and People*. University of Georgia Press, Goergia.

Peterson, Michael (2007) 'The Animal Apparatus: From a Theory of Animal Acting to an Ethics of Animal Acts'. *The Drama Review*, vol. 51, no. 1, Spring 2007, pp. 33–48.

*Pittsburgh Post-Gazette* (1946a) 'Operations Crossroads in Post-Mortem Stage'. 5 July 1946, p.4.

—— (1946b) 'Atom Test Animals Melt Away'. 15 July 1946, p.3.

—— (1951) 'Tamba, One of Hollywood's Top Comics, Is Dead'. 6 March 1951, p.12.

—— (1952) 'New Film: "Fearless Fagan", A Soldier and His Lion at Ritz'. 17 October 1952, p.27.

*Pittsburgh Press* (1952) 'Epidemics Rage in Korea: "Panic" Blamed for Red Lies of Germ War'. 8 March 1952, p.1.

Porter, B.A. (1952) 'Insects Are Harder to Kill'. *Yearbook of Agriculture 1952: Insects*, US Department of Agriculture, Washington, pp. 317–320.

*Prescott Evening Courier* (1959) 'Pandora's Box'. 24 November 1959, p.3.

Quittner, Joshua (1948) 'Animals in Films Handsomely Paid: Humane Society Keeps Eye on Productions'. *Reading Eagle*, 19 December 1948, p.45.

—— (1950) ' "Bonzo", Chimp, Hailed as Film Scene Stealer'. *Reading Eagle*, 24 September 1950, p.33.

—— (1951) 'Chimpanzee Fails Intelligence Test, But Retains Movie Contract'. *Reading Eagle*, 1 February 1951, p.12.

—— (1998) 'Big-Game Hunting'. *Time*, 7 December 1998, online at http://www.time.com/time/magazine/article/0,9171,989745,00.html.

Rayner, Jay (2008) 'Sure It might be Cruel but Intensive Farming Saves Lives'. *The Observer*, 13 January 2008, online http://www.guardian.co.uk/commentisfree/2008/jan/13/lifeandhealth.ruralaffairs?INTCMP=SRCH.

*Reading Eagle* (1952a) 'Reds Reject Germ Probe'. 26 March 1952, p.21.

—— (1952b) 'Lion Is Signed as Answer to Talking Mule by MGM'. 8 July 1952, p.14.

Regan, Tom (2004) *The Case for Animal Rights*. University of California Press, Los Angeles.

Responsive Management/National Shooting Sports Foundation (2008) *The Future of Hunting and the Shooting Sports*. US Fish and Wildlife Service, Harrisonburg, VA.

Ritvo, Harriet (1987) *The Animal Estate: The English and Other Creatures in the Victorian Age*. Harvard University Press, MA.

Rivers, Thomas M. (1954) 'The Story of Research on Poliomyelitis'. *Proceedings of the American Philosophical Society*, vol. 98, no. 4, 16 August 1954, pp. 250–54.

Rollin, Bernard E. (2008) 'Foreword'. In Armstrong, Susan & Richard G. Botzler (eds), *The Animal Ethics Reader: 2nd Edition*. Routledge, London, pp.xiv–xvii.

*Rome News-Tribune* (1951) 'Bonzo the Acting Chimp Stars in First Avenue Comedy Today'. 18 March 1951, p.10.

—— (1958) 'Chemicals for Fire Ants Kill Wildlife'. 25 June 1958, p.2.

Rothfels, Nigel (ed.) (2002) *Representing Animals*. Indiana University Press, Indiana & Bloomington.

Rowan, Andrew N. (1984) *Of Mice, Models and Men: Critical Evaluation of Animal Research*. State University of New York Press, New York.

Rupke, Nicolaas (1990) *Vivisection in Historical Perspective*. Routledge, London.

Sabrosky, Curtis W. (1952) 'How Many Insects Are There?'. *Yearbook of Agriculture 1952: Insects*, US Department of Agriculture, Washington, pp. 1–7.

Salt, Henry (1894) *Animals' Rights Considered in Relation to Social Progress.* Macmillan & Co., New York and London.

*Sarasota Herald-Tribune* (1951a) 'Homeless Leo'. 30 March 1951, p.1.

—— (1951b) 'Fearless Fagan Finds a Home'. 2 April 1951, p.1.

—— (1956) 'Lloyd's Finally Hedges Policy – On Actor's Blush'. 15 April 1956, p.11.

*Sarasota Journal* (1953) 'Three Polio Cases Here'. 21 July 1953, p.16.

Sarma, Daisy (2008) 'Entertainment: United States'. *The Money Times*, 23 April 2008, online at http://www.themoneytimes.com/articles/20080422/disney_returns_to_roots_launches_disneynature-id-1020856.html.

*Saturday Review of Politics, Literature, Science and Art,* March 1884, p.800.

Sax, Boria (2000) *Animals in the Third Reich: Pets, Scapegoats and the Holocaust.* Continuum, London & New York.

*Schenectady Gazette* (1952a) 'Fakes Exposed'. 5 April 1952, p.5.

—— (1952b) 'Doctors Making Progress on Cure for Korea Fever'. 27 November 1952, p.15.

Scott, John L. (1950) 'Irma and Her Friends Take Zany Journey'. *Los Angeles Times*, 30 June 1950, p. A6.

Serpell, James (1999) *In the Company of Animals.* Cambridge University Press, Cambridge.

—— (2002) 'Anthropomorphism and Anthropomorphic Selection – Beyond the "Cute Response"'. *Society and Animals*, vol. 10, no. 4, pp.437–454.

Shaw, Gaylord (1972) 'Great Lakes Clean-Up Set'. *Tuscaloosa News*, 16 April 1972, p.8.

Shirley, Bill (1975) 'U.S. Visitor'. *Los Angeles Times*, 14 June 1975, pp.19–21.

Sicart, Miguel (2009) *The Ethics of Computer Games.* MIT Press, MA.

Simross, Lynn (1980) 'The Gentle Jungle: Animal Trainers Replace Whip and Chair With Affection'. *Pittsburgh Press*, 1 July 1980, p.9.

Singer, Peter [1975] (1995) *Animal Liberation: Second Edition.* Pimlico, London.

SkyNews (2009) 'Big Cat Keeper: Lion King of South Africa'. *SkyNews*, 20 March 2009, online at http://news.sky.com/skynews/Home/World-News/Lion-King-Kevin-Richardson-Treated-Like-One-Of-The-Pride-By-The-Big-Cats-At-His-South-Africa-Reserve/Article/200903315245291.

Smith, Charles (2009) 'Daily Telegraph Writer Mauled after Entering Lion's Enclosure'. *Daily Telegraph*, 4 September 2009, online at http://www.telegraph.co.uk/travel/travelnews/6139806/Daily-Telegraph-writer-mauled-after-entering-lions-enclosure.html.

Smith, Merriman (1970) 'President Would Make Our Peace With Nature'. *Lodi News-Sentinel*, 23 January 1970, p.1.

Sontag, Susan (1982) *Susan Sontag: A Reader.* Penguin Books, London.

*Southeast Missourian* (1950a) 'Hollywood Talk of Movies, Stars'. 16 February 1950, p.11.

—— (1950b) 'Don't Laugh at Chimpanzee; He May Be Smarter Than Your Child'. 15 March 1950, p.20.

—— (1951) 'Famous Movie Monkey Dies of Suffocation'. 6 March 1951, p.4.

—— (1958) 'Report Insects Would Survive If Radiation Disaster Hit World'. 19 March 1958, p.2.

Spear, Ivan (1950) 'Hollywood Report'. *Billboard*, 7 January 1950, p.20.

*Spokane Daily Chronicle* (1946) 'Bikini Animals Comfy and Cozy'. 3 June 1946, p.6.

—— (1951) 'Relatively Speaking'. 9 April 1951, p.24.

—— (1952) 'Criminal Trials Urged'. 13 March 1952, p.48.

—— (1953) 'Circus to Show Fearless Fagan'. 19 June 1953, p.40.

Sporting Conservation Council (2008) *Strengthening America's Hunting Heritage and Wildlife Conservation in the 21st Century: Challenges and Opportunities.* Sporting Conservation Council.

Stallwood, Kim (2004) 'A Personal Overview of Direct Action in the United Kingdom and the United States'. In Best, Steven & Nocella, Anthony J. (eds), *Terrorists or Freedom Fighters? Reflections on the Liberation of Animals.* Lantern Books, New York.

*St. Petersburg Times* (1946a) 'H-Hour for Bikini Can Come Any Day'. 29 June 1946, p.77.

—— (1946b) 'Science on the March Heralds Atomic Age'. 14 September 1946, p.95.

—— (1947a) 'Moviemakers Cut Production Cloth to Tastes of Every Nation'. 24 August 1947, p.29.

—— (1947b) 'Atom Energy Helps Treat Human Ills'. 3 August 1947, p.44.

—— (1948) Peninsula Telephone Company advertisement. 13 October 1948, p.3.

—— (1949a) 'Hey! Get off the Line'. 24 April 1949, p.1.

—— (1949b) Peninsula Telephone Company advertisement. 27 April 1949, p.21.

—— (1951) 'A Ham at Heart, Bonzo Is Star'. 27 May 1951, p.45.

—— (1975) 'Sharks Attack for Other than Hunger Reason'. 26 July 1975, p.4.

Steinke, Jocelyn (2005) 'Cultural Representations of Gender and Science: Portrayals of Female Scientists and Engineers in Popular Films'. *Science Communication*, vol. 27, no. 1, September 2005, pp. 27–63.

Sterba, James (1975) 'Sharking: New Interest in Sport Since Movie "Jaws"'. *Ocala Star-Banner*, 29 July 1975, p.28.

*Sunday Herald* (1949) 'Pig No. 311 Is Well Again: But A-Bomb Survivor Can't Have Piglets'. 3 April 1939, p.23.

—— (1950) 'Martin and Lewis Fans'll Love It'. 24 September 1950, p.38.

—— (1952) 'Insect Poisons Can Injure User; Care Always Needed'. 1 June 1952, p.112.

*Sydney Morning Herald* (1946) 'Atom Bomb Tests Grimly Awaited'. 4 June 1946, p.2.

—— (1951) 'The Long Shooting Arm of the Law'. 17 March 1951, p.2.

*Sydney Morning Herald Garden Supplement* (1950) 'How to Beat Pests'. 28 August 1950, p.8.

Tait, Michael (2010) 'Stalking Deer in the Scottish Highlands: "Make Sure You've Got the Wind in Your Face"'. *Guardian*, 24 May 2010, online at http://www.guardian.co.uk/environment/video/2010/may/21/scotland-highlands-stalking-wild-deer.

*Telegraph* (1959) 'Water Pollution Danger Increases: Hundreds of New Chemicals Now Taint Water'. 30 December 1959, p.4.

—— (2009a) 'Jonathan Ross's Dormouse Joke Prompted Police to Raid Animal Sanctuary'. *Telegraph*, 25 March 2009, online at http://www.telegraph.co.uk/

news/newstopics/celebritynews/5049693/Jonathan-Rosss-dormouse-joke-prompted-police-to-raid-animal-sanctuary.html.

—— (2009b) 'Animal Charity Saves 60 Elephants Amid Controversy'. *Telegraph*, 19 June 2009, online at http://www.telegraph.co.uk/news/worldnews/africaandindianocean/malawi/5578422/Animal-charity-saves-60-elephants-amid-controversy.html.

—— (2009c) 'Wildlife Photographer of the Year Wolf Picture at Centre of Fakery Claims'. *Telegraph*, 22 December 2009, online at http://www.telegraph.co.uk/earth/wildlife/6859434/Wildlife-Photographer-of-the-Year-wolf-picture-at-centre-of-fakery-claims.html.

Terzian, Sevan G. & Grunzke, Andrew L. (2007) 'Scrambled Eggheads: Ambivalent Representations of Scientists in Six Hollywood Film Comedies from 1961 to 1965'. *Public Understanding of Science* 16 (2007), pp. 407–419.

*The Day* (1939) 'Cruelty in Films'. 24 January 1939, p.3.

—— (1954) 'Behind the Hollywood Scene'. 14 June 1954, p.7.

*The Science News-Letter* (1932) 'Chimpanzee Excels Baby in Several Mental Tests'. vol. 22, no. 597, p.175.

*The Times* (2006) 'Where Little Monkeys Can See Big Beasts'. 4 December 2006, online at http://www.timesonline.co.uk/tol/travel/holiday_type/family/article659802.ece.

Thomas, Bob (1953) 'Hollywood Report'. *Daytona Beach Morning Journal*, 20 August 1953, p.4.

*Times Daily* (1951) 'Bonzo The Chimp Steals Stars' Thunder'. 15 March 1951, p.8.

—— (1957) 'Fire Ant Fight Bill to Be Asked'. 20 March 1957, p.8

*Times-News* (1951) 'Develop Weapon for Attack on Insects in Korea'. 28 November 1951, p.4.

—— (1952a) 'Ask Germ Warfare Inquiry'. 12 March 1952, p.6.

—— (1952b) 'No Money Wasted on Monkey Business'. 15 July 1952, p.4.

—— (1957) 'U.S. Ready for Aerial Warfare on Fire Ant'. 9 April 1957, p.3.

—— (1975) '"Jaws" May Be Adversely Affecting Coastal Economy'. 2 August 1975, p.21.

*Toledo Blade* (1950a) 'There's Big Money in Training Wild Animals'. 25 June 1950, p.74.

—— (1950b) 'Army Guarding Against Korean Disease Threat'. 11 August 1950, p.2.

—— (1950c) 'Chimp Insured for Thousands'. 15 October 1950, p.89.

—— (1952) *'Fearless Fagan* advertisement'. 17 September 1952, p.23.

Travel Foundation (2008) *Responsible Safari Guiding*. Online at http://www.thetravelfoundation.org.uk/index.php?id=249.

*Tri City Herald* (1949) 'It Shouldn't Happen to A Pig, But It Did'. 3 April 1949, p.37.

—— (1951) 'Gave Him a Hand and He Bit It'. 28 January 1951, p.61.

Triggs, John (2009) 'The Albino Bounty Hunters'. *The Daily Express*, 7 April 2009, online at http://www.dailyexpress.co.uk/posts/view/93750.

Troup, John (2008) 'Lion Terror of Holiday Briton'. *The Sun*, 2 February 2008, online at http://www.thesun.co.uk/sol/homepage/news/754044/Kate-Drew-Savaged-by-lion-Zimbabwe.html.

Tschinkel, Walter, R., (2006) *Fire Ants*. Harvard University Press, Cambridge, Massachusetts.

Tudor, Andrew (1989) *Monsters and Mad Scientists: A Cultural History of the Horror Movie*. Blackwell, Oxford.

*Tuscaloosa News* (1953a) 'Fly Clean-Up Campaign Well Worth Effort'. 22 June 1953, p.3.

—— (1953b) 'Insecticides Posing Threat to Public Health'. 19 August 1953, p.3.

—— (1958) 'Conservation Leaders Say Any Chemicals Peril Wildlife'. 20 April 1958, p.2.

Urry, John (2002) *The Tourist Gaze*. Sage, London, California and Delhi.

Van de Water, Marjorie (1933) 'An Ape for a Baby Sitter'. *The Science News-Letter*, vol. 24, no. 646, pp. 133–135.

Vogel, H. Gerhard, Hock, Franz Jacob, Jochen Maas and Dieter Mayer (2006) *Drug Discovery and Evaluation: Safety and Pharmacokinetic Assays*. Springer, New York & Berlin.

Wallace, W (1892) *Pall Mall Gazette*. 7 November 1892, p.246.

Watson, James & James More (1949) *Agriculture: The Science and Practice of British Farming*. Oliver & Boyd, Edinburgh & London.

Watts, Jonathan (2010) 'Not Just for Dinner: China's Pet Lovers Seek Ban on Eating Dogs'. *The Guardian*, 27 January 2010, pp.1–2.

*Weekly Dispatch* (1886a), 'Topics of the Day'. *Weekly Dispatch*, 30 May, 1886, p.1.

—— (1886b), 'Letters to the Editor'. *Weekly Dispatch*, 6 June 1886, p.9.

Weingart, Peter with Claudia Muhl & Petra Pansegrau (2003) 'Of Power Maniacs and Unethical Geniuses: Science and Scientists in Fiction Films'. *Popular Understanding of Science*, vol. 12, pp. 279–287.

Witmer, Lightner (2010) 'A Monkey with a Mind'. *New York Times*, 30 January 1910, p. SM7.

Wolch, Jennifer & Jody Emel (eds) (1998) *Animal Geographies: Place, Politics and Identity in the Nature-Culture Borderlands*. Verso, London & New York.

Wolf, William (1980) 'The Ronald Reagan Follies'. *New York*, vol. 13, no. 9, 28 July 1980, p.46.

Wolfson, Lisa (1987). 'Humane Society Keeps Film Set Abuse Down'. *Lawrence Journal-World*, 11 July 1987, p.51.

Yerkes, Robert (1963). 'Creating a Chimpanzee Community'. *The Yale Journal of Biology and Medicine*, vol. 36, December 1963, pp. 205–223.

Zanuck, Darryl (1939). 'Zanuck's Answer: Letter to the Editor'. *Pittsburgh Press*, 1 February 1939, p.10.

# Index